# Asylum Seekers

# Asylum Seekers

## AUSTRALIA'S RESPONSE TO REFUGEES

Don McMaster

MELBOURNE UNIVERSITY PRESS

MELBOURNE UNIVERSITY PRESS
PO Box 278, Carlton South, Victoria 3053, Australia
info@mup.unimelb.edu.au
www.mup.com.au

First published 2001
Reprint with new Preface 2002

Designed by Jo Waite
Typeset by  Syarikat Seng Teik Sdn. Bhd., Malaysia in 11 point Garamond 3
Printed in Australia by RossCo Print

National Library of Australia Cataloguing-in-Publication entry

McMaster, Don.
Asylum seekers: Australia's response to refugees.

  Bibliography.
  Includes index.
  ISBN 0 522 84961 X.

  1. Refugees—Australia. 2. Refugees—Government policy—Australia.
  3. Refugees—Legal Status, laws, etc.—Australia. 4. Detention of
  persons—Australia. 5. Australia—Emigration and immigration—
  Government policy. I. Title.

325.210994

For my parents Frederick and Laurel

# Contents

Preface 2002                                              ix

Abbreviations                                            xiv

1    Australia's 'Other'                                   1

2    The Wretched of the Earth                             8

3    Australian Immigration and Its 'Other'               38

4    The Politics of Detention                            66

5    International Comparisons                            98

6    The Politics of Race                                127

7    The Politics of Belonging                           161

8    Detention, Exclusion and the 'Other'                189

Notes                                                    192

Select Bibliography                                      232

Index                                                    246

# Preface 2002

## Lies, Boats and Videotapes: Politics of Deception

Since the first publication of this book in 2001, issues about asylum seekers have been headline news on a weekly, if not daily, basis. The most notable have been the *Tampa* crisis in August 2001, the so-called Pacific Solution and the 'children overboard' saga (the last two continuing as I write). In Australia, racist rhetoric and action against Muslims and Middle Eastern people were fuelled by the terrorist attack on the United States of America in September 2001. The majority of asylum seekers arriving in Australia at that time were from Afghanistan, Iraq and Iran, and unfortunately were wrongly perceived as either terrorists or 'the enemy'. Ironically, the asylum seekers from Afghanistan were escaping persecution from the very same forces that the West declared war on.

Since that time, protests by detainees in detention centres, particularly Woomera, have continued, with the government retaliating by tightening control. At the Woomera Centre, protesting detainees were sprayed with water from fire trucks, the media was distanced from the camp perimeters and exaggerated charges of child abuse by detainee parents were released. These reactions by the Howard Government have highlighted a crisis in their (mis)management of refugee and asylum policy.

The government introduced a number of Bills during 2001 including a Bill to allow strip searches of refugees, to increase prison terms for
those who flee detention and to further restrict visitor access to detention
centres (which are much harder to access than ordinary prisons)[1]. They
also introduced the Border Protection Bill and the Migration Amendment Bills 1 and 2. These attempt to excise from Australia's migration
zone certain territories such as Christmas Island and Ashmore Reef. The
Border Protection Bill and the Migration Amendment Bills authorise the
expulsion of asylum seekers from Australian territory, with the Migration
Amendment Bill 2 allowing removal of an individual to a country that
the Immigration Minister deems appropriate. This allowed the government to instigate the 'Pacific Solution' of interning asylum seekers on
neighbouring Pacific Islands—at a cost to Australia.

The Border Protection Bill also allows the Australian Navy to inter-
cept boats before they land on Australian soil. This enables any asylum
seekers on them to be either taken outside Australian territory or brought
into the migration zone.[2] The *Tampa* incident illustrated that such detention may be lengthy, potentially involving people being detained in poor
conditions during protracted negotiations with other states and international institutions. The indeterminacy of this situation may breach
Article 9 of the International Covenant on Civil and Political Rights.

In late 2001 and with a federal election imminent the Howard
Government used asylum seekers for the basest of political motives: to
win votes. A master of strategy, John Howard saw the asylum seekers
aboard the *Tampa* and the public fear this produced as a vote winner—and
it worked. The government was prepared to deploy the armed services,
and the Australian public saw the SAS board the Norwegian freighter
*Tampa*, take control of an non-Australian ship and, with the Australian
navy, escort it out of Australian waters to deposit the asylum seekers on
neighbouring Pacific islands.[3]

However, by February 2002 the strategy of dehumanising asylum
seekers came back to haunt both Howard and his government. A month
before the 2001 election, the government released media reports of
asylum seekers throwing their children from a boat in protest at being
boarded and shipped out of Australian territory. A few days later, photos
were released as confirmation. The photos were disputed at the time as
not being of children thrown overboard by their parents but rather of
asylum seekers escaping from their sinking boat in an incident a few
days later.

A Senate inquiry into the 'children overboard' deception continues as I write, already with unsettling examples of the political uses to which photographs and videotapes have been put. So far, the inquiry has uncovered blatant government manipulation of the armed forces and the public service, as well as of asylum seekers. The Australian public has been provided with an insight into the underhanded strategies used by the Howard Government to control the asylum seeker issue for its own, and not the national, interest.

With what they perceived as a mandate in their treatment of asylum seekers after the November 2001 election (70 per cent of the Australian public appeared to support the government's treatment of asylum seekers for much the same reasons as I outline in this book), the Howard Government has strengthened its resolve to maintain the draconian and inhumane detention system, regardless of criticism from organisations such as the United Nations High Commissioner for Refugees (UNHCR), Amnesty International and the Human Rights and Equal Opportunity Commission. It was predicted that the government would spend over $200 million on locating, removing and detaining asylum seekers during the financial year 2001/02.[4] However, with the latest system of interdiction by naval boats and transfer (or dumping) of asylum seekers to poorer Pacific islands, this figure could easily double or treble.

On the other hand, Australia will contribute to the UNHCR refugee fund only around US$12 million (not including the money proposed for Afghanistan relief).[5] The money spent on detention centres and the use of the navy in the interdiction of boats could be better used by the UNHCR to alleviate some of the root causes of the displacement of asylum seekers. Until those causes are addressed, people will continue to flee life-threatening situations. These people are desperate: they seek asylum for their very existence and will continue to do so until conditions are safe within their homelands.

We need to let asylum seekers know that only certified refugees will remain in Australia; we need orderly programs with quotas; and we need to stop people smugglers. However, Australia must uphold the human rights treaties it has ratified and is obliged to provide asylum for those in need. Dialogue and cooperation with countries the asylum seekers traverse (such as Indonesia and Malaysia) as well as with the UNHCR is essential, yet the present political situation risks Australia being ostracised. The root causes of people movement are major and complex, and will not be resolved quickly. Leadership is needed to move from our present stubborn, obstructionist and militarist policies to more proactive bi- and multilateral responses.

The move for alternatives to detention has grown over the last year. Since *Tampa* there has been a public groundswell against the government's draconian interdiction and detention policies. The mandatory detention policy is expensive, costing $104 a day per head, and many groups are calling for a more appropriate and humane method of managing asylum seekers, such as community based programs. Community systems have been costed by a Select Committee of the New South Wales Parliament at these average costs per head, per day: parole system, $5.39; probation $3.94; home detention, $58.83. Clearly this would be more economically efficient and much more humane.

Australia's management of asylum seekers is abysmal and is not respected in the international community.[6] Introduction of the Border Protection Bill and Migration Amendment Bills 1 and 2, as well as implementation of anti-terrorist legislation in response to September 11, indicate serious moves to restrict civil liberties and human rights. These are major concerns for all Australians, as they minimise citizens' democratic rights while creating broader powers for governments to exclude targeted groups and individuals. Howard and the cultural right of the Coalition have shown not only general indifference to multiculturalism but also overt cruelty in their treatment of Muslim asylum seekers— treatment that would be inconceivable if they were European. International condemnation continues, with the United Nations High Commissioner for Human Rights (Mary Robinson) and the Secretary General of Amnesty International (Irene Khan) both publicly denouncing the Howard Government's treatment of asylum seekers and the continued use of mandatory detention.

Australia needs a humane and sustainable approach to refugee and asylum policy; this requires an end to mandatory detention and a closing of the 'hell holes' such as Woomera Detention Centre. Humane treatment of asylum seekers is the mark of a civilised society. We are failing ourselves as a nation as well as those we detain. In forty to fifty years from now, historians will look back on a dark period in Australian history. It will resonate with other dark periods such as the exclusion of Australia's Indigenous peoples and the Stolen Generation. It is not too late to change—Australia needs action and leadership to draw on the tolerance and 'fair go' that symbolises an Australia we can be proud of.

I acknowledge all asylum seekers for the courage and initiative to leave their country and place their lives at risk to escape persecution, trauma and torture. Their stories need to be told, especially by themselves, to change the distorted views and attitudes held by many Australians. I thank the asylum seekers whom I spoke to and interviewed, for their openness and courage to speak of events that still hold much trauma. Acknowledgements also go to the many refugee support groups formed since the *Tampa* event—their social activism will make a difference.

Greg McCarthy and Clem Macintyre provided much-valued encouragement, patience and productive criticism during the supervision of my PhD thesis, which became the basis of this book. Members of the Politics Department at the University of Adelaide, Glenda Mather, Patrick Allington, and Cally Guerin, offered thoughtful comments, editing advice and support, while Tina Esca and Chris McElhinney provided invaluable technical help, all much appreciated. I also acknowledge the valuable editorial and production assistance provided by Janet Mackenzie, Gabby Lhuede and Jean Dunn at Melbourne University Press.

Finally, I must express my deep thanks to my partner, Rosemary Warmington, and my daughters Simone and Shae, for patience and unflagging support through years of research and endless hours in front of computers.

**March 2002**                                    **Don McMaster**

[1]   *Migration Legislation Amendment (Immigration Detainees) Act 2001*. The strip search provisions were rejected, but reintroduced on 27 June 2001 in the Migration Legislation Amendment (Immigration Detainees) Bill (no. 2) 2001.

[2]   HREOC, 2001. *Human Rights and International Law Implications of Migration Bills*, Briefing Paper, 21 September, www.humanrights.gov.au/ human_rights/ asylum/migration_bills.html.

[3]   The captain, crew and owners of the *Tampa* were awarded the Nansen Refugee Award by the UNHCR on 19 March 2002 for their humanitarian act of rescuing the 438 stranded asylum seekers.

[4]   RCOA Media Release, 20 June 2001.

[5]   *Ibid*.

[6]   See Seth Mydans, 'Which Australian Candidate has the Harder Heart?', *New York Times*, 9 November 2001; Kathy Marks, 'Shame on Australia', *The Independent*, www.independent.co.uk, 11 November 2001, Norwegian Refugee Council, Media Release, 30 August 2001; 'Australia Migrants Land in Troubled Camp', *New York Times*, 2 December 2001.

# Abbreviations

| | |
|---|---|
| CPA | Comprehensive Plan of Action |
| DIEA | Department of Immigration and Ethnic Affairs |
| DIMA | Department of Immigration and Multicultural Affairs |
| DORS | Determination of Refugee Status |
| ECRE | European Council on Refugees and Exiles |
| HREOC | Human Rights and Equal Opportunity Commission |
| INS | Immigration and Naturalization Service (USA) |
| OAU | Organisation of African Unity |
| OFPRA | Office for the Protection of Refugees and Stateless Persons (France) |
| RCOA | Refugee Council of Australia |
| UNHCR | United Nations High Commission for Refugees |
| US INS | United States, Immigration and Naturalization Service |

# 1
# Australia's 'Other'

## A White Australia

*When the good God gave us this continent*
*To love and live in as our Fatherland,*
*Was it not in his counsels planned,*
*And His intent*
*That we for ever should unite*
*To keep it white?*

*He saw the homeland filled to overflowing,*
*And marked the empty spaces of the new,*
*And by His patient guidance drew*
*Thousands to going*
*Where on a white land they should light*
*And keep it white.*

*Not that He loved the black, and brown, and yellow*
*Less than our own—for all He did create*
*And set them living separate*
*Each from his fellow*
*That black should not with yellow fight,*
*Nor brown with white.*

*And how shall we such purpose best fulfil*
*True to our destiny, and just to all?*
*Is not that destiny a call*
*To labour till*
*From Perth to Brisbane, Gulf to Bight*
*The whole is white.*

*To hold the land in trust for God and others,*
*To rule it wisely, and to work it well;*
*At home in unity to dwell*
*As friends and brothers,*
*To live for Justice, Truth, and Right*
*Will keep it white.*

Percy Henn[1]

Kosovar refugees were sipping tea at Hobart cafes . . .
but why are we not so generous towards Asian
asylum-seekers?

R. Eccleston, 1999[2]

The coincidental arrival of both Chinese boat people and Kosovar refugees in Australia in the first half of 1999 attracted considerable media attention, but the reaction to the two events could not have been more different. On one hand, the boat people were greeted with headlines such as 'Invaded' and 'Outcry over illegals', and they were placed in detention.[3] The underlying fear of the Asian 'other' had surfaced, creating a perceived threat of invasion. On the other hand, the Kosovar refugees were invited to Australia and then greeted, in a show of much positive emotion and humanitarian concern, with headlines such as 'Sanctuary' and 'Safely into Our Arms'.[4] They were welcomed; they were European and not the 'other'. These events highlight the discriminatory manner in which Australian refugee policy and citizenship have been used to exclude its 'other'.

Since 1989 the detention of asylum-seeking boat people has evoked debate. Boat people are predominantly South-East Asian asylum-seekers who come to Australia by sea without authority. They come for various reasons: many are escaping persecution, some are seeking better economic conditions, others are queue-jumpers, and some are part of human trafficking. They are all unlawful non-citizens and, although the number of people involved is minor, Australia's treatment of them 'raises significant and fundamental human rights issues'.[5] The first arrived in 1976 and, while attracting attention, were not detained. The controversy aroused by their arrival was disproportionate to the actual number of people arriving.

Although Australia had a detention clause in its immigration policy, it had been used only for specific cases and only for individuals until the arrival of the boat people. It was activated to incarcerate this particular group. This discriminatory response arose out of the fear of Australia's 'significant other': Asia.

The 'significant other' is a group or race that is perceived as the most important threat to the existence of a nation or national identity. The 'Asian', 'the yellow peril' and 'the hordes from the north'[6] have been constructed as the threat to the Australian nation and national identity. Edward Said, in his influential work *Orientalism,* argues that the West constructed the Orient by a system of ideas that structure power in such a manner as to dominate and appropriate the Orient as the 'other'.[7] The term 'Asian' is contentious (there is no people that calls itself 'Asian'); it is an Orientalist and racist construction. I use it here for convenience, while recognising that power relationships operate within it. In the Australian context the meaning of 'Asian' has shifted; it meant people of Chinese descent during the nineteenth century, but was expanded to include people of Japanese and South-East Asian descent in the twentieth century. The Orientalist perspective denotes Asia as demographically located between the Bosporus in the west and the Pacific rim in the east, thus including any 'coloured' peoples. In official Australian policy terms this held true for the White Australia policy. Although this policy was instituted in the late nineteenth century to exclude Chinese, it eventually excluded all Asians and other non-Europeans from citizenship and belonging to the Australian nation. Thus, these peoples came to be represented as the 'other'.[8]

The White Australia policy effectively excluded most Asians until its demise in 1973. Following the end of the Vietnam War there was a gradual introduction of Asian people as refugees and migrants into Australia. However, when this number began to increase, mainly due to family reunion, it evoked resistance from some Australians and a divisive public debate. The so-called 'immigration debates' influenced government policy and led to the detention of boat people. This prolonged detention is a human rights violation committed by Australia and an inhumane method of managing a 'perceived problem'.[9]

Refugee detention policy is interlinked with debates on citizenship, which in turn are framed by the context of identity politics. The discrimination against boat people is based on fear of the 'significant other'. A more humane approach would allow asylum-seekers, such as the boat people, rights existing in social citizenship, as applies to 'denizens' in European countries and in the community parole system in North America. This form of discrimination is analysed by examining the construction of identity within a framework of immigration, human rights and citizenship. This framework is valuable because identity encompasses legal, national and cultural categories that determine who 'belongs' and who is excluded from citizenship. For non-citizens, or aliens, the term denotes exclusion and a valuing of citizenship; conversely, aliens are devalued, creating an area where discrimination against a nation's 'other' can occur. As Alastair Davidson says, 'citizenship and migration have always been confused in Australian history' where citizenship has been used by successive governments to exclude Australia's 'other'.[10]

This book examines the historical construction of Australia's 'other' and the political and legal structures that have evolved to maintain exclusionary and discriminatory policies. Successive Australian governments have used these structures, the White Australia and detention policies, in a discriminatory way, often at an unconscious and administrative level hidden from the public gaze, to exclude a specific group of people because of their race.

Throughout white history, Australians have feared invasion by 'the hordes from the north'. Racist attitudes are not unique to Australians; what is unique is the fear of invasion and especially of being overrun by Asians. The poem at the beginning of this chapter captures the attitude of white settler society that promoted 'a white Australia'. This attitude still exists and has found consistent expression in the White Australia and detention policies. Immigration, and more specifically refugee, policies are indicators of the attitude of a country to strangers, and the management of strangers reflects the sense of insecurity of a country in relation to others. Australia's response to strangers, and especially to its 'significant other', has been highly discriminatory, revealing both a fear of the 'other' and a fragile Australian identity.

Australia's treatment of migrants is inconsistent. On one hand, it has accepted migrants from Britain enthusiastically, and migrants from Europe with tolerance, sometimes reluctantly. On the other hand, migrants from Asia have been excluded for the greater part of settler history.

The Australian colonies first moved to exclude Asians during the nineteenth century when Chinese workers were perceived as a threat to Australian labour, particularly in the goldfields. The Chinese were treated as an inferior race and a threat to national identity, which at that time meant being a British subject. The White Australia policy, incorporated in the *Immigration Restriction Act 1901,* one of the first laws enacted by the new Australian Federation, was the culmination of this ideology. Australia was not alone in this exclusionist policy; Canada, the United States and New Zealand engaged in similar, though less fierce, methods of exclusion during this time and maintained discriminatory immigration policies until the 1960s.[11]

Australia is an 'immigrant society' with immigration playing a pivotal part in the nation-building process.[12] Australian immigrant society is relatively young compared to most European and Asian societies and constitutes a developing and insecure identity. White Australian identity is interlinked with colonisation and the establishment of a settler society in Australia. During this period of colonising, Australia's link to Britain was seen as paramount and unbreakable. Australian national identity was formed on the foundation of an Anglo-Celtic heritage, a white heritage defended by means such as the White Australia policy, and which remains strong in areas of Australian society today.

Australian identity has two main strands. The first, developing out of the white settler foundation, is romantic and nationalistic in character, espoused by a group of conservatives such as Geoffrey Blainey, John Howard and Pauline Hanson. The second is cosmopolitan and multicultural in character, a more liberal and inclusive identity that has come to the fore since the 1970s and is articulated by academics and public commentators such as Mary Kalantzis, James Jupp and Phillip Adams.

After World War 2, immigration changed considerably with the introduction of European migrants, initially Northern, and then Southern Europeans. They were encouraged to come to Australia to increase the population and service a newly industrialised society. They entered under policies of assimilation where new migrants were expected to discard the culture of their former country and to blend into, and become part of, the British-based Australian society. The philosophy underpinning this policy was one of social cohesion and 'sameness', the giving over of 'otherness'. Asians, as the 'significant other', were still excluded.

During the 1960s this discriminatory policy was replaced by the integration policy, which allowed new migrants to retain their former culture while integrating into Australian society. Although this was a shift in accepting cultures other than the dominant British heritage, it included only cultures from European derivations; Asian people were still not included. In the 1970s Australia implemented a 'multicultural' policy that recognised and celebrated cultural diversity within the Australian nation and identity. However, acceptance of multiculturalism was neither uniform nor smooth.

The White Australia policy, which did not officially end until 1973, effectively excluded most Asians and other non-Europeans from Australian society, citizenship and identity. Even after its demise there was a reluctance to accept them. Australia's immigration programs are both highly regulated (with set numbers and constituents) and expansive, contributing to almost trebling the Australian population since 1945.[13] In this remarkable expansion the number of Asian migrants entering Australia is, by any measure, small (but increasing). However, increased Asian immigration has, at times, raised a storm of controversy. The immigration debates and the detention of boat people both highlighted this reaction, illuminating Australia's fear of its 'significant other'.

During the 1990s, controversy surrounding the detention of boat people highlighted the inadequacies of Australian immigration and refugee policy. More importantly, the detention controversy demonstrated the discriminatory manner in which refugee policy and citizenship structures are used to exclude specific individuals and groups, such as a nation's 'other'. The detention of boat people, who are predominantly Asian, will be examined in the framework of identity —in terms of citizenship and belonging. The question of who belongs and who is to be excluded in a nation hinges on citizenship, and immigration policy has a pivotal part in this construction.

A survey of the theoretical perspectives of what constitutes a refugee and what are human rights violations shows that Australian governments have discriminated against boat people. Connecting these revelations about discrimination to citizenship in turn uncovers the gaps that asylum-seekers, such as the boat people, can fall into; they are at the mercy of the nation-state without any sufficient recourse to natural justice. A nation-state can discriminate against its 'other' by enacting policies that, unjustly and contrary to human rights, exclude targeted groups. A comparative analysis shows that, although operating within the framework of liberal democracy, nation-states are relatively free to formulate policy regulating the introduction of strangers and to target those whom they wish to exclude.

A central concern here is to identify racist attitudes and discriminatory practices and relate them to national identity. Analysis of immigration debates in Australia confirms Asia as the 'other'; this clarifies the fear of invasion by 'the hordes from the north' and explains why these fears are periodically triggered by rhetoric or events.

My argument is that rights of social citizenship should be granted to asylum-seekers waiting refugee determination. Comparison with Europe, Canada and the United States reveals the discrepancies in Australian refugee and detention policy. The contribution of this book is its analysis of identity in terms of the 'other'. In the case of Australia this exposes the underlying racist attitudes that have resulted in government measures such as the refugee detention policy.

# 2
# The Wretched of the Earth

The world is full of refugees. There are refugees fleeing hunger;
there are refugees fleeing war. They run for their lives or for their
freedom: they run from invaders or from their own governments,
from natural disasters or from man's inhumanity to man, woman
and child. They have been bombed in their shelters and
machine-gunned on the roads, they have been hunted, starved,
raped and murdered, betrayed and vilified, driven out of one
country and refused admission into another. They are, some for a
period, some for the rest of their lives, among the wretched of the
earth.

Eugene Kamenka[1]

Refugees are truly the wretched of the earth. The word 'refugee' produces
a melange of bleak images: overcrowded detention camps, a teeming
boat depositing passengers on foreign shores, a bloated child in Africa, a
war-torn section of Belgrade. These images pervaded the closing years of
the twentieth century. Refugees, especially asylum-seekers, are vulnerable to the goodwill of the receiving country, as it is the nation-state
which controls and determines who enters their country and society. The
plight of the refugee raises profound moral questions for governments in

terms of foreign policy, as well as the practical implications of inclusion or exclusion.[2]

With the advent of the 'global village', travelling time between continents and the social distance between people has diminished. Boundaries and borders are both more fluid and guarded. Electronic media and telecommunications have few boundaries and connect the majority of the world's population with events happening in the rest of the world. The plight of the refugee is increasingly reported from many parts of the world: scenes of starving, emaciated and homeless people fleeing natural or human disasters are common on prime-time television news.[3]

Most mass migration is taking place in the developing world, although larger numbers of people are migrating from developing countries to industrialised nations.[4] Both 'sending' and 'receiving' countries have had great difficulty coping with the disruptive effects of massive flows of migration; examples are Afghanistan and Pakistan, Eastern and Western Europe, and movements of people in the Horn of Africa and Central Africa.[5] States, or governments, remain the major actors in relation to forced migrants. They create the conditions that cause people to become refugees, or displaced within their country; and they have the power to receive refugees as well as assisting the internally displaced to return after reconciliation has taken place.

The magnitude of mass migration and refugee flows in the last few decades has generated global concern. In 1951, when the United Nations High Commission for Refugees (UNHCR) was established, there were an estimated 1.5 million refugees in the world; by 1980 numbers were estimated at 8.2 million, and by 1999 at 21 million. Exact numbers are not known, and displaced people are not included in these figures; they may number another 50 million. Official figures relate to refugees who are specified as 'persons who are outside their country because of a well-grounded fear of persecution'. Excluded from this definition are the vast majority of people displaced within their own country for political reasons or uprooted by natural catastrophes such as famine or floods.[6]

On one hand, these flows have produced humanitarian concern for the millions of people dispossessed. On the other hand, host states fear that their social, economic and political stability is threatened by the streams of unwanted strangers. States are struggling to form a proper balance between the need to maintain control over their borders and the need to protect refugees who seek asylum within those borders.[7]

Some states grant asylum to refugees, or fund the support of refugees in asylum countries in order to solve refugee problems permanently through systems of resettlement.[8] Following World War II and the formation of the United Nations, Australia has participated in this system. However, Australia also has stringent methods of control, such as detention. Asylum-seekers are vulnerable if discriminatory practices are part of the refugee determination system, which is controlled primarily by the nation-state.

## Historical Perspective

Refugees, broadly defined as those people who seek and obtain sanctuary and protection, have existed from the earliest times. Mass movements of people have changed the demographic maps of the world during every century and the main causes remain the same: war, intolerance and persecution of religious, ethnic or political minorities. The movement of individuals, families or groups between neighbouring and distant lands has characterised non-industrial as well as industrial societies throughout the world. However, until the advent of the nation-state, little attention was paid to the boundaries of sovereign states and the people who crossed them.[9]

Open borders and open societies with free movement existed in pre-industrial times with few marked borders for people to cross. Territories were ruled under jurisdictions with attitudes and interests strikingly different from those that prevail today. The church granted asylum during ancient times, while the granting of asylum by monarchs, republics and free cities was a consequence of territorial sovereignty. These societies were not necessarily more humane than those of today: prior to the development of the welfare state, most refugees had to rely upon charity offered by the church, municipality or sovereign.

Refugees were lucky if they received such support and often perished if they did not. Although conditions varied widely, pre-modern rulers generally tended to view population as an asset rather than a liability in an era of relatively low population. Rulers favoured the movement of people into their jurisdictions, expecting to add to the production of wealth and to increase the number of taxpayers and those who could serve in the army. As a result, those expelled or fleeing from one place could often find ready refuge and acceptance in another.[10]

Permanently displaced people were practically unknown in premodern times; there were no camps to detain people in a suspended state between the flight from their original homes and full admission to the receiving state. Refugees were regarded as assets rather than liabilities where societies granted refuge to people of religious or cultural backgrounds similar to their own. Rulers of the time viewed control over large populations, along with natural resources and territory itself, as an index of power and status. Most movements were undertaken, however, with enormous difficulties; travel was mainly on foot, and refugees often met a hostile reception along the way.[11] Nonetheless, people in every age moved around, and most were accepted as assets in their new communities.

Tensions have arisen, resulting in restrictive legislation, when national priorities have come to predominate over those of the migrant poor or displaced refugees. The oppression and expulsion of religious, political or ethnic minorities have been recurrent themes in history, gaining momentum in contemporary times, but asylum in the past did not necessarily require formal permission as it does today. Significantly, the escape routes that were available to refugees or asylum-seekers have effectively been barred through the development of fixed, closed borders. A political matrix has been enforced upon most refugee movement and legislation, with the majority of the world's population requiring documents to cross borders, effectively fixing national identities.[12]

History is full of narratives describing movements of people escaping persecution or oppressive forces, such as the biblical story of Moses and the Jews fleeing Egypt. Prior to the fifteenth century, movements of people were unrestricted, freer and, with a smaller world population, much easier to contemplate. In China internal movement and voluntary migration were common, despite the strong cultural bonds of family and government, which helps explain the emergence of a relatively homogenous Chinese people over such a large area. There is a strong tradition of free movement in Africa and also in the Middle East, where the concept of *Dar-al-Islam* (House of Islam) stressed the unity of Islamic civilisation and of free movement within its geographic regions. Mass population movements are not adequately recorded until the fifteenth century, when the emergence of the powerful European states inaugurated a distinctive era in the history of human migration.[13]

European colonising of the New World and the associated aggressive imperial pursuit of commercial hegemony had the effect of incorporating the world's population into a single migratory system, bringing about unprecedented encounters between very different groups widely separated geographically and culturally. Aristide Zolberg distinguishes three epochs, each producing distinctive patterns of economic and political migration.[14]

## First Epoch: Religious Persecution

During the sixteenth to eighteenth centuries, an era of absolutism and mercantilism, population increased slowly and was considered a scarce economic and military resource. Refugees were seen as a valuable commodity as European rulers sought to contain their subjects within their territory and at the same time boost the population from 'the external world'. Within this era there was little international movement of labour within Europe. However, outward expansion produced two large transoceanic migrations. Firstly, there was the migration of some two to three million Europeans to the New World colonies, most as bound labourers. Secondly, up to the nineteenth century, there was the importation of up to 15 million West Africans as plantation slaves, initially to countries adjoining Europe and then to the New World of the Americas. Africa was already the major source of slave labour for the Islamic world and continued to play this role well into the twentieth century, with an estimate of 17 million slaves taken from Africa between 650 CE and 1920.[15]

Independent migrants from the middle classes of European society were attracted to the New World. European governments attempted to restrict these movements to prevent both the loss to their own society and colonial competition with the metropolis. Although this movement was mainly voluntary, occasionally rulers ejected groups. If not ejected, non-conforming groups were persecuted until they fled, as happened to the unconverted Jews and the Arab-descended Moriscos of Spain.[16]

Generally, refugees expelled during this period were religious minorities, held to constitute some challenge to existing political authority. In addition to the Jews and the Moriscos driven out of Spain, Protestants from France and the Spanish Netherlands were similarly exiled, along with Protestants or Catholics from states and principalities in Central Europe during the Reformation era. Other refugees included

Serbs fleeing Ottoman rule from the seventeenth century, crossing the Danube into Hungarian lands; English, Irish, and Scottish Catholics following their Stuart monarch into exile after 1688; and various Protestant sects leaving Scandinavia and Central Europe in the eighteenth century, seeking free religious expression. There were also refugees displaced by war: for example, the population temporarily displaced by the Thirty Years War, the campaigns of Louis XIV, and the wars of the seventeenth century. The last massive wave consisted of some 200 000 Huguenots who fled France when Louis XIV revoked the Edict of Nantes in 1685.[17]

The word 'refugee' was first recorded in France in 1573 in the context of granting asylum and assistance to foreigners escaping persecution. The same year, saw the arrival of Calvinists in France from the adjacent Low Countries (Belgium and the Netherlands); the Reformation had gained support in the Low Countries but the Spanish rulers were engaged in an all-out repression of religious dissent. The English interpretation of 'refugee' is derived from the French, first used by them about a hundred years later when, ironically, the Huguenots, originally persecuted Calvinists from France, had settled in Britain.[18]

The case of the Huguenots illustrates the plight of the refugee clearly within that historical context. So what made the Huguenots refugees? They were a Calvinist Protestant minority in a country where the majority were Catholic. They coexisted peacefully due to the Edict of Nantes, a political compromise enacted in 1598, whereby Catholicism was established as the state religion. However, shortly after seizing power in 1661, Louis XIV set out to eliminate Calvinism from France and to unify the Catholic populations in an undertaking of absolutist ideology to achieve what he conceived to be a perfectly unified polity. Louis made it impossible to be born, marry, work or die a Calvinist. The aim was not to exile the Calvinists from France but to convert them to Catholicism. However, at least one-quarter of the Protestants fled France between 1681 and 1720.

They were refugees in the classic sense, fleeing life-threatening danger. They would certainly qualify as statutory refugees under the current definition. This historic movement of Huguenot exiles 'had features in common with the situation of refugees today: emergency assistance, protection, refoulment, pirate attacks on "boat people" at sea, integration problems, resettlement, repatriation ... and they also brought great benefits to their countries of asylum'.[19]

However, the Huguenots' relationship with the receiving countries contrasts with the position refugees and asylum-seekers find themselves in today. The Huguenots were widely accepted and welcomed as assets, whereas the majority of refugees today are seen as a problem or a burden in their receiving country. Zolberg illuminates a simple but crucial point for migratory practice, pointing out that, although the Huguenots were persecuted in their country of origin, they were recognised and accepted in their countries of asylum. They were granted asylum because the receiving countries were in sympathy with their religious and political ideologies. Zolberg argues that for a refugee flow to begin, certain conditions must be met in the states of destination as well as in the state of origin: 'People cannot leave their country if they have no place to go—a truism that holds for all types of international migration—and the availability of such a place is in turn largely determined by those who control the places of destination, usually governmental authorities'.[20]

This is not the case today. To the contrary, people *do* leave their country even if they know they have no secure destination. Holding camps in Hong Kong, on the Thai–Cambodian border and Australian detention camps testify to this fact. If people are under threat of death they will, and do wherever possible, leave their place of origin and hope to find a hospitable destination. Tensions and problems arise when the receiving countries do not wish to welcome displaced persons, as in the Rwandan crisis of the mid-1990s, and the refugee flows in South-East Asia and the former Yugoslavia. In the sixteenth to eighteenth centuries, with low population numbers, an influx of new people was an asset; in present-day Africa and Asia the population factor is now a major reason for non-acceptance of refugees and displaced people.

Asylum was available to the Huguenots because the condition that deemed them unacceptable to their state of origin was, on the contrary, supported by politically powerful groups in other states. It was an astute move in the game of statecraft, to gain a population renowned for its skills and wealth in the dawning era of mercantilism. However, by the middle of the seventeenth century movement of people affected by religious persecution halted, partly because most states had achieved a degree of religious homogeneity by that time and also because the Catholic–Protestant differences had lost their significance in regard to international political conflict.

## Second Epoch: Political Opposition

The conflicts of this era, which was inaugurated by the industrial, democratic, and demographic revolutions of the late eighteenth century, fostered a new category of refugee based on political rather than religious grounds.[21] This transformation extended into the political, cultural and economic spheres. It was the age of democratic revolutions that resulted in the emergence of industrial capitalism as the dominant mode of economic organisation: 'A distinctive feature of the conflicts of this period is that they were fought in the nascent language of political ideology, with the object of preserving or achieving a particular regime and with status groups—the aristocracy, the bourgeoisie—as the most relevant social categories'.[22]

Overseas there were now a number of independent countries or self-governing colonies under the control of European descendants, eager to secure settlers and workers. For Europe, these developments prompted governments to relinquish traditional prohibitions on emigration, a way of lowering welfare burdens and a safety valve for social unrest. 'Freedom to leave' was recognised as a human right, but existed at the discretion of the state. In a situation similar to the pre-modern and non-Western worlds, the ideal of free movement between states in Europe and America was realised in the nineteenth century, a period that Dowty classified as the 'Liberal Interlude'.[23]

The nineteenth century was an era preoccupied with exiles, individuals who had left their native country for political reasons, usually having engaged in revolutionary activity.[24] As political activists these revolutionaries frequently appeared to their host countries as troublemakers. A literary example is provided in the mysterious character in George Eliot's 1876 novel *Daniel Deronda,* who was 'a Pole, a Czech, or something of that fermenting sort, in a state of political refugeeism'. Karl Marx has been described as a refugee who had imposed exile upon himself and family.[25]

Although exiles gained notoriety, most migration was voluntary. Emigration from Europe grew from a mere 120 000 in the first decade of the nineteenth century to about 8.5 million in the last decade, with a total of some 29 million emigrants throughout the century. During the nineteenth century movement of peoples within the Western world was virtually unhindered. Britain allowed emigrants to leave freely and assisted some in their departure, such as 339 000 emigrants sponsored to Australia and elsewhere.[26]

Along with economic transformation and the growth of a large consumer market came an increase in the demand for tropical commodities in Europe. Most of these were produced on plantations in the colonies or countries in the developing world. The processes of colonisation enforced major influxes of people into areas not physically or culturally akin to them. For example, British plantation owners in the Indian Ocean and the Caribbean recruited workers under indenture from India. Imperial authorities in India welcomed this transfer as a way of reducing population and social conflict. This type of migration was extended to South-East Asia, southern and eastern Africa, and to colonies of other European powers. After the conquest and partition of Africa, the European colonists also instigated large intra-African migration, usually involving coercion, to provide labour for their plantations and mines.[27]

Democratic and national revolutions during the eighteenth and nineteenth centuries produced a distinctive type of refugee based on political opinion and class affiliation. Until the second half of the nineteenth century international treaties made no mention of refugees, and states made no distinction between those fleeing criminal persecution and those escaping political repression. Émigrés who escaped the French Terror are the best known of the early waves of revolutionary refugees, but the American Revolution triggered an even larger flow of people in relation to population size. Political refugees became commonplace throughout the nineteenth century, predominantly from the ranks of defeated nationalist and revolutionary movements. These exiles, mostly educated professionals and intellectuals, easily found asylum among the emerging liberal regimes of America and Europe.[28]

During this epoch refugees were generally not problematic among states and rarely preoccupied people in positions of authority. As there was no generally accepted obligation to protect and harbour strangers who arrived from distant territories, few people worried about the economic or social burdens that refugees might impose. Rarely did refugees threaten social or public order, so they were not seen as a threat to social stability. Workers and peasants in various parts of Western Europe participated in radical social and political movements, which sometimes lead to their arrest, incarceration and transportation to penal colonies in Australia and Algeria. Usually it was the affluent who sought the luxury of refuge; many of the poor simply perished before even becoming refugees or engaging the attention of people in power.

With the increased availability of cheap long-distance sea transport it became possible for poor refugees to flee as well. Movement between states was relatively easy as there were still few barriers or borders.

## Third Epoch: Towards Mass Movements

The final decades of the nineteenth century signalled the beginning of a protracted crisis, which pushed refugee issues to the centre of international concern and gave rise to the institutional apparatus for dealing with refugees that exists today. A major aspect of the third epoch was the ever-widening gap that separated the capital-rich, technologically advanced and militarily powerful countries of Europe or European origin, plus Japan, from the rest of the world.[29] Human mobility was further facilitated by the development of mechanised travel, while the spread of written, and later electronic, media provided information about world conditions to most of the world's population. Boundaries were stretched and redefined in geographical as well as personal terms, creating a space for potential migrants from diverse backgrounds to entertain the idea and possibility of movement.

From the beginning of the twentieth century 'waves of refugees'[30] appeared throughout Europe. Hundreds of thousands of people were displaced by war, or fled persecution and devastation by the post-war realignment of territories after the collapse of four great European empires. Affluent states instituted more effective border controls in response to the threat of poor strangers, categorising them as 'undesirable or racially inferior groups'.[31] Border control effectively imposed limits on entry for purposes of permanent settlement and had far-reaching implications for citizenship, nationality and identity.

By the end of the twentieth century refugees were presented with the dilemma of nowhere to go. Borders are much more clearly defined, nationality laws surrounding citizenship are more strenuously enforced and movement across borders is restricted in most areas. During the twentieth century migration patterns reversed: movement from developed countries to new or undeveloped territories was replaced by movement from less-developed countries to the developed. Refugees are now presented to the international community as the 'stock figure of the unwanted supplicant . . . awkward, confused, powerless, and often utterly demoralised'.[32] The beginning of the twentieth century denoted the emergence of a new variety of collective alienation, one that becomes a 'hallmark of the time'.[33] This continues for the rest of the century, a point illuminated by Hannah Arendt and Edward Said.[34]

During the early twentieth century the growth of the modern nation-state played a significant role in the position of refugees.[35] The formation of the nation-state led to the naming of certain groups as enemies of the nation, the 'significant other'. Specific groups for whom the nation-state would not, or could not, assume responsibility became targeted as the 'other' in a form of discrimination that sometimes resulted in expulsion. During World War I this became explicit when nation-states expelled unwanted or menacing groups who were seen as threats. At this time immigration controls such as passports were introduced.[36]

These migratory groups were welcomed nowhere and could be assimilated nowhere. Having left, or being evicted from, their home-land, they were 'homeless'; having left their state, they were 'stateless'. Hannah Arendt forcefully points out that now they were deprived of their human rights and were regarded as 'the scum of the earth'.[37] In the early part of the twentieth century the landscape of displacement resembled that of the closing years of the century with mass displacements in the Balkans and parts of Africa. By 1922 over 1.5 million people had fled from Russia, inflicting a dilemma upon surrounding and receiving countries. This migration was a response to the economic devastation resulting from World War I, the collapse of the Russian empire in the 1917 Russian Revolution, and the onset of famine. However, as a result of the hardships of reconstruction following the war, growing unemployment and political unrest, receiving countries were reluctant, and often refused to admit large numbers of refugees.[38]

Questions of sovereignty became predominant in geopolitics. Whereas before the twentieth century migration had been mainly un-regulated, it now became highly regulated and restrictive as new states were formed. With the turmoil and displacements of World War I, the Russian Revolution and the dissolution of the Hapsburg and Ottoman Empires, the number of people who were classed as refugees soared. Refugee 'problems' became a matter of international concern, transcending national and bilateral interests. In August 1921 the League of Nations appointed Dr Fridtjof Nansen as High Commissioner for Refugees in Europe, recognising the gravity and scope of the refugee situation. Foundations for international responsibility for refugees were in place, and the subsequent conventions on refugees became the basis for international recognition of refugees.[39] The predicament and vulnerability of refugees were intensified by the growth of the nation-state. The nation-state had structures that could legitimately exclude those it did not want, opening spaces for policies that could discriminate against its 'other'.

Two terms to designate these new refugees were deployed after World War I and the ensuing peace treaties: the German *heimatlosen* or 'homeless' and the French *apatrides* or 'stateless'. These synonymous terms support Arendt's assertion that stateless people form the 'most symptomatic group in contemporary politics',[40] a symptom of the nation-state and the borders that are now well defined. A new sense of identity has grown whereby anyone not within state borders was classified as 'stateless'—they simply did not belong or exist. Refugees who flee their country have lost their national protection and identity and have no claim on the protection of other states. They are a legal anomaly. The absence of national protection has been the basis for refugee status and 'the *raison d'être* of international concern'[41] from 1921 to the present time.

The movement of people in the early twentieth century was connected to the political upheavals caused by the consolidation of nation-states. The modern state, with a few exceptions, is an association that claims not only territorial integrity but also a specific national identity. Before the twentieth century the formation of a nation-state consisted, in most cases, of a process of assimilation rather than expulsion: for example, the formation of British and French national identities was also tied to empire-building and colonisation. When decolonisation began in the mid-twentieth century the process of exclusion gained dominance, especially in Central, Eastern and South-Eastern Europe, in the Caucasus and Asia Minor, where nation-states were formed out of the break-up of far-flung empires.[42] Here nation-state formation took the form of exclusion and expulsion, with a growing number of displaced persons becoming both homeless and stateless.

During the years between World War I and World War II international arrangements were constructed to limit the scope of responsibility for refugees by defining them in terms of specific national or ethnic groups. This categorisation meant that groups such as the German

Jews, Assyrians, Turks and Russians, who were in need of international protection on the basis of the objective situation in their country of origin, could be recognised as *bona fide* refugees. It was only after the horrific episodes of World War II had been exposed that refugees came to be seen as individuals who require protection from the excesses of the state, thus becoming a universal concern. A universal mandate to protect refugees was bestowed on the UNHCR in 1951, thus changing the legalities concerning refugees. This mandate, established in the United Nations 1951 Convention Relating to the Status of Refugees and amended by the 1967 Protocol Relating to the Status of Refugees, contains a definition of a refugee that is recognised by most countries.[43]

The terminology applied to stateless people changed during World War II when the term 'displaced persons' came into use. Arendt argues that the term 'stateless person' acknowledged that these people had lost the protection of their government and required international agreements for safeguarding their status. Its replacement with 'displaced persons' designates, for Arendt, a deterioration in the understanding and position given to these people, as the term 'displaced' expresses a purpose of liquidating statelessness once and for all by ignoring its existence.[44] 'Displaced person' denotes a more general, non-geopolitical figure than 'stateless person'. As Arendt points out, 'displaced person' implies the expectation of repatriation. However, the hard facts were, and still are, that most refugees cannot be repatriated, if only because they face persecution if returned. They are then, to substantiate Arendt's argument, 'stateless' persons, without citizenship, outcast in a space of non-identity.

Many people have left their homes and the community in which they had lived in exchange for a 'homeland', an identity attached to a nation-state, such as Israel. In the logic of the nation-state, people must identify with a homeland in order to belong to the only community that counts, the nation and its own state: 'for those who find themselves excluded from the national identity amidst which they live, this exclusion is a perilous one because homelessness is the constant threat, no matter how long they or their ancestors have been resident in a particular bit of geography'.[45] Kurds and Palestinians represent this predicament, as people with homes but no homeland, nomads without identity.[46]

In contemporary times refugees represent a symptom of the homelessness or uprootedness of the modern and (so-called) postmodern age. The refugee, in many cases, is denied not only a homeland but also the possibility of establishing a home, of making roots and securing identity. The hegemony of modern nation-states over questions of identity and its insistence on the principle of sovereignty create this dilemma for the refugee. Principles of human rights are meant, in liberal democratic states at least, to fill the spaces left by the hegemonic structure of sovereignty. This is not always achieved, as we will see in Chapter 4.

Refugees thus encapsulate the contemporary political identity crisis. In their homelessness and statelessness refugees are the unwilling representatives of a cosmopolitan alternative to the idea of a homeland. The ideal homeland can be seen as unrealisable, or alternatively recognised as the site of struggle against the reductionism of national identity.[47] Although this romanticised ideal is similar to that espoused by exiles during the nineteenth century, it does not describe the position of desperate, emaciated refugees struggling to survive, such as the displaced peoples of Africa and Asia in the 1980s and 1990s.

The political crisis for refugees lies in their recognition and processing by International Conventions and sovereign laws that determine identity and allow them the label 'refugee'.

## Who are Refugees?

Millions of displaced people from diverse national backgrounds now exist on all populated continents. They have fled from political or religious persecution, racial or social discrimination, wars or territorial conflicts, economic deprivation or natural disaster.

Determining conceptually, if not politically, who qualifies as a refugee seems straightforward. A refugee is a person fleeing life-threatening circumstances. For general, and indeed journalistic, purposes this is roughly the meaning of 'refugeehood', to appropriate a term from Andrew Shacknove. The definition becomes more circumscribed when used in legal and political circles among officials who formulate refugee policies for states and international agencies. The predominant historic conception advanced by international instruments, municipal statutes, and scholarly treatises identifies the refugee as 'a person who has crossed an international frontier because of a well-founded fear of persecution'.[48] This concept of a refugee is not a definition. Dozens of definitions exist under various jurisdictions; most states have their own, usually following the construction of the United Nations Convention.[49] Even the United Nations has not, up to this time, succeeded in adopting a satisfactory definition of who precisely qualifies as a refugee among the displaced people of the world. Although the United Nations has instituted agencies such as the UNHCR, it has not been sufficient and effective in dealing with the enormity of the refugee situation.[50]

As we have seen, the UNHCR records some 21 million refugees dispersed over the globe, with the largest number of displaced people being in Asia and Africa.[51] This large population consists of Afghans, Indochinese from Vietnam, Cambodia, and Laos, plus substantial numbers of refugees from the Sudan, Uganda, Rwanda, East Europe, Nicaragua and Chile. Currently, the largest number of refugees is located in the Asian area, with a known 4.8 million refugees, some 1.7 million internally displaced persons and 1.2 million returnees assisted by the UNHCR.[52]

This estimated 21 million includes only those who have registered as refugees with the appropriate UN and governmental agencies, in fulfilment of a specific definition of refugee incorporated in the UN 1951 Convention Relating to the Status of Refugees and its 1967 Protocol. According to the 1951 definition, a person is a refugee who

> as a result of events occurring before 1 January 1951 and owing to a well-founded fear of being persecuted for reasons of race, religion, nationality, membership of a particular social group or political opinion, is outside the country of his nationality and is unable or, owing to such fear, is unwilling to avail himself of the protection of that country; or who, not having a nationality and being outside the country of his former habitual residence as a result of such events, is unable or, owing to such fear, is unwilling to return to it.[53]

The temporal limitation was removed by Article 1(2) of the Protocol, which in effect deletes the words 'as a result of events occurring before 1 January 1951', and 'as a result of such events', from the Convention definition.[54]

A set of 'rights of refugees' compliments the definition in the Refugee Convention; significantly, they include the right not to be forcibly repatriated to the country of origin, known as non-refoulment.[55] However, the definition remains narrow in its legal-political disposition. Such concrete definitions assume that only the politically and socially persecuted can be awarded refugee status, and only when they have been forced to take up refuge outside their countries of origin. The definition implies that a bond of trust, protection, loyalty and assistance between the citizen and the state has been severed. Persecution and alienage are always the physical manifestations of this severed bond and provide the necessary and sufficient condition for determining 'refugeehood'.[56]

James Hathaway presents five essential elements in the composition of the Convention definition.

- *Alienage* includes only persons who have left their country of nationality, or country of habitual residence in the case of stateless persons.
- *Persecution* is the risk of serious harm against which the state of origin 'is unwilling or unable to offer protection'. Serious harm is defined as 'the sustained or systemic violation of core, internationally recognised human rights'.
- *Genuine Risk:* the refugee claimant must be *genuinely at risk* and with objective facts existing to provide a concrete foundation for the concern for which the claimant seeks protection in another state.
- *Genuine connection* must exist between the perceived risk of persecution faced by the refugee claimant and their race, religion, nationality, membership in a particular social group, or political opinion.
- *Protection* must be genuinely needed and legitimately claimed. This element incorporates the cessation clauses and the exclusion clauses of the Convention. Cessation clauses provide that refugee status is not warranted if the refugee can either reclaim the protection of their own state, or has secured an alternative form of enduring protection. The exclusion clauses ensure that serious criminals and persons whose actions have exhibited disregard for basic norms of human dignity cannot invoke international protection.[57]

'Persecution' is the element in the Convention definition that determines refugee status. Shacknove says it asserts both a moral and an empirical claim: 'moral, because it posits the existence of a normal, minimal relation of rights and duties between the citizen and the state, the negation of which engenders refugees; and empirical because it asserts that the actual consequences of this severed bond are always persecution and alienage'.[58] The Convention definition leaves out a range of displaced people whose plight has been, if not more arduous than, then at least similar to those who qualify as refugees.

Amin Saikal categorises dispossessed and displaced people into three groups:

- Internal refugees, millions of people displaced within their own countries resulting from either adverse social, political and economic conditions, armed conflicts or natural disasters. These displaced people, as refugees, suffer serious violations of human rights or social and economic deprivation as their externally displaced counterparts but for a variety of reasons have not been able to seek refuge outside their countries.
- A category of dispossessed people who have not been specifically persecuted, but have suffered as a result of generalised violence or economic deprivation within their country, and succeeded in escaping to another country.
- Another category of dispossessed people from a 'well-off' urban background who have not felt it appropriate to register with the UN agencies as refugees.[59]

None of these categories fits the Convention definition of a refugee, and such people have been left out of the UN registration. Many displaced persons, including boat people, who fail the persecution criterion would not be granted refugee status should their applications be considered under the 1951 Convention or 1967 Protocol.[60] Many, if not most, internal refugees have little or no access to outside relief agencies who can supply humanitarian aid. Assisting internally displaced persons is the responsibility of the country of origin; however, if that country is unwilling or unable to meet the minimum criterion set by human rights law, then protection and provision of humanitarian aid becomes a matter of international attention.

It is recognised that displaced persons, outside the original definition of refugees, are within the scope of UN and international concern. The General Assembly of the United Nations affirmed, in Resolution 46/182 of December 1991, 'that humanitarian assistance for victims of natural disaster and other emergencies was a matter of international import'.[61] Circumstances do not always allow the United Nations or the international community to follow these emergency procedures; for example, the threat to the safety of personnel carrying out such aid, as in the case of the former Yugoslavia, has restricted aid delivery to displaced persons and refugees.[62]

Why has the United Nations not been able to revise the strict Convention definition so that the non-registered categories of refugees could also be enumerated and helped? Saikal presents an answer that lies within the political and economic games that are played within and between the world's states. Most states that create refugees are not interested in seeing the definition of refugee expanded.

> This is largely because the creators of refugee movements fear the political and economic damage which may result from international awareness of persecution of their subjects, and the recipients want to evade legal obligations which they would be forced to assume towards a wider category of refugee than the 1951 Convention currently embraces.[63]

In the 1951 Convention and the 1967 Protocol the United Nations created an apolitical instrument for co-ordinating international action for refugees, under the 'good offices procedure'.[64] In effect the resulting definitions avoid any connection of a given group of refugees, such as displaced persons, with any political event. UN instruments were designed with the individual refugee in mind, the individual with a sound reason to believe that their basic human rights will be violated in their country of nationality because of a particular characteristic of that individual. Many other individuals or groups with vaguer, though well-founded, fears are not included in the Convention definition, leaving them with no protection or formal recognition.

Sadako Ogata, the High Commissioner for Refugees, argues that the UNHCR mandate has been extended in specific circumstances on behalf of particular groups, especially for large groups in Asia and Africa and later for groups in the conflict in Bosnia-Herzegovina.[65] In these cases, despite the extended mandate, the UNHCR was unsuccessful in protecting and assisting the internally displaced.

The UNHCR, non-government and voluntary agencies recognise and act for people who fail to meet the Convention refugee status, for example, stateless people, migrant workers and exiles who are unable to return to their countries of origin because of fear of persecution or civil disturbance. People in these categories have benefits similar to Convention refugees under the mandate of the UNHCR which, when it was established in 1950, called upon governments to provide protection by the High Commissioner for refugees not excluding those in the most destitute categories. This mandate allows the High Commissioner, under extenuating circumstances, to extend protection to people who are externally displaced and to those who are internally displaced and require protection.

The mandate is wider than the Convention but, unless people have removed themselves from their own country, generally the UNHCR will not protect them. Rarely does the UNHCR go beyond its mandate. However, within its mandate, agreements with governments to deal with returnees have been made and the UNHCR has been invited to supervise or aid nationals who are refugees in every way, except that they are internally displaced. The UNHCR's inclusion of displaced peoples in Lebanon, Angola, Cyprus and Southern Sudan has extended services provided to many who do not fit the narrow Convention definition. The breadth of the UNHCR's mandate, together with the delay in ratification of conventions and protocols, and individual reservations, enable both the Convention and mandate refugees to cohabit in a specific country for a specific time.[66] However, this is not common.

There are limits to the supports that developing countries of first asylum can provide for refugees, but is this true of the rich industrial countries? Many of the developed countries have deployed this argument to justify only limited refugee intake, along with other arguments about the complexities and difficulties that refugees from developing countries, the 'other', allegedly face in being included in Western societies. This is the Janus nature of refugee discourse, the interaction of the domestic interest and international responsibility which decides who is excluded.[67] In practice, the nation-state, sovereignty and borders remain dominant and continue to dictate who crosses them.[68]

Inadequacies in the institutional mechanisms that the United Nations has constructed to deal with the refugee situation are well recorded and extensively debated. Although the UNHCR has provided invaluable service from its inception, it has been constrained by numerous factors such as dependence on the co-operation of the UN member-states with which it must work. Power plays and conflicts make some states reluctant to antagonise their neighbours by characterising them as human rights violators or as states from which refugees flee. Australia's relationship to Indonesia concerning the situation in East Timor is an example: Australia, to maintain a stable relationship with Indonesia, turned a blind eye to human rights violations by the oppressive Indonesian political regime.[69]

UN refugee relief agencies are dependent for their operational funding on the goodwill of the member states. This goodwill does not always meet the demands of the services that agencies attempt to provide. Since the early 1980s a funding crisis has affected the UNHRC in a number of different spheres. Aid from donor countries has dropped as the number of explosive situations around the world and the numbers of refugees and displaced people have grown. In 1989 contributions to the United Nations amounted to US$325 million, but even after massive cost-cutting measures there was a funding shortfall of US$65 million, placing the United Nations in a precarious financial situation.[70]

Funding in these circumstances is at the mercy of shifting priorities in governments' economic and foreign aid policies. When foreign aid is determined by political and economic rather than humanitarian and moral considerations, refugees are easy victims. They are hidden, invisible and usually non-voters; they can be easily overlooked. For example, the Australian annual contribution to support the UNHRC fell dramatically during the 1980s from A$29 million in 1981 to A$4.7 million in 1988.[71] There is no mechanism for extracting a set proportion of a country's real gross domestic product that is dedicated to coping with refugee crises or situations.

Saikal suggests a global Refugee Fund under the control of the UNHRC and accountable for its actions only to a judicial body such as the International Court of Justice, free from the political pressures to which UN agencies are frequently subjected. Such a framework would enable the world community to discharge more effectively its political and moral obligations towards a wider range of displaced people. I agree with Saikal and Shacknove that the 1951 definition of the refugee needs to be altered to complement this institutional process and to alleviate the plight of the refugee.[72] We will now look at some amendments to the definition.

The 1951 Convention definition was positively amended by the Convention on Refugee Problems in Africa, a regional instrument adopted by the Organisation of African Unity (OAU) in 1969, to include 'people fleeing external aggression, internal civil strife or events seriously disturbing public order' in African countries.[73] This challenges the proposition that persecution is the essential criterion for refugee status. We need to note that the UN and OAU definitions reflect markedly different historical contexts. The UN definition was a response to the European experience after World War II when refugees were primarily people persecuted by highly organised predatory states. In the context of the 1960s, the OAU definition recognised that the normal bond between the citizen and the state can be severed in diverse ways, persecution being but one. The OAU definition extended beyond the persecuted individual to include whole groups fleeing from dangerous situations.

The Cartagena Declaration of 1984 developed the definition of a refugee further, once again reflecting the historical context in which it was made. This Declaration, approved by representatives and experts from Central American nations and specifically covering that region, includes 'persons who have fled their country because their lives, safety or freedom have been threatened by generalised violence, foreign aggression, internal conflicts, massive violation of human rights or other circumstances which have seriously disturbed public order'.[74]

The OAU and Cartagena definitions are much more inclusive and in keeping with specific events and occurrences in the regions concerned. My argument is that the Cartagena Declaration is the appropriate definition for refugees. Contemporary refugee movements originate primarily in developing regions such as Africa, Asia, Central and South America, Eastern Europe and the Middle East. This is in contrast to the period immediately after World War II when the key international instruments were formulated.

The 1951 Convention definition, with its focus on individuals and persecution, determines refugee status from an act of government against individuals, thereby excluding those fleeing from generalised conditions of violence, insecurity and oppression. It thus excludes countless people in Asia, Africa, South and Central America, Eastern Europe and the Middle East and the former Soviet Union, who cannot count on their governments to provide basic political, economic and physical security. The Convention definition does not recognise the situation where a government, or indeed a society, has ceased to exist; it refers only to the absence of state protection under predatory governments. It does not match current realities. As Shacknove says, neither persecution nor alienage captures all that is essential for refugees or about 'refugeehood'.[75]

As used here, the term 'refugee' refers to people who have been displaced, dispossessed of their home/land, because of violence or persecution, regardless of whether they have departed their country of origin or whether they are recognised as refugees by the government of their host country or by the UNHCR.

The UNHCR has formulated three categories of Populations of Concern: stateless persons, Convention refugees, and de facto refugees. A separate Convention concerning stateless persons was ratified in 1954 by those countries party to the 1951 Convention. 'A stateless person may, for example, be a victim of territorial re-alignment and not necessarily qualify under the "well founded fear of persecution" clause of the 1951 Convention.'[76] Examples are the residents of Uganda expelled by Idi Amin who had neither British nor Ugandan passports. Thus they were regarded as stateless persons but also qualified as 'refugees'.[77]

Under international law the second category, Convention refugees, have the right to seek asylum and a guarantee against forcible repatriation, 'non-refoulment'. However, the expulsion of aliens is equally a sovereign right of states. In practice, therefore, the rights of a Convention refugee only apply once she or he has been granted permanent asylum. Temporary asylum does not usually entitle a refugee to the full economic and social benefits embodied in the main provision of the 1951 Convention. These are:

(i) Treatment as accorded to nationals of the Contracting State;
(ii) Treatment as accorded to nationals of the state of habitual residence of the refugee;
(iii) The most favourable treatment accorded to nationals of a foreign country;
(iv) Treatment as favourable as possible and in any event not less favourable than that accorded generally to aliens in the same circumstances.[78]

For Convention (or *de jure*) refugees, when asylum has been granted, the Convention rules that: travel documents will be issued; the individual may move within and outside the country and earn a living wage, or if necessary receive welfare payments as deemed eligible by the state; and education must be provided for the individual and any children, along with access to counselling services and language instruction. After a certain period, the Convention refugee and his or her children are eligible to apply for citizenship. The Convention includes access to the legal system and, when outside the country of asylum, the individual must be treated as a national of the host country.[79]

De facto refugees differ from Convention refugees by reason of not having crossed a national border, or are rejected as being eligible for Convention status by the host country in which they reside. Although these individuals or groups are not eligible for Convention status, it is considered that they cannot be returned to their country of origin because of political disturbances there.[80] De facto refugees include those who still have their passports, also known as 'crypto-refugees'. Examples are foreign students unwilling to return to their native country for fear of political persecution, such as the Chinese students in Australia after the 1989 Tiananmen Square uprising.

Exiles are included in the de facto category, but their status becomes apparent only when they need to renew a passport or work visa or when they are recalled to their country of origin. Many de facto refugees fear that an application for Convention will affect the safety of relatives in the country of origin, or they may fear future discrimination because of refugee classification or, if the application is unsuccessful, added retribution on return to the country of origin. The de facto refugee group explicitly excludes, by international consensus, illegal migrants and migrant workers in search of better living standards. However, the increasing populace of migrant workers from less-developed countries residing in affluent countries often constitutes another anomalous crypto-refugee group.

De facto refugees suffer specific legal and social disabilities compared to Convention refugees, depending on the laws and procedures of the host country. For example, restrictions on employment and access to benefits such as language classes or vocational training are often critical in obtaining employment and entering courses at secondary and higher levels of education. A scholarship may require a recommendation from the country of origin, which is usually not forthcoming.

Most pertinently, de facto refugees are not always fully protected from 'refoulment'. The major benefit in certain countries in being a Convention, rather than a de facto, refugee is protection under the non-repatriation clause. Usually Convention status that is conferred after asylum has been sought takes considerable time. Refugees who are eligible for Convention status but are waiting for that status to be granted can be forcibly repatriated.[81]

Thus there is a discrepancy between the theory and practice of international rulings on refugees. Theoretically, any individual who fulfils the criteria of the Convention is recognised as a refugee, but in practice the individual can only benefit from that status once it has been recognised by the potential country of asylum. This anomaly produces the 'transit refugee' or 'refugee in orbit': the individual presenting at a point of entry is refused admission, detained or returned to the point of exit (which may or may not be the country of origin), where, once again, entry is refused and the individual is shuttled away (Chapter 5).

Given these discrepancies, Convention refugees clearly have the easiest passage towards settlement and regaining a life and identity. Although international instrumentalities have a major role in the determination process, and in creating agreed standards for the protection and treatment of refugees, both in law and in practice, it is ultimately the sovereign nation-state that determines who is a refugee. The 1951 Convention and 1967 Protocol have been signed by 134 states including the major Western powers, Japan, China, South Korea and Cambodia. Countries from the Indian subcontinent and the Association of South-East Asian Nations, for example, have not yet signed.[82]

This leaves a shady area in which asylum-seekers and displaced persons are at the mercy of the receiving country, its national asylum law, and the practices by which it determines who fits. Such determinations are affected by political factors, including domestic public opinion regarding 'foreigners'.[83] UNHCR instrumentalities can service these categories only under extenuating circumstances, and although the UNHCR has included them as persons who are of concern,[84] they are still vulnerable and at the mercy of receiving states.

## Mass Movement Towards . . .?

Migration on an international scale is not specific to the late twentieth century, or even to modernity in its double guise of capitalism and colonisation. Migratory patterns have been part of human history from the earliest times, but the twentieth century was 'the age of the refugee, the displaced person, mass immigration'.[85] International migration has grown in significance and volume since 1945, especially since the mid-1980s. In the early twenty-first century, rising migration will remain one of the most important factors in global change.

Castles and Miller give several reasons for on mass movement and migration in general. Political, demographic and ecological pressures impel people to seek refuge in other countries. Ethnic and national conflict, as in the former Yugoslavia, former Soviet Union, Palestine, Cambodia and Rwanda, is increasing due to factors such as the end of the Cold War and the movement of people moving in search of better living standards. The creation of new free trade areas produces movements of labour, in this case as migrants rather than refugees.[86]

Whatever the reasons for uprooting, those involved share some experiences as they attempt to re-establish themselves in strange places among people who regard them as intruders. It is the refugee who is likely to feel the extremes of alienation, especially those refugees caught in the limbo of camp or detention life,[87] where everything is seen as temporary and unrelated to both past and future, a state of non-identity.

People who leave their home and country, for whatever reason, feel the tragedy of uprooting and the loss of identity, home and community. States around the world are increasingly affected by international movements and migration of people, either as receiving states or as societies of emigration or both. Refugees and migrants alike run the risk of being rejected, left in the 'perilous territory of not-belonging where in the modern era, immense aggregates of humanity loiter as refugees and displaced people'.[88]

International migration is part of a transnational revolution that is reshaping politics and societies around the world.[89] Immigration in the twentieth century took the form of mass movements of people to states such as Australia, Argentina, Canada, New Zealand and the United States. The populations of these nations consist predominantly of British and European immigrants and their descendants who have, generally, displaced the indigenous populations of their land.

In the 1980s and 1990s Australia, New Zealand and the United States experienced immigration from new source countries, especially from Asia. Large-scale migration occurred in this period in most areas of the world, with Africa, Asia and the Middle East experiencing mass movements of people. In these areas colonisation and white settlement established migrant labour systems for development purposes. Since decolonisation, migrations of people in these areas have increased due to political unrest and ecological disasters. In Asia large-scale migrations are frequent; Iran and Pakistan house 2.6 million Afghan refugees, and India has received inflows of immigrants from Bangladesh, Nepal and Sri Lanka.[90]

Large-scale migration and high refugee numbers have resulted from the break-up of the former Soviet Union; outflows of refugees from Indochina have greatly affected Thailand, Malaysia, Hong Kong and Australia. Virtually all Latin American countries experience movements of refugees or migrant workers. Migrant and refugee flows are global, diverse and increasing.

Castles and Miller identify particular tendencies in migration movement around the world that are likely to play a major role in the first twenty years of the twenty-first century:

- *Globalisation:* There is a tendency for more countries to be affected by migratory movements at the same time. Further, the diversity of the countries and areas of origin are also increasing, so that most immigration countries having entrants from a broad spectrum of social, economic and cultural backgrounds.
- *Acceleration:* People are moving in greater numbers and from increasingly diverse geographical areas. This quantitative growth increases the urgency and the difficulties of government and international policy-making.
- *Feminisation:* Greater numbers of women are migrating in all regions and all types of migration. This is especially noticeable in labour migration, which traditionally has been male-dominated. Increasing numbers of women become refugees after their spouse or male relatives have been killed in wars.
- *Differentiation:* Most countries now experience more than one type of migration, including labour migration, refugee or permanent settlement, and internal displacement. Typically, migratory claims that start with one type of movement continue in other forms, despite (or because of) government efforts to stop or control the movement. As Castles and Miller point out, this differentiation presents a major obstacle to national and international policy.[91]

It is the last point, the differentiation of migration, that we focus on here, but all points have a bearing on the reasons and outcomes for displaced people and in particular the plight of the refugee. Governments now see international migration as a central political issue. Previously migrants were divided into categories such as permanent settlers, foreign workers and refugees, and dealt with by a variety of special agencies such as immigration departments, labour offices, welfare authorities, education departments and alien police. The increase in mass international movement of people began to receive high-level, systematic attention in the late 1980s. The European Union is an example, for its member states removed or loosened internal boundaries, they became increasingly concerned about strengthening external boundaries to prevent an influx from the south and east.[92]

Old distinctions between types of migration are losing their validity, for now a migratory chain that commenced with labourers might continue with family reunion or refugees. The early 1990s saw a backlash against the open and liberal movement of people that had taken place in the preceding decades. Extreme right-wing groups, such as the neo-fascists in Europe, perceived the new and rising immigration as a threat to national identity, national sovereignty and ethnic purity. This resulted in political violence and attacks on migrants, refugees and their property, with states such as Germany and Britain struggling to find satisfactory solutions.[93]

During the mid-1980s authorities realised that mass immigration was escalating and the character of the migrants and the method of movement were changing. In 1985 the Schengen Agreement between Germany, France and the Benelux countries instigated a series of conferences and treaties between Western European countries, culminating in the Maastricht Treaty in 1993, all of which were designed to improve controls on migration. Changes were also occurring in the United States, Canada and Australia where, as in Western Europe, government commissions of inquiry were set up and new legislation was enacted.[94] Migration and especially asylum-seekers were perceived as a 'problem'.

In 1991 the leaders of the seven major industrial democracies, the G7 Group, declared that '[International] migration has made and can make a valuable contribution to economic and social development and that . . . there is a growing concern about worldwide migratory pressures, which are due to a variety of political, social and economic factors'.[95]

This declaration was a watershed; international migration was recognised as a major determinant of global politics against the backdrop of the massive changes associated with the end of the Cold War and 'groping efforts' to inaugurate the so-called New World Order, or, as Castles and Miller designate it, 'Disorder'.[96]

International migration in all its forms is now an integral part of world development. Along with the increasing pressures for global integration in the guise of globalisation and global capitalism, migration is increasing in the categories of business, labour migration and economic refugees. These pressures are mainly economic as the processes of globalisation and transnational companies compete on the open world market. However, in many areas, as we have seen in the last decade, specific groups are going against this trend in the guise of nationalism with the formation of new states from the break-up of larger states, such as Yugoslavia and the Soviet Union. It seems unlikely that international and national governmental measures will significantly reduce migration. At best they can hope to regulate movements and ensure that these take place under humane conditions, without resorting to practices such as detention.

Increasing migratory movements and ethnic diversity will require significant changes in central political institutions such as citizenship, as well as affecting the very nature of the nation-state. Already this can be seen in parts of Western Europe and Asia, and will intensify if mass migration continues on its present scale. As Castles and Miller point out, one of the most pressing challenges for highly developed countries today is finding ways of coping with and processing 'unwanted' migratory flows.[97]

> The blanket term 'unwanted migration' embraces:
> - illegal border-crossers, boat people
> - legal entrants who overstay their entry visas or who work without permission
> - family members of migrant workers, prevented from entry legally by restrictions on family reunion
> - asylum-seekers not regarded as genuine refugees.[98]

Western European countries have had an enormous increase in unwanted immigrants in the last two decades; Australia, Canada, the United States, and regions in Asia and Africa are also affected. These people are not as 'unwanted' as it first appears; many supply cheap labour, as in the United States.[99] Unwanted immigration is often at the forefront of public fears of mass movements and refugee influxes, and therefore acts as a catalyst for racism and extreme right agitation by groups such as the Front National in France and One Nation in Australia. Governments see that they must halt unwanted immigration in order to safeguard social peace and maintain social harmony in an era of economic hardship and high unemployment. Attitudes have hardened, as shown in the rise of 'Fortress Europe' and the hostility to immigration and Asians in Australia. In Western Europe, the response has been a series of agreements designed to secure international co-operation in stopping illegal entries, and to expedite the processing of applications for asylum.[1]

However, as the European experience has shown, such agreements are hard to introduce and even harder to implement; some agreements have still not been ratified by member governments years after the initial signing. Australia, Canada and the United States have taken measures to improve border control and to speed up refugee determination, but this has not prevented a steady increase in the number of entrants who do not fit into official quotas, such as boat people (Chapters 4, 5).[2] It is not difficult to understand why contemporary control measures are problematic. They work against the powerful forces that are leading towards greater economic and cultural interchange. In an increasingly international economy, borders are open for movement of information, commodities and capital, but closed to people. Global circulation of investment and knowledge creates movement of people and this has been increasingly obvious with business migration. However, borders are not so fluid when migration is not connected to economics or business, and the 'right to seek asylum, one of civilisation's oldest and most honoured principles, is under threat almost everywhere'.[3]

A range of factors complicate the implementation of migration policy, such as the difficulty of adjudicating asylum claims and distinguishing economically motivated migrants from those deserving of refugee status, and the inadequacies or insufficiencies of immigration law. Employers are eager to hire foreign workers for manual and low-paying jobs when nationals are unwilling to take such positions. However, despite the apparent desire of Western governments to stop illegal migration, many of the causes are to be found in the political and social structures of the receiving countries and their relationship to the countries of the developing world. Until the root causes of mass movements are alleviated, there will always be displaced persons and refugees.

## Conclusion

We have examined the historic development of refugee movement and migration and analysed the definition of refugees. The question 'who are refugees?' has enormous implications for the refugee and displaced person. The answer determines the amount of support and protection they receive, as well as the long-term resolution of their plight. The UN definition, set out in the 1951 Convention and the 1967 Protocol, does not cover all refugees in contemporary times and situations. A redefinition of the refugee along the lines of the Cartagena Declaration would be more inclusive, allowing persons who are internally displaced to claim refugee status.

The refugee has been represented as the 'significant other' throughout history but, as shown in this chapter, this has been more pronounced since the advent of the nation-state and legalised boundaries. Displaced persons and refugees are the 'other' in the realm of national politics; they represent all that is foreign, strange and alien. This discourse assumes that refugees present a problem: 'they are not ordinary people, but represent, rather, an anomaly requiring specialised correctives and therapeutic interventions'.[4] Refugees are suspects in their new lands, perceived as amoral criminals or even terrorists. This politics of fear separates refugees from citizens.

# 3
# Australian Immigration and Its 'Other'

*For those who've come across the seas*
*We've boundless plains to share.*

'Advance Australia Fair'[1]

Australia is a nation of immigrants, all having come from somewhere else, the Indigenous peoples arriving over forty thousand years ago and European settlers just over two hundred years ago. The majority of the first white European settlers were criminals, evicted from their homeland by a regime that banished its unwanted, a type of refugee in forced exile from their homeland. In comparison, the majority of contemporary refugees are law-abiding citizens forced to flee their country of origin. The settlers of two hundred years ago were boat people, having traversed the oceans under harsh conditions. Many migrants since have made similar journeys, although under more hospitable conditions. However, the boat people from Indochina in the latter part of the twentieth century faced conditions that paralleled the journeys of the early settlers, journeys that involved hardship with lack of food and water, in wooden boats with few resources.

The history of Australian immigration policy highlights its role in the construction of the nation's 'significant other'. The fear of strangers has shaped immigration policy. Although economic factors contribute to this fear, cultural factors and political identity are at its core.

Australia is an isolated island surrounded by diverse cultures and peoples who, Australians are convinced, have their eyes on the boundless plains. This has manifested in a fear of 'hordes' invading Australia's northern shores and, for certain groups, the 'boundless plains' are not available to all 'who've come across the seas' to share.[2] Asians have been, and still are, targeted as the 'other' and excluded. In the late nineteenth century Chinese labourers were targeted as a group. Reaction against them culminated in legislation that enshrined the White Australia policy. Thus, the beginnings of Australian immigration policy were explicitly racist in the exclusion of Chinese foreigners.

White Australia had, as a basic tenet, a British society; initially it imported British migrants and then accepted Northern Europeans, expanding to all Europeans after 1945. Non-Europeans were discriminated against until the 1970s, when small numbers of refugees, primarily boat people, were accepted after the Vietnam War. After the demise of the White Australia policy in 1973, Asians were included as part of the immigration program. Asian immigrants have not been readily accepted by all Australians. The perceived threat of the Asianisation of Australia came to public debate first in 1984, and again in 1996, with attitudes and rhetoric that exemplified the underlying tension of white Australia and its 'other' (Chapter 6).

## White Settler Immigration and Exclusion

Settler Australia had its origins in a penal system; remnants of the penal attitude can still be seen in exclusionary politics such as the White Australia and the detention policies. White settler immigration began in 1788 with the transportation of convicts from Britain, lasting until 1852 in eastern Australia and 1868 in Western Australia. During this period 180 000 convicts, mainly of English and Irish descent, were sent to Australia. Free settlers first arrived in New South Wales in 1793, Western Australia in 1829 and South Australia in 1836. British subjects were part of a scheme of assisted passage, which, between 1831 and 1982, became the most important single incentive scheme for attracting immigrants to Australia. Only rarely were assisted passages extended to non-British persons, signifying a policy of preference for Anglo-Saxon and Celtic.[3] Thus initial immigration policy focused on assisted passage schemes for British, predominantly English, immigrants. Free or part-paid passages and free land were offered between 1905 and 1914 to British migrants. Empire still played a significant role in British politics after World War I, and between 1921 and 1930 the Empire Settlement Scheme sought to settle or redistribute the white population of the British Empire. Australia was a major participant in the scheme, and two-thirds of the 300 000 migrants settling in Australia in the 1920s were assisted. The first recorded refugees were Germans who had left their homeland to escape religious persecution by King Frederick William of Prussia, settling in South Australia in 1838.[4]

In 1848 the first arrival of significant numbers of Asians occurred when Chinese 'coolies' arrived in Australia, as indentured labour and freely, to work on the Victorian goldfields. By 1861 the population of Chinese had grown to 55 000 residing in Chinese quarters on the New South Wales, Victorian and Queensland goldfields. The Chinese and European migrants remained separate and antagonism grew between them, resulting in riots between 1857 and 1877.[5]

These riots were racially motivated in an atmosphere of extreme economic competition and racial hostility. By 1857 negative views of Chinese civilisation were widespread throughout the eastern states. Apprehension of an imminent and enormous influx of Chinese grew, characterised as the 'swamping' of the 'handful' of white people by swarming Asians and 'the hordes from the north'. The growing numbers of Chinese migrants prompted both cultural and economic insecurity among the British and their Australian-born descendants. During this era the white colonists, desiring to keep Chinese immigration in check, came to believe that the only feasible policy was one of exclusion.[6]

Between 1891 and 1901 the White Australia policy was developed. The initial focus was on culling Chinese immigration, later expanded to include immigrants from all 'peoples whose presence was, in the opinion of Australians, injurious to the general welfare'. Immigrants from India and Japan who had begun to arrive in the Australian colonies during this time, and the Melanesians or Kanakas who were used as cheap labour in Queensland,[7] were included in the new category.

## A White Australia

The White Australia policy had its basis in the *Commonwealth of Australia Constitution Act 1900*, passed by the Parliament of the United Kingdom in July 1900, which came into force on 1 January 1901. Under the terms of this Act:

> the powers of the Commonwealth parliament included the power to make laws for the peace, order, and good government of the Commonwealth with respect to naturalisation and aliens; the people of any race, other than the aboriginal race in any state, for whom it was deemed necessary to make special laws; emigration; and the relations of the Commonwealth with the islands of the Pacific.[8]

Thus the new Commonwealth Parliament could pass laws to ensure that, with few exceptions, non-whites would not be permitted to settle, work, or live (temporarily or permanently) in Australia. 'White Australia' became the catchphrase in immigration. During its first year, the government passed the *Immigration Restriction Act 1901,* which embodied the White Australia principle.[9] This policy justified institutional racism in Australia. The *Bulletin,* aligned to federation Australian nationalism, justified the policy in 1901, claiming:

> It is impossible to have a large coloured alien population in the midst of a white population without a half-caste population growing up between the two. India proves that; would prove it much more conclusively only the white population isn't large enough to be a very extensive parent to the Eurasian mongrel . . . and Australia thinks highly enough of its British and Irish descent to keep the race pure.[10]

As one of the first acts of the new Commonwealth government, the White Australia policy instilled the racist tone of immigration policy. Any non-Europeans already in Australia, or able to obtain entry via 'certificates of exemption' allowing temporary stays in Australia, were denied naturalisation and the right to vote. Thus, excluded from social welfare, they were denied access to old age and invalid pensions and the maternity bonus.[11] Historian Keith Hancock argues that every national policy choice in Australia was conditional, either consciously or unconsciously, upon the relationship with the White Australia policy or the maintenance of a white, preferably British, society. He identified it as the 'indispensable condition of every other Australian policy',[12] with obvious consequences for the Australian identity founded on a white British 'self' juxtaposed against its Asian 'other'.

During the next fifty years the *Immigration Restriction Act* was amended on a number of occasions (in 1905, 1910, 1912, 1920, 1935, 1940 and 1949), mainly to incorporate concessions relating to specific events and to strengthen its provisions in relation to illegal entry. From 1901, Asian or 'coloured' immigration was controlled by certificates of exemption that allowed specific categories of non-Europeans to enter Australia, while also giving the minister powers to cancel that exemption at any time. This certificate applied to merchants and students and was primarily directed at excluding Chinese people who were the least favoured of the Asian peoples.[13] At the same time, it could be applied to any other 'coloureds'.

The collective national desire to remain British in political principles and institutions, and more importantly to remain white, was the underlying ideology of the White Australia policy. Critics of the policy asked whether many non-Europeans would choose to settle in Australia, implying that only a small number would want to and, in practical terms, could afford to.[14]

By the 1930s refugee intakes and their inclusion in immigration policy became an issue, with the arrival of several thousand Jewish refugees fleeing from Nazi domination of their homelands. This was a significant development in migration and foreshadowed the post-war refugee intakes. Australia had agreed to accept 15 000 Jewish refugees at the 1938 Evian Conference but the outbreak of war intervened and only 7500 of the refugees arrived. Other Europeans persecuted in Germany arrived as refugees and more than 2000 German 'aliens' were transported to Australia in 1940, adding to the diversity of European settlers in Australia. Jewish refugees suffered prejudice during the late 1930s and the war years, and were given the derogatory label 'reffos'. The Jewish refugees were explicitly 'not British' and this appears to be the basis of the prejudice against them, rather than pure anti-Semitism. British migrants were still the largest group to be welcomed and accepted into Australia,[15] but this was soon to change.

From the 1920s it was considered that Australia had to increase its population. However, a polarity arose between pro-immigration groups, expansionists who favoured large-scale immigration, and anti-immigration groups who opposed all immigration.[16] There were arguments for filling Australia's wide open spaces with people, as a buffer against the teeming millions of Asia. Others, such as the trade unions, argued that a large immigration intake posed a threat to full employment and the standard of living.

These arguments highlighted the refugee as a new factor in Australian attitudes toward immigration. The acknowledgement and acceptance of refugees from European countries was a breakthrough in immigration policy. Conditions were imposed on the immigrants: they had to be of European descent, good health and character, and able to guarantee their maintenance in Australia. However, the introduction of non-British immigration was initially based on refugee intake. A reassessment of immigration policy took place during and after World War II, recognising that power relationships with the rest of the world had altered and that new skills were needed in Australia to facilitate economic expansion.

Immigration from Southern and Central Europe was necessary to increase the population and supply the numbers that Britain and the Scandinavian countries could not. The principle of public support was introduced by the Chifley Labor Government, showing a drastic change in attitudes of the trade unionists to immigration. Programs were established to persuade Australians that the 'aliens' would make good Australians—or, as they were called, 'New Australians.' Organisations such as the Commonwealth Immigration Advisory Council and government agencies were established to assist in planning for the assimilation of non-British immigrants.[17]

In 1945 Arthur Calwell was appointed the first Minister for Immigration in the Chifley Labor Government. On 2 August he announced a large-scale immigration program with the slogan of 'Populate or Perish'. Its objectives were to 'strengthen national security and economic development by increased population growth; meet post-war labour shortages; and fill the serious gaps in the age structure of the existing population'.[18]

Calwell stated, in November 1946, that 'it is my hope that for every foreign migrant there will be ten people from the United Kingdom'.[19] Thus he explicitly excluded the British from the category 'foreign', reinforcing the connection of the Australian national identity to Britain. Calwell strongly believed in racial exclusivity. His administration made no exceptions on entrance to aliens in the belief that exceptions would 'open the floodgates' to Asian immigration. He was the only Immigration Minister to voice his racism so blatantly. However, Calwell's hope that British immigrants would outnumber other immigrants by ten to one did not materialise: immigration from other sources continued to grow.[20]

In 1947 Australia entered into an agreement with the Preparatory Commission for the International Refugee Organisation to accept an annual quota of 12 000 displaced persons, with a provision to increase this number to 20 000 if the international body could transport the refugees to Australia. Migrants with skills had first priority, with preference given to Baltic persons and later Czech, Slavs and Poles. The Australian economy quickly absorbed these refugees and more displaced persons were provided with passage assistance. More than 170 000 refugees came to Australia under the Displaced Persons Scheme between 1947 and 1954.[21] They were not all Convention refugees, but most had a reasonable fear of persecution upon returning to their homelands.

Australia tapped a much broader geographical area to recruit migrants and refugees in the 1950s, including all European nations; there was even some limited recruitment in parts of the Middle East. Between 1952 and 1961, 70 000 refugees were accepted, including 30 000 Yugoslavs and Italians leaving Yugoslavia, 19 000 German and Dutch, 14 000 Hungarians after the 1956 Revolution, and 7000 White Russians from China.[22] There was a decline in immigration from Britain, although it continued to be the largest source of migrants. However, the main feature of the White Australia policy still operated: the non-European, the 'other', was not accepted.

After World War II, the United Nations 1951 Convention Relating to the Status of Refugees and the 1967 Protocol Relating to the Status of Refugees, which Australia signed, set the framework for Australian immigration and refugee policy. The arrival of displaced persons and refugees paved the way for community acceptance of increased numbers of Europeans as well as the traditional British migrants, although very few Asian or non-white migrants were accepted.

Asian students were admitted temporarily during the 1950s, numbering almost 5500 by 1958. By 1964 numbers had increased to 12 366, comprising 10 814 private students and 1552 sponsored under the Colombo Plan and other programs.[23] By this time Australia needed to counteract the continuing ill-feeling in Asia about the White Australia policy, and the Colombo Plan was seen by the External Affairs Minister, Percy Spender, as a means of building goodwill. Immigration Minister Downer (senior) pointed out in 1958 that the 'reconciliation between Australian foreign policy in Asia and the White Australia policy was relying very largely on the Colombo Plan'.[24] This plan provided some impetus for the abolition of the dictation test in 1958 and liberalisation of migration policy. However, A. Markus argues that a reading of confidential government records show that the Colombo Plan and reforms of 1956 were a half-hearted attempt to appease criticisms coming from Asia about the continuing exclusive immigration policy.[25]

During the 1960s new wars broke out, mainly in response to independence movements in the post-colonial thrust for national identity and the Cold War. Numbers of refugees soared throughout the world. Australia, in this period, was a receiving country of first rank for refugees. The nature of immigration policy had changed with the inclusion of Southern and Eastern Europeans, including 'reffos' and 'DPs' (displaced people). Australia was still of overwhelmingly British stock in 1945 but by 1971 one-eighth of the population was made up of those born overseas or of non-British origin.[26]

Immigration policy after World War II was guided by the 'one per cent rule' where immigrant intakes 'were targeted to increase Australia's population by one per cent, with "natural increase" contributing one per cent as well'.[27] This resulted in 70 000 immigrants per year, predominantly British. The settlement strategies, based on assimilation, proved ineffectual as most refugees were located in remote areas or former military camps and did not mix with native-born Australians.[28] Refugees during this period were bonded for two years as directed workers, many located in industrial areas such as Port Kembla and major industrial projects such as the Snowy Mountain Scheme, at times separated from family and living in camps. Strict discipline was maintained by the threat of deportation. Many refugees had experienced holding camps and detention centres in Europe and discovered conditions in Australia just as unbearable, having exchanged one form of forced labour for another.[29]

Calwell's immigration policy for receiving displaced persons from Europe proclaimed selection without discrimination of race or religion, but this was not the case in practice. Initially there was a ban on Jews, and eventually a hierarchical order of the various European ethnic and national groups was imposed. Baltic immigrants were the most popular; once their supply diminished, other groups such as Poles, Ukrainians, Slovenes, Czechs and Yugoslavs were admitted and by 1949 virtually all European refugees were regarded as acceptable.

Australia was accused of selective immigration because it took single, fit men before family units, elderly or disabled refugees. This high rate of single males produced isolation, loneliness, alcoholism and mental breakdown among an already vulnerable group.[30] Immigrants, including refugees, were seldom accepted as social equals by Australians, and experienced intense alienation during the immediate post-war period. Kovacs and Cropley conclude that Australians have never fully accepted immigrants into their society. They argue that attitudes toward immigrants have not changed since immigration began, despite the perceived toleration of immigration from the public and active encouragement by government agencies.[31] Chapter 7 considers their argument in the context of multiculturalism.

Calwell introduced the *Nationality and Citizenship Act 1948,* which recognised Australian citizenship as separate from the status of British subject. British subjects could become Australian citizens, if they wished, after one year of residence; non-British migrants had a five-year qualifying period and were required to 'renounce previous allegiances in public at naturalisation ceremonies. Non-Europeans could not become naturalised at all.'

The citizenship provisions were part of the assimilation policy that required migrants to jettison their language, customs and allegiances. As Lack and Templeton point out, this requirement appears insensitive and objectionable today but 'the challenge is to understand why it could be made so readily' during that time.[32] It was a social experiment in which ethnic groups would give over their traditional and inherited identities and adopt a new one. In hindsight, this was an unreasonable and unrealistic expectation.

In 1949 Good Neighbour Councils were established to assist immigrants and refugees to resettle. They emphasised white Anglo cultural norms and de-emphasised cultures of the non-British immigrants and refugees as part of the assimilation policy. In 1951 the National Advisory Committee was formed to act as a liaison between the Good Neighbour Council and the various national minorities among the refugees. Problems arose within the Good Neighbour Council. The new arrivals, predominantly, became industrial workers and looked to the trade unions and labour movements, whereas many of the organisers of the Good Neighbour movement were conservatives in sympathy with the Liberal and National (Country) parties with the goal of assimilation of the new arrivals. By the early 1970s Southern Europeans revolted against the paternalism and assimilation of the Good Neighbour movement. Commonwealth support was withdrawn from the Good Neighbour Councils in 1978, and charities assumed a major role in refugee settlement and advocacy issues. Refugee camps were closed, the last being Bonegilla in 1971, and refugees were processed through reception centres in the capital cities, thereby removing the last vestiges of post-war immigration strategies.[33]

## Dismantling the White Australia Policy

Australia was able to maintain a direct racialist control policy until the 1970s and still does indirectly today. Freeman and Jupp relate this change to the relative insignificance of Australia on the global stage. While White Australia had some embarrassing overtones, it caused few serious consequences for Australia.[34] The geographical isolation and the dominant trading patterns with Britain and the United States meant that the White Australia policy went virtually unnoticed until the progressive integration of the Australian economy into the Asian region started in the 1960s.

For seventy-two years the White Australia policy remained in force, finally being abolished by the Whitlam Labor government in 1973. The *Immigration Restriction Act* was replaced by the *Migration Act 1958* which left the policy unchanged apart from scrapping the dictation test as the method of exclusion. Ministerial discretion was substituted as the preferred strategy. Within Australia, politicians and the public accepted the White Australia policy almost universally. However, the policy was criticised outside Australia and by the late 1950s and early 1960s internal criticism began to appear. Initially, this criticism came from the Immigration Reform Group, the Association for Immigration Reform and Student Action. The Immigration Reform Group was formed in 1959 at the University of Melbourne, producing a set of recommendations for a more liberal immigration policy. It disclosed that there was a virtual prohibition of non-white immigration These groups became part of a successful movement for change late in the 1960s.[35]

In 1966 significant changes to the Restricted Immigration Policy set in motion the dismantling of the White Australian policy. New regulations were adopted under which non-European spouses, children and parents of Australian citizens were admitted to Australia, qualifying for naturalisation under the same conditions that applied to European immigrants. Policy on eligibility for naturalisation of non-Europeans who had resided in Australia for fifteen years and restrictions for family entrance became less severe. A new category of immigrant was incorporated into the policy, namely Distinguished and Highly Qualified Asians, thus providing an avenue for professionally qualified, English-speaking Asians who had been offered a job in Australia to obtain permanent settlement. Although this was a breakthrough for Asian immigration, it was explicitly selective. The Immigration Minister emphasised that, even though the number of Asians entering Australia would be 'somewhat greater than previously, [it] will be controlled by the careful assessment of the individual's qualifications, and the basic aim of preserving a homogenous population will be maintained'.[36]

The censuses of 1947 and 1966 show that migrants provided 73 per cent of the increase in Australia's total workforce during that period.[37] This highlights the success of post-war immigration achieved with the introduction of European, especially Southern European, migrants. They were important to the manufacturing industries, especially the motor industry in Melbourne and Adelaide. Increases in non-European immigrants followed when Australia expanded its economic and political links with Asia, making it increasingly difficult to bar Asians from settlement. Chinese nationals who obtained citizenship in 1966/67 numbered 1086, up from 325 in the previous financial year, and in 1971 1832 independent Chinese immigrants arrived.[38]

Against this background of a gradual easing of restrictions on the entry of Asians, especially refugees, into Australia, the Vietnam War played a prominent role. It became a benchmark in Australian foreign policy, with divisive and polarising effects on the Australian public's perceptions. The very large refugee movement produced by this war raised problems for Australian refugee policy, especially in relation to boat people.

While the incumbent Liberal–Country Party Coalition favoured Australian involvement in the war, the Labor Party eventually opposed Australia's military involvement in Vietnam. A new generation of left-wing students and academics protested against it 'with all the fervour of crusaders battling the greatest of moral evils'.[39] To the dismay of the activists, the general public supported the pro-Vietnam stance of the government. The average voter regarded the Vietnam War as a renewed threat of 'the hordes from the north', justifying the racist attitudes of the Australian public. However, by the early 1970s, after passionate demonstrations and the unfolding disaster and futility of the war were portrayed by the media, the anti-war message had reached a wider public.

The election of the Whitlam Labor Government in late 1972 set in motion a shift in immigration policy, based on commitment to the 'avoidance of discrimination on any grounds of race or colour of skin or nationality'.[40] Al Grassby, the Minister for Immigration, offered a new image of a 'united family of the nation'. Cultural pluralism became the ideology that underpinned national identity. This included the preservation of ethnic traditions and languages, and their perpetuation into an indefinite future. 'Multiculturalism' was a term for a policy that sought restitution for the wrongs that immigrants had suffered, and it also applied to diversity in cultural attributes such as films, food and customs. Multiculturalism began as a descriptive term for 'the demographic reality of an Australia made ethnically diverse by a broadening entrance policy, and a mere  acknowledgement of the peaceful co-existence of diverse ethnic cultures'.[41]

In practice multiculturalism also became a policy that delivered services to migrant constituencies in line with the new access and equity principles and programs. This dualism between multiculturalism as an ideology of society and multiculturalism as a principle of social policy explains how the label of multiculturalism could be maintained by such diverse governments as those of Whitlam, Fraser, Hawke and Keating.[42]

The Whitlam Labor Party's commitment to ethnic equality was accompanied by a policy that would markedly reduce immigration. With high unemployment, increasing population was not a priority any more, and Australia became more selective. Family reunion was the major criterion, with an explicit rejection of ethnic origin as a factor in selection. In line with the Labor Party's 1972 policy, discrimination between prospective migrants on any ground of race, colour or nationality was renounced with the passage of the *Racial Discrimination Act 1975*. However, this did not result in a sudden transformation in the ethnic make-up of the immigration intake; on the contrary, the new emphasis on family reunion helped preserve the status quo.[43]

Asian governments were reassured by the dismantling of the White Australia policy in 1973 and the introduction of immigration policies that were aimed at improving rather than exacerbating Australia's foreign relations in the Indo-Pacific region.[44] In Australia the ingrained attitudes of White Australia surfaced with the arrival of the Indochinese refugees. The latest refugees, mainly from Vietnam, were racially different and this rekindled the attitudes and language that fuelled the White Australian debate. The opening up to Asian immigrants coincided with the reduction of overall numbers. Immigration intakes fell from 170 000 in 1970/71 to 140 000 in 1972/73, continuing to fall to 50 000 with the Labor government in 1975.[45] The post-war target of increasing immigration at a rate of one per cent of population per annum was gone.

The Whitlam Labor Government eliminated race-based selection criteria for immigration and dismantled the White Australia policy, increasing the numbers of non-European immigrants; the Fraser Liberal–National Party Coalition Government that followed applied most of those non-discriminatory principles to refugee settlement. During its term in government the Labor Party cut back on immigration intakes; it was the Coalition that increased immigration quotas, especially refugee numbers, in response to the arrival of boat people from Asia.[46]

The 'Green Paper; Immigration Policies and Australia's Population' was tabled in Parliament on 17 March 1977, inviting an exploration of the complex issues of population and immigration. This paper became an important guide for policy-making; its aim was to inform public opinion and create policies in accord with the times.[47] In a policy statement of 24 May 1977, Immigration Minister MacKellar clarified that 'Australia fully recognises its humanitarian commitment and responsibility to admit refugees for resettlement', and agreed to help with the resettlement of refugees in other countries.[48] The government produced a refugee policy of controlled intake, highlighting to prospective boat people that it was not an open-door policy but one of controlled entrance. In effect, it was a deterrence policy, but it was also based on humanitarian concerns.

The refugee policy took account of Australia's international legal obligation as a signatory to the UNHCR Convention and Protocol. The Coalition recognised the development of Australia as a mature society with an obligation to provide sanctuary for asylum-seekers. It realised that the domestic situation and absorptive capacity must be taken into account for a refugee policy to be successful and acceptable to the Australian public.[49] MacKellar affirmed the government's refugee policy and the underpinning four principles as:

- Australia fully recognises its humanitarian commitment and responsibility to play its part with the rest of the world in the resettlement of refugees.
- The decision to admit refugees must always remain with the government of Australia.
- Special assistance will often need to be provided for the movement of refugees in designated situations or for their resettlement in Australia.
- It may not be in the interests of some refugees to settle in Australia. Their interests may be better served by resettlement in countries elsewhere. [50]

This instituted a clear distinction between immigration policy and refugee policy, with the distinguishing feature being 'human need'. The statement recognised that immigration policy was 'pragmatic and self-interested' with the principal motivation of the 'economic, social and cultural enrichment of a society and its people both home-born and migrants'. In contrast the motivation for a refugee policy 'is a response to situations of human misery by providing refuge, security, freedom and hope . . . recognising that a refugee policy presents the challenge of accepting people who will have problems and involve costs'.[51]

By late 1977 the focus had switched from the number of refugees to be brought to Australia to the constant stream of arrivals on Australia's northern coastline. One response to this was to increase the number of official settlers from the overcrowded refugee camps in Asia, especially in Malaysia, which were the main departure points for boats en route to Australia.[52] Despite such measures, critics were still warning of the 'invasion' from the north and estimating the cost of deploying the navy to control the northern coastline to apprehend boat people. Headlines reflected the emerging unease within the community about the increasing numbers of Asian refugees and boat people, predicting 'floods' and 'invasions'. For example the *Courier Mail*, 29 November 1977, fuelled the racist debate with the headline 'It's the Yellow Peril Again'.[53]

Although immigration policy had bipartisan support during the 1970s, fractures began to occur in the early 1980s when the admission of non-Europeans became policy.[54] This surfaced publicly with the Great Immigration or Blainey Debate of 1984. Geoffrey Blainey was, and still is, opposed to a large intake of Asian immigrants, perceiving it as contributing to the 'Asianisation' of Australia.

In 1978 MacKellar had visited refugee camps in Thailand, Malaysia and other parts of Asia. He saw that refugees had not left their homeland purely for economic reasons, as was being asserted in some quarters in Australia. He found most refugees were desperate to return to their homes if safety and conditions permitted. This visit affirmed MacKellar's commitment to Indochinese refugees, and his influence on refugee policy was significant. This personalisation of refugee policy by the implementation of ministerial discretion surfaced over the next decades and is examined in detail in the next chapter.

The arrival of boat people presented a dilemma for the Fraser Government. The initial arrivals in 1976 were given permanent status, but after March 1978, when the Government established the Determination of Refugee Status Committee, boat people were granted refugee status (Chapter 4). This procedure was devised to assure applicants of the protection of and adherence to the UN Convention on Refugees. However, it was also intended 'more for domestic consumption following widespread allegations at the peak of the boat flow in 1977 that many of the boat people were not "genuine refugees"'.[55]

With the arrival of independent refugee boats to the northern coast, emphasis shifted from stigma and symbolism back to harder realities 'and a new formulation of the old defence argument acquired some currency'.[56] The argument diverged from defending Australia and repelling 'the hordes' and invoked 'morality' arguments, with claims that a generous migration policy signalled Australian commitment to a sharing and altruistic policy.

Jerzy Zubrzycki states that this argument is based on the notion that 'morality could serve as a form of defence, disarming hostility by correct behaviour, but, if Australians were "selfish", others would come and force them to share their country anyway'.[57]

Katherine Betts contends that in the late 1970s and early 1980s refugee lobby groups fostered this altruistic concept of the immigration program. It was not the view of the politicians and officials responsible for immigration at the time, who supported the economic rationale. Betts argues that immigration, in this altruistic mode, 'was to be a means, not of meeting Australia's own needs for defence or economic growth, but of expressing humanitarian, internationalist and anti-racist values and, in so doing, meeting other people's needs'.[58] On the contrary, these values were becoming 'our needs' and part of the formation of the Australian identity, with this cosmopolitan definition for immigration matching multicultural settlement policies and sentiments. Later we will see that this marked a turning point for Australian identity, breaking with the past British-oriented establishment, which was 'tainted with British colonialism, racist immigration policies, and the Vietnam war'.[59]

In the 1980s a refocusing on economic factors and a push to establish links with Asia influenced immigration and refugee policy. Trading ties were strengthened with the fast-growing economies of the Asian and Pacific Rim countries, and the accompanying rhetoric espoused the need to forge stronger links with the rich rather than a moral obligation to share with the poor. This 'new talk' came from the economic rationalists who were re-establishing an economic focus for immigration and refugee programs.[60] The Labor Governments of Hawke and Keating reduced immigration numbers, but they maintained and at times increased humanitarian and family reunion intakes of both refugees and immigrants.

Major changes occurred in the early 1980s, first in attitudes towards refugees fleeing Indochina, and then in policies instigated by a new Minister for Immigration and Ethnic Affairs, Ian Macphee. The blanket recognition of refugee status given to those fleeing Indochina was reviewed and refugees were strictly scrutinised. Those who failed to fit the UN Convention and Protocol definition were refused refugee status. A clear distinction between political and economic refugees was made, following the example set by the United States.[61] A reassessment of refugee policy was part of a general review of migration, which widened of family reunion and emphasised skilled migration; this narrowed migration of unskilled workers without family links in Australia.

Macphee explained to the House of Representatives on 16 March 1982 that the criteria for refugee entry would be tightened significantly by applying the criteria of the UN Convention on an individual basis rather than relying on the group mandate status accorded by the UNHCR previously. This policy was instigated to deter those leaving Indochina for economic reasons; the result was a fall in Indochinese refugee entry in 1982 of nearly one-third compared to the previous three years. As Nancy Viviani contends, Australia's refugee entry policy had come full circle from the restrictive entry of the 1975–77 period, through the cautious but expansionist period of 1978–81, to the tightening of refugee entry criteria of 1982.[62]

The admission of 170 000 Indochinese refugees had signalled the demise of the White Australia policy and the 'Vietnamese boat people, by their unorthodox direct arrival in Australia, appeared to challenge many fundamental tenets of Australia's migration, quarantine, customs and even defence policy'.[63] The initial fears of an 'invasion' from the north dissipated as fewer than 2500 Vietnamese and Cambodians arrived by boat from 1976 until 1991. This was only 1.58 per cent of Vietnamese and Cambodian migrants who had arrived in Australia, indicating that the media and public attention the boat arrivals generated was far out of proportion to the actual number of arrivals.[64]

Viviani contends that, apart from the adverse media attention and the resultant misconceptions of the public, refugee policy between 1978 and 1982 was, for the most part, a success. This was an improvement on the period between 1975 and 1977, when neither the Labor Party nor the Coalition had successfully dealt with the problem of boat arrivals. The latter period was one of successful control and resettlement policy, maintaining stable international relations and diffusing internal fears and debates. This was largely a consequence of the work of MacKellar and Macphee who established a 'consensus of elite opinion favourable to refugee entry, one that would offset the political effects of a divided community opinion'.[65]

This consensus relied on bipartisan support, with credit given to Bill Hayden as Opposition Leader and the Labor Party as well as the Government, who managed to confine debate to strict agendas instead of fuelling the racist fears. Both had realised that it was not a party issue and had great consequences for Australia, both nationally and internationally, which significantly assisted positive policy-making. Viviani perceived the Vietnamese refugee entry as the first real test of the dismantling of the White Australia policy, 'and a test successfully passed'.[66]

The Global Special Humanitarian Program, established in 1981, provided flexibility in Australia's humanitarian response to refugee and refugee-like situations, enabling Australia to operate outside its restrictive migration program. The program made provision for Australia to accept people who hold a fear of gross discrimination amounting to substantial violation of their human rights but not persecution.[67] Australia could now respond positively to those not classified as refugees under the 1951 Convention but nonetheless in need of resettlement opportunities.

Immigration policies of the Hawke Labor Government, which came to power in March 1983, differed considerably from those of the Coalition. The main difference became apparent with the Labor Party's commitment to the Refugee and Special Humanitarian Program and emphasis on family reunion as opposed to economic immigration. Immigration levels fell in the first two years of the Hawke Government, but the Refugee and Special Humanitarian categories remained relatively stable.[68] Australia's settlement policies under both Coalition and Labor Governments in the late 1970s and early 1980s had considerable success, and compare favourably with those of many other countries, especially Canada.

Immigration policy during the Hawke era was as controversial as it had been under Whitlam and Fraser. Faultlines opened between the economic and social aims of immigration, due to factors such as economic rationalism, increasing ethnic diversity, the influence of ethnic lobby groups, and diverging views of economists. The economic focus, which highlighted skills-based intakes, challenged the humanitarian and family reunion focus. This was exacerbated by a failing Australian economy in the late 1980s and early 1990s.

Immigration policy oscillated under Hawke's leadership. He allowed ministers responsible for immigration free rein in policy formulation, so the debates were renewed with each ministerial appointment.[69] Fluctuations in intakes were a regular feature under Hawke, mirroring controversies over immigration. In 1985 the Government altered the policy of using immigration for population expansion, a radical break with the directions of its first two years. In a statement to Parliament, Immigration Minister Chris Hurford explained the serious problems facing Australia because of low fertility rates and an ageing population.

> Immigration must now be seen in the context of Australia's population and economic development needs . . . with a vision for the future of a managed, gradual expansion of the immigration programme . . . immigration had contributed to economic growth and development and, in the short term, does not adversely affect

the employment prospects of the Australian resident population
. . . an understanding must be that immigrants carefully selected
create more jobs than they take.[70]

A new Independent and Concessional Category of immigrants was
created to attract a wider range of people with the potential to contribute
to Australia's economic and social needs. In a politically damaging
budget in 1986, the Government cut immigrant services, upsetting
ethnic lobby groups. Mick Young replaced Hurford in early 1987, and
proceeded to establish the Committee to Advise on Australia's Immigration Policies, which became known as the Fitzgerald Review. Its
report, released in June 1988, stated that the public saw multiculturalism as driving immigration policy, and that community attitudes to
immigration 'reflect confusion, anxiety, criticism and scepticism . . . and
that public support in some quarters is faltering and community consensus in favour of immigration is at risk'.[71]

Multiculturalism, with the original ideals of justice, equality and
esteem, became obscured by a multiplicity of meanings, rendering the
term a liability. The Fitzgerald Report exposed a polarity: one side, seen
to be inhumane, advocated immigration purely on economic grounds;
the other was seen as foolishly charitable. The report recommended a
'middle-ground' approach, stressing the compatibility of the three objectives of immigration policy: 'economic, humanitarian and compassionate
as expressed in the three components: general immigration, refugee intake and family reunion' with a convincing economic rationale.

The report aroused controversy, particularly from conservative sections of the community who used the critique of multiculturalism to
extend the Blainey Immigration Debate of 1984. John Howard, Leader
of the Opposition, seized the report as 'a stick with which to beat the
Hawke Government', publicly supporting its critique of multiculturalism. Howard introduced the 'One Australia' paper, which proposed a
decrease in Asian migration in the interests of 'social cohesion'.[72]

Robert Ray, as Immigration Minister, responded to the Fitzgerald
Report, rejecting the committee's proposal for a single open category.
This category placed restrictions on the extended family immigrants at
the expense of increasing 'young, skilled, entrepreneurial' migrants, a
shift from Labor's focus on family reunion. In 1989 Ray introduced
important legislative reform, relieving the Immigration Minister of

ministerial discretion, a move regarded by some experts as the most significant change in immigration administration since 1945. This clarified, in written form, who could or could not come to Australia 'rather than allowing it to be subject to a large degree of arbitrariness'.[73]

Ray also reformed the systems of review to reduce applicants, appeals to the court system, and introduced mechanisms for ensuring that targets were not exceeded. A two-tier review system was introduced: the first tier was a separate, independent Migration Internal Review Office within the Department of Immigration, Local Government and Ethnic Affairs; the second was the Immigration Review Tribunal, an independent statutory authority. Although this was a fairer system, including representatives from independent and non-government sources, decisions still remained at the discretion of the government and the incumbent Immigration Minister, a point discussed in the next chapter.[74]

Immigration intake was cut by 25 per cent in a response to an economic recession in the early 1990s. Consultative meetings were held with industry, state governments, unions and ethnic lobby groups before the 1992 decision on the intake, but the recession created irresistible pressure for reducing numbers. Numbers dropped from 123 500 in 1990/91 to a projected 80 000 in 1992/93, with a change to the points system to focus on skills and occupations in demand.[75] Labor was compelled by its constituency and its opponents to act accordingly.

Immigration policy during the late 1980s and early 1990s was controversial. Hawke's decision to allow Chinese students already in Australia at the time of the Tiananmen Square massacre of June 1989 to stay provoked criticism from other ethnic groups about the special treatment. This highlighted inconsistencies in refugee policy, especially in regard to the several hundred Cambodian boat people who arrived in 1989–91. Hawke condemned the boat people, as he had done in 1977, as queue-jumpers and economic refugees.[76] He declared: 'let no one think that we're just going to stand idly by and allow others, by their autonomous action which reflects perhaps some unhappiness with the circumstances in which they find themselves in their own country . . . to determine our immigration policy'.[77]

The Government, particularly Immigration Minister Gerry Hand, was adamant that boat people would not breach policy, and if 'these people turned up they would stay confined until they were assessed'.[78] This highly reactionary stance reflects the underlying fear of 'the hordes from the north', with boat people as the vanguard of an Asian invasion. Minister Hand appeared uncompromising and heartless, which provoked protests from the incarcerated boat people, their lawyers, supporters and human rights activists.

The Global Special Humanitarian Program, instituted in 1981 and the dominant element in determining humanitarian intake, was replaced by the Special Assistance Program in 1992. The new category recognised that only a minority of displaced persons could be categorised within the Convention and Protocol definition. In 1989 the UNHCR argued that most refugees in developing countries did not fall within the Convention category but belonged to 'a wider category of persons who had left their countries because of danger to their lives and security emanating from armed conflicts or other grave forms of violence and danger'.[79]

As discussed in the previous chapter, national governments decide who enters their country and Australia, like most countries, opted to stick with the UN Convention definition for refugee determination. Australia allowed a small number of entrants under the Special Humanitarian and Special Assistance Programs, who were eligible for all the services available to permanent settlers. This Special Assistance Program, according to the Minister, allowed Australia

> flexibility in helping people who had a special need to resettle here, but who do not fit the United Nations definition of a refugee. The category may, for example, be used to assist individuals or groups who are suffering severe distress and/or displacement within their own countries . . . the Special Assistance category is designed to allow us to reach people who are in situations of real need but who do not fit neatly into our traditional programs.[80]

Most of the initial 4000 places were allocated to ethnic minorities from the former Soviet Union, former Yugoslavia, East Timor and Lebanon; few were given to displaced persons from Indochina. While the Government can be commended for the humanitarian concern in creating this category, it can be criticised for excluding from it displaced persons, including the boat people, from Asia. Double standards and discriminatory policy were at work in the exclusion and control of certain groups, especially, once again, those of Asian derivation. Critics of the

Special Humanitarian and Special Assistance Programs claimed that they were really disguised immigration programs. The predominantly European nature of the entrants within these categories exemplifies exclusion of non-Europeans from the immigration program[81] and a continuation of excluding the 'other'.

This rationale of control behind migration reform in Australia, particularly since 1989, resulted in the minimisation of the judicial review of government procedures concerning refugee status determination and the increasing detention of asylum-seekers. The National Population Council's *Refugee Review* of 1991 recommended that policy be based on two concerns: humanitarianism, and migration control within the pursuit of national interests. However, these perspectives are antithetical to the aims of a national refugee policy as they are ambiguous in the claim for pursuing national interests. This allowed the government to shift the emphasis for entrance criteria from humanitarianism to one of control.[82]

Distinctions between 'lawful non-citizens' and 'unlawful non-citizens' became the new signifier of categories; all persons without visas were classified as 'unlawful non-citizens'. This was a clear strategy by the bureaucracy and government to regain control over immigration, and especially detention. The judicial system often appeared in conflict with the administrative system; claims that the courts were overriding the policy-making role of parliament, and thus fracturing immigration control, were heard from both sides of the Parliament. The Government struck a blow in this ongoing conflict between the judicial and administrative processes of immigration by passing legislation that denied courts the right to order the release of a designated person from detention.[83] This was devastating for refugees, especially boat people, who lost an avenue of appeal and, in specific cases, access to human rights. As Mary Crock states: 'the courts were seen to be letting in people that the government, acting through its bureaucracy, wanted to keep out. They [the courts] were threatening the legal structures erected to keep the invading hordes at bay'.[84]

However, the courts were upholding international law and human rights treaties to which Australia is a signatory. The *Migration Amendment Act 1992* that set up these two categories was a blatant political strategy to forestall bail applications by Cambodian boat arrivals who had been in detention for almost two years pending a decision on their refugee claims. These detention arrangements, human rights lawyers argued, breached the requirements set down in various international treaties such as the International Covenant on Civil and Political Rights and the Convention Relating to the Status of Refugees—treaties that the Australian Parliament has signed and is obliged to follow. For refugee and immigration policy, this was a highly contentious time, encapsulated by Cronin as 'a culture of control'.[85] In fact, it was 'out of control', as the people in detention ultimately suffered in the political and legal quagmire.

Under the regime of control (which still exists[86]) all refugee applicants for resettlement in Australia are assessed against the definition of the UN 1951 Convention and 1967 Protocol after their cases have been registered with a local UNHCR representative, or equivalent authority, in the country of first refuge. A refugee who chooses Australia as the country of first refuge may be detained or turned around at the port of entry by immigration officers. These practices stress control more than is necessary purely for humanitarian considerations.

In July 1993 the establishment of the Refugee Review Tribunal indicated a move from the 'culture of control' to conciliation in decision-making processes.[87] Although the establishment of the tribunal helped to diffuse the mentality of control in refugee assessment, control still remained a primary tenet for immigration policy. Advocates called for a refugee policy that was not an appendage to an immigration policy based on control. Hosking and Murphy argue that, although the focus of policy is on control, refugees risk a return to persecution, 'a result not acceptable in legal, ethical or moral terms'.[88]

Asylum-seekers arriving without legal documentation are classified as 'unlawful non-citizens' and cannot seek humanitarian classification, showing that control takes precedence over humanitarian considerations. Illegal immigrants and 'unlawful non-citizens' challenge national control of borders and commitment to human rights conventions.[89] In February 1994 the Joint Standing Committee on Migration reaffirmed Australia's sovereign right to determine the eligibility of non-citizens to enter and remain in the country and the right to detain such entrants as an appropriate means of processing refugee applicants.[90] Thus the control mentality is entrenched as deeply in refugee policy as in immigration policy.

Australia has an administrative model for refugee policy and determination that has focused on control and emphasised the advantages of efficiency and cost, denying social rights such as welfare benefits, employment permits and medical care to refugee claimants.[91] These disincentives for asylum-seekers to apply for refugee status are strategies of control. The rationale of control underlying the administrative model is in conflict with humanitarian interests, subjecting selected groups of refugees (such as unlawful non-citizens) to different procedures. Hence some refugees do not receive the benefit of the doubt, an essential guideline of the UN code of ethics for refugees, while their status is being determined. Australian detention of refugees has been under scrutiny; international coverage and reports of human rights violations concerning long-term detainees have exposed the inequities in Australian refugee policy.[92]

Immigration policy was less controversial in the final years of the Keating Labor Government. Nick Bolkus, the last of the Hawke–Keating Ministers for Immigration, supported a Family Reunion Program and the Refugee Review Tribunal. This ended in March 1996 with the election of the Howard Coalition Government, with Philip Ruddock as the new Minister for Immigration. Headlines such as 'Howard slashes immigration' and 'Ruddock targets refugee logjam' heralded new immigration and refugee policies. Deputy Prime Minister Tim Fisher railed against the 'immigration industry' and blamed the previous Government for allowing the immigration program to get out of control. These initial statements set the tone for Coalition immigration policy. [93]

As Opposition Leader in 1988, John Howard had made controversial remarks about immigration, and particularly its ethnic make-up, upsetting immigration lobby groups as well as ethnic groups. Howard came under attack from what he saw as the politically correct lobby, as well as sections of the public. As Prime Minister in 1996, Howard sought to restore immigration policy to what he perceived as the correct course for Australia. Immigration was cut by 10 000 places to 86 000 for 1996/97, with skilled migrants given priority over those entering under the family reunion categories. Family reunion was cut by 13 500, while the skilled migrant category was boosted by 4400. The focus of the migration program shifted to become 'more closely aligned to Australia's economic interests by delivering people with needed skills and expertise'.[94]

Priorities for migrant intakes focused on business and English-language skills, in line with the economic directions advocated by the 1988 Fitzgerald Report (which Howard had supported). Migrant groups criticised these moves, slamming the policies as racist and lacking humanity.[95] For the first time, a federal government had set a quota for refugees arriving in Australia without prior application. Previously refugees had been assessed on the basis of need rather than on the number of places available. The language test introduced in 1996 had similarities to the discriminatory dictation test abolished in 1958, thus raising concern from migrant groups. Sydney-based solicitor Anne O'Donaghue pointed out that the pass mark used by the Australian Immigration Department for skilled candidates was already very high, and if it were increased again, many people would simply choose destinations other than Australia.[96]

Along with these concerns, the Government's proposals to abolish the Refugee Review Tribunal and introduce a $30 000 bond for new migrants made, and continue to make, immigration groups uneasy and uncertain.[97] Immigration and refugee policies under the Howard Coalition Government have a very different focus from the Coalition Government of Malcolm Fraser, which supported balanced immigration and multicultural policies. In one of the first changes in his new Government, Howard transferred the Office of Multicultural Affairs from the Prime Minister's Department to a separate Department of Immigration and Multicultural Affairs (DIMA). No extra funding was provided, so in effect it was abolished. The Bureau of Immigration, Multicultural and Population Research, often seen as pro-immigration, was axed in the August 1996 budget, signalling the differing and oppositional stance taken by the Coalition on multiculturalism.[98]

The Howard Coalition Government has maintained a non-discriminatory immigration policy, 'which means that anyone from any country can apply to migrate, regardless of their ethnic origin, sex, race or religion'.[99] The immigration policy designates two major categories in which people may enter, or apply to enter, Australia: the Migration Program and the Humanitarian Program.

The Migration Program has two components, skilled migrants and family reunion. Skilled migrants must satisfy a points test, have particular work skills, be nominated by particular employers or have other links to Australia, or have successful business skills and/or significant capital to bring to Australia to establish a business of benefit to this country. Family migrants are selected on the basis of their relationship to a sponsor in Australia: essentially they are spouses, fiancés, and dependent children, as well as parents who meet the 'balance of family' test (designed to indicate how strong the family links are with Australia compared with other countries).

Those accepted under the Humanitarian Program must satisfy the criteria concerning refugee or humanitarian cases. The three categories are:

- *Refugee:* persons who meet the Convention definition of a refugee
- *Special Humanitarian:* those with close links to Australia who, while not refugees, have suffered gross violation of their human rights
- *Special Assistance:* those with close links to Australia who are displaced or otherwise in situations of hardship and special need.

Planning levels released by Immigration Minister Ruddock for 1998/99 contain 68 000 entrants in the Migration Program, and 12 000 places in the Humanitarian Program. Both programs retained the same numbers as the previous year but with differing configurations.

The Migration Program consists of: Skill Stream: 35 000; Family Stream: 30 500; Special Eligibility Category: 2500. The Humanitarian Program consists of: Refugee: 4000; Special Humanitarian Program: 4250; Special Assistance Category: 1750; Onshore Protection Visa Grants: 2000.

Major changes in the Migration Program are the decrease in Family Stream from 44 580 in 1996/97 to a level of 30 500 in 1998/99, with an increase in the Skill Stream from 27 550 in 1996/97 to 35 000 places in 1998/99. A new focus on skilled and business entrants is indicated with a weakening in the Family Reunion category. The immigration detention policy under the Howard Coalition remains in line with the report of the Joint Standing Committee on Migration (1994), which supported mandatory detention.[1]

Although John Howard and his Government produce the rhetoric of a non-discriminatory immigration policy, it is often hollow. Howard has not supported multiculturalism or high immigration levels. This is apparent in the dismantling of institutions devoted to multiculturalism and the drop in immigration intakes following recommendations from the 1988 Fitzgerald Report. However, Howard was upstaged by a newcomer with anti-immigration and anti-Asian rhetoric, Pauline Hanson, as we will see in Chapter 6.

## Exclusion Continues

Australia's history of immigration is also a history of exclusion. This chapter began with the history of racism and exclusion of the Chinese in the late nineteenth century and finishes with the rhetoric of racism and exclusion towards Asians a hundred years later. During this time, immigration policies changed considerably. The first immigration policy in 1901 instituted the exclusionary White Australia policy with the focus on white, and preferably British, migrants. Acceptance of non-British European migrants took place after World War II, followed by the gradual introduction of non-European migrants after the Vietnam War. Attitudes towards Asians seemingly changed and barriers between 'them' and 'us' came down: but did they?

The rise of the One Nation Party and public support for its anti-Asian policies highlight the fear of the 'other' that still exists in Australian society. In times of economic recession the 'politics of blame' takes the form of discrimination against the 'other', in Australia's case the Asian.[2] The attitudes towards the Chinese of the nineteenth century appear little different from the attitudes towards Asian migrants, and especially the boat people, of the 1990s. Australia has a non-discriminatory immigration policy and is signatory to international treaties binding it to be 'just' in the acceptance of migrants. Yet Australia's refugee administrative system allows discrepancies and discrimination to occur, as the following chapter will demonstrate.

Current Australian immigration and refugee policies have a historical precedent in the fear of uncontrolled migration. This has manifested as an irrational xenophobic concern that Asian 'hordes' are poised to invade Australia seeking land and economic opportunity. This fear first surfaced in the colonial model of restricted Chinese entry, explicitly racist in its exclusion of foreigners.[3] On the other hand, Australia has developed immigration policies that are emulated by other countries of the world. The post-1945 immigration and the ensuing multicultural policies have been recognised as great successes that provide Australia with rich economic and cultural resources.

In contemporary times it is more feasible to promote policies of social harmony and mobility among ethnic groups in Australia than to rely on a strategy of control against a formidable trend of worldwide population movement. The increased demand from asylum-seekers is a substantial part of this population movement; reliance on barricades and detention processes to preserve the state is a tactic suited to an old world order and is futile even in the short term. The challenge for present and future governments is to build on the successful components of Australian immigration and formulate policies for immigration and refugees that are innovative, humane and just.

# 4
# The Politics of Detention

The right to liberty is a fundamental right, recognised in all major human rights instruments, both at global and regional levels. The right to seek asylum is, equally, recognised as a basic human right. The act of seeking asylum can therefore not be considered an offence or a crime. Consideration should be given to the fact that asylum-seekers may already have suffered some form of persecution or other hardship in their country of origin and should be protected against any form of harsh treatment.

As a general rule, asylum-seekers should not be detained.[1]

To the Private Secretary,
. . . Are you aware of the plight of the 'boat people' in Australia? To date there are up to 300 Cambodian refugees who are being held in detention camps, in Villawood and Port Headland[sic]. Some of them have been behind barbed wire for almost 4 years now. There are children born in custody . . .

The Cambodian refugees are suffering. Please Sir, it is a modern day concentration camp . . .

David Chang[2]

In January 1994 David Chang, a Sydney university student obsessed by the plight of the Cambodian boat people, fired a starter's pistol near

Prince Charles at an Australia Day celebration in Sydney. Although at that time boat people had been detained for almost four years, attracting considerable media coverage, this act by David Chang highlighted a serious failing in Australian refugee policy, the harsh, inhumane and prolonged detention of Cambodian and other Asian boat people.

Unauthorised persons known as boat people have arrived on the northern coastline of Australia since 1976 and have been detained from 1989. Predominantly from Asia, they come for many reasons; some seek better economic conditions, some are queue-jumpers, but many come seeking protection from persecution.[3] The detention component of Australia's immigration policy makes it one of the severest of Western liberal democracies (Chapter 5). The arrival of the boat people aroused the fear, ingrained in the Australian psyche, of 'the hordes from the north' and Australia's 'significant other'. Detention as a policy and in practice is a political act of deterrence; however, this chapter shows that it is also an act of discrimination.

In 1989, in response to an influx of boat people, Australia invoked the detention provision in the immigration policy, which applies to unlawful non-citizens who seek to enter or remain in Australia without a valid visa or entry permit. Under the *Migration Act 1958,* such non-citizens can be 'detained, and in some circumstances must be detained, while their claims to enter or remain in Australia are determined . . . and, if their claim is unsuccessful . . . they must be removed from Australia as soon as practicable'.[4]

This practice conforms to legal principles of national sovereignty, accepted in Australian and international law, where the state designates which non-citizens are admitted and also the conditions under which they may be removed. It also conforms to Australia's universal visa system, which both facilitates and controls the movement of people into Australia.[5]

In Australia, detention for all unauthorised arrivals is mandatory until the determination process is resolved; this process can be prolonged, resulting in detention periods of up to five years for some applicants. Since 1992 detention, for all practical purposes, has been unreviewable by the courts, a situation which is highly political and cotentious. Although the policy of mandatory detention of most unauthorised arrivals breaches international human rights standards, successive Australian governments allowed this policy to remain. Boat people represent less than 0.01 per cent of all arrivals in Australia, yet they have created headlines and controversy out of all proportion to their actual numbers.[6]

Immigration policy and refugee policy are technically distinct, but in fact immigration control overrides the obligations and objectives of refugee protection. Australia's first officially administered refugee policy was introduced in 1977 in response to the influx of boat people from Indochina. The administrative system, relying heavily on ministerial discretion, has opened up avenues for discriminatory processes to be utilised against Australia's 'other'. Although there had been provision in Australian immigration policy for detention since 1901, it was only from 1989 that detention was widely used; these events highlight Australia's lack of political maturity and confusion in refugee policy.

## Overview of Detention Policy

The first significant immigration case, in 1891, concerned the detention of a Chinese immigrant, Chung Teeong Toy. In this case (*Musgrove v Chung Teeong Toy*, 1891 A.C. 272), the Privy Council held that Chung Teeong Toy, as a non-citizen, had no right to recover damages for false imprisonment when detained and refused entry into Victoria.[7] This and other incidents of detention attracted little attention from the public until the advent of asylum-seekers in the 1970s, intensifying from 1989 with the detention of the boat people.

Under the *Migration Act 1958,* any person who arrives in Australian territory without a visa will be detained until refugee status is determined. Detention can continue, at times for years, until refugee status is obtained or the applicant is refused and removed from the country. In contrast, people who enter Australia on tourist visas and overstay the period allowed on their entry permits and then make application for refugee status are not generally detained.[8] At 31 December 1997, there were about 51 000 people unlawfully in Australia, having overstayed the length of their visas. Most arrived as visitors (76 per cent) and about 24 per cent have been unlawfully in Australia for nine years or more. The highest numbers of overstayers came from the United Kingdom (11 per cent), United States (9.3 per cent), Philippines (6.9 per cent), and China (5.4 per cent).

Illegal non-citizens are treated differently from legal non-citizens,[9] although neither have authorised permits to stay or reside in Australia. Why are unlawful non-citizens such as boat people detained immediately, while lawful non-citizens who become overstayers, if apprehended, are rarely detained? It is the origin and manner of arrival of the boat people that arouse fear of invasion. Overstayers, mainly British or Americans arriving as visitors, do not present such a threat, since they are not perceived as the 'other'. However, both categories are non-citizens. Not only is it against humanitarian considerations to detain either group, but it also highly discriminatory to detain one group (the boat people), and not the other.

The *Migration Act 1958* guides the government's intentions regarding immigration and detention policy, while providing the framework within which the Department of Immigration and Multicultural Affairs (DIMA) operates. The legislation distinguishes between people who have permission to enter Australia (having obtained some sort of visa), and people who have not obtained permission to enter Australia (unauthorised entrants). Mary Crock explains:

> Australia's immigration system is predicated on the notion that all non-citizens who come to this country should obtain some sort of permission before being allowed to enter. The first line of our immigration 'defence' was and is the device of visas. These allow for pre-screening from overseas of people wishing to come to Australia for specific purposes. The second line of defence has been a series of provisions in the *Migration Act 1958* which allow for the removal of non-citizens who come to Australia without a visa or other permission to enter.[10]

'Removal' may mean deportation or detention. This is undertaken under the guidance of the United Nations and international law. The UNHCR Executive Committee noted 'with deep concern that large numbers of refugees and asylum-seekers in different areas of the world are currently the subject of detention . . . by reason of their illegal entry or presence in search of asylum, pending resolution of their situation'. It expressed the opinion that:

> in view of the hardship which it involves, detention should normally be avoided. If necessary, detention may be resorted to only on grounds prescribed by law to verify identity; to determine the elements on which the claim to refugee status or asylum is based;

to deal with cases where refugees or asylum-seekers have destroyed their travel and/or identity documents or have used fraudulent documents in order to mislead the authorities of the state in which they intend to claim asylum; or to protect national security or public order.

The UNHCR also insists on 'importance of fair and expeditious procedures for determining refugee status or granting asylum in protecting refugees and asylum-seekers from unjustified or unduly prolonged detention'.[11]

In theory, Australian government policy for detention is in accordance with the recommendations of the UNHCR. In practice the experience of asylum-seekers detained in Australia breaches the UNHCR guidelines, which stipulate that asylum-seekers should be detained only when it is necessary and reasonable to do so, and without discrimination, and for a minimal period.[12] The guidelines explicitly state that the use of detention to deter future asylum-seekers is contrary to the principles of international protection.[13] Australia is clearly in breach of these guidelines, both by detaining asylum-seekers for prolonged periods and by using detention as a policy of deterrence.

## The First Wave: The Vietnamese

In April 1976, a small boat with five Indochinese on board arrived in Darwin. During the following year six other boats came, bringing a total of 204 people, who were initially housed in government hostels and, significantly, given permanent residence.[14] These asylum-seekers had been granted refugee status. Initially the numbers were small but by June 1979 a total of fifty-one boats had reached northern Australia bringing a total of 2011 asylum-seekers. There was much public debate as to whether the boat people were genuine refugees and the fear of 'the hordes from the north' was reinvoked.[15]

Flows of people, including boat people, from Vietnam swelled after the end of the Vietnam War, alerting governments in the region, including Australia, to a possible flood of refugees.[16] There were calls for Australia to 'send the boats back' and to take a harsher stand on the perceived influx of Asian refugees. The Fraser Coalition Government introduced Australia's first officially administered refugee policy in 1977, not an open-door policy but one of controlled intakes. Although the introduction of the refugee policy was a positive move, it is ironic that the first official refugee policy was implemented in a response to the influx of the 'other' and the perceived threat of invasion.

The refugee policy was administrative; in contrast, as we will see in the next chapter, the Canadian refugee policy was adjudicative, that is, anchored in law and incorporated in the Canadian *Immigration Act 1976*. Australia's administrative model has proved burdensome for subsequent Australian governments as the *Migration Act 1958*, with later minor amendments, vested complete authority and discretion in the hands of the Immigration Minister, and therefore has been susceptible to change.

The Fraser Government had responded speedily and efficiently to the refugee situation. Presenting the new refugee policy, Immigration Minister MacKellar stated that 'the government was committed to the most effective role in refugee settlement, in the belief that there was a community willingness to assist the dispossessed and displaced from overseas in a sensible and realistic way to seek sanctuary and a new life in Australia'.[17]

The Fraser Government acknowledged Australia's legal obligation as a party to the UNHCR Convention and Protocol Relating to the Status of Refugees, which includes the detention clauses, while making it clear that the decision to admit refugees must always remain with the government of Australia.[18] In recognising the interests of the boat people, MacKellar complied with the UN Declarations and Protocols but incorporated fair and humanitarian procedures of control. As we have seen, the Determination of Refugee Status (DORS) Committee was established in March 1978 to bring administrative order in verifying the status of the arrivals. During this time most asylum-seekers who arrived on Australian shores were given refugee status by the DORS Committee. Before this 1043 refugees had been granted permanent residence and this policy was generally continued after, with the DORS Committee recommending refugee status for most boat people.[19] The DORS Committee was an inter-departmental advisory body that considered written (but not oral) requests for refugee status. It made recommendations to the Minister, who had final say on the request. The committee had no statutory basis and had no direct role in the decision of the application; it could only make recommendations. This system opened the way for more accountable and public refugee processing.[20]

Nancy Viviani contends that the DORS Committee was instituted as an assurance for adherence to the UN Convention on Refugees. There were widespread allegations, especially at the peak of the boat arrivals in 1977, that many were not genuine refugees and the DORS procedure was a strategy to counter these allegations.[21] Of the 11 872 Indochinese refugees admitted to Australia to June 1979, only 2011 were boat people. They were admitted under the strict procedures of the refugee policy and not part of a huge influx or invasion from the north.[22]

No issues of detention arose at this stage. Asylum-seekers were grouped with refugees as a component of immigration policy. The incumbent minister, MacKellar, was sympathetic to the plight of refugees and asylum-seekers from Indochina. However, implementation of policy depended upon the whim or discretion of the minister. The next Minister of Immigration and Ethnic Affairs, Ian Macphee, had a more restrictive approach to refugees. He instigated a review of Indochinese asylum-seekers. A refugee who failed to fit the UN Convention and Protocol definition was refused refugee status. There was stricter scrutiny of perceived economic refugees (that is, refugees fleeing for economic gain). This was to counteract the previous *carte blanche* acceptance of Indochinese fleeing 'adverse' regimes, such as Vietnam. Macphee emphasised defence of Australia's northern coastline against an invasion from the north, setting the scene for the 'defend, deter and detain' mentality of the following decade.[23]

Macphee, in a statement to the House of Representatives on 16 March 1982, clarified the Government's position: the criteria for refugee entry would be tightened significantly by applying the refugee criteria of the UN Convention on an individual basis rather than relying on the group mandate status accorded by the UNHCR.[24] This policy was planned to deter economic refugees leaving camps in Indochina for Australia. Statistics for 1982 show that the numbers of Indochinese entrants had fallen by nearly one-third from the previous three years,[25] indicating that this 'deterrence' measure did have an effect.

The first wave of boat people was a new phenomenon for Australia. Previously, few asylum-seekers had come, and very few in the manner of the boat people. The arrival of the boat people exposed the lack of policies and procedures to deal with influxes of asylum-seekers.

The Government was under internal and external pressure: domestic opinion, fuelled by media reports, opposed entry for boat people and was reluctant to accept large numbers of refugees from South-East Asian camps; and South-East Asian governments requested that Australia accept more refugees from holding camps. The Australian Government had belatedly realised the connection between the overcrowding in the holding camps and the number of refugees setting out by boat from these camps to Australia. Viviani contends that 'there seems little doubt that if Australia had taken more substantial numbers of refugees, especially from Malaysia, in late 1976 and 1977 and had sought agreement from the regional governments to hold boats embarking for Australia, the numbers of these boat arrivals would have been smaller'.[26]

This lack of foresight resulted in public disquiet. The media accentuated the misconception of 'invasions'; stories about the 'yellow peril' and 'the hordes from the north' fuelled fears to unrealistic proportions.

Detention was not an issue for the first wave of boat people. An interregnum followed, with no boat arrivals from 1982 until the second wave in 1989. The main reason for this was the continuation of the Cold War politics of accepting refugees from communist countries. Refugee intake continued under the controlled resettlement program, with Australia in the top five countries admitting Indochinese refugees in the offshore refugee program.[27] Just over two thousand boat people entered Australia between 1976 and 1989, while over a million migrants entered in the regular migration program. The number of boat people was minute compared both to the migration arrivals and to the level of controversy and fear.[28] Detention of unauthorised people, and especially the boat people, became an issue with the arrival of boat people, categorised as the second wave, from 1989.

## The Second Wave: The Cambodians

Most of the first wave of boat people had been granted permanent residence or refugee status without suffering the stigma and hardship of detention. The second wave, arriving between November 1989 and January 1994, were less readily accepted. On 28 November 1989 twenty-six Cambodian nationals on the *Pender Bay* were the first boat people to arrive in Australia since 1982. Together with 119 people on the *Beagle,* which arrived on 31 March 1990, they were denied refugee status by the Immigration Department.[29]

From the time of their arrival until they were rejected as refugees in April 1992, these people were all detained. Almost two years later, on

27 January 1994, three of the *Pender Bay* asylum-seekers and forty-four of those from the *Beagle* remained in custody, a prolonged period breaching international human rights standards and violating Australia's human rights commitments. Between November 1989 and January 1994, eighteen boats arrived in northern Australian. Most of the arrivals were from the Kompong Som region of Cambodia, mainly Cambodian, Vietnamese and Chinese nationals. One-third of them remained in detention to the end of that period.[30]

In 1989 and the early 1990s Australian migration law did not have adequate provisions, and immigration officials did not have suitable experience, to deal with unauthorised entrants who were detained for prolonged periods.[31] The *Migration Act 1958* made provision for illegal entrants to be detained until the return of the vessel upon which they arrived. Given the isolated geographic position of Australia, people had not 'just turned up' without authorisation except as stowaways on ships and planes, and thus could be easily returned to the vessel in which they had arrived.

The boat people presented a new challenge. The boats they had arrived in were mainly fishing trawlers, small wooden boats that were classified as a quarantine risk by the authorities and subsequently burnt. Legislation decreed that the boat people, as illegal entrants without authorised visas or entry permits, could be detained until their boat could be turned around.[32] With their boats destroyed, boat people could be detained indefinitely.

The Immigration Department feared that Australia's northern coast-line would be inundated with asylum-seekers, mainly Cambodians fleeing the inhospitable refugee camps in Malaysia and Indonesia.[33] It sent strong messages that boat people were not welcome. Gareth Evans, Minister for Foreign Affairs, prejudged the outcome of refugee claims by stating that the Cambodians were unlikely to be accepted as refugees, although he did add that each case would be looked at individually.[34] This caused an outcry about ministerial interference.

Immigration officials went to Cambodia to liaise with Cambodian government officials for the return of the boat people, thus negating Senator Evans' rhetoric about looking at individual claims by attempting to have the Cambodians, as a group, sent home. This presented consequences in terms of international obligations relating to refoulement, questioning the safety of the Cambodians if they were returned to Cambodia. It was expected that the Cambodians would be returned home after the political settlement was reached in Cambodia in 1991, a process in which Senator Evans took a leading role.

A claim of institutional bias was brought in the Federal Court against the Immigration Department on the basis of Senator Evans' announcements and a statement made by Prime Minister Hawke. He said:

> these people [the Cambodians] are not political refugees . . . we have an orderly migration programme. We're not going to allow people just to jump that queue by saying we'll jump into a boat, here we are, bugger the people who've been around the world . . . no qualms about it . . . I will be forceful in ensuring that that is what's followed.[35]

Justice Keely upheld the case and determined that it was 'grossly improper' for the Prime Minister to make such statements, which were likely to prejudice the Minister's delegates against the Cambodian boat people and their application for refugee status.[36] This was a clear message from the Federal Court that asylum-seekers were not being given fair and equitable treatment on their arrival in Australia. Hawke and Evans presented a hard line on the boat people, using them as an example that Australia was taking a tough stand against the 'invasion' of 'the hordes from the north'. This case highlights both the political interference in the Cambodians' quest for asylum and the importance of foreign policy in relation to refugee status. Australians feared the spectre of a repeated outflow of refugees from Indochina, similar to the flows from Vietnam in the late 1970s, and the Hawke Government acted tough to deter Cambodian boat people. However, the strategy also ignored humanitarian considerations, breached obligations to international treaties, and introduced a system that discriminated against a specific group, the Cambodian boat people.

In the early 1990s Australia took a major role in the Paris Peace Agreements.[37] Gareth Evans, as the Australian Foreign Minister, figured prominently in negotiations with the ruling factions of Cambodia and their international supporters who were working to resolve the internal problems of Cambodia and the resulting exodus of refugees. It was considered that the agreements would be undermined if Australia accepted refugees from Cambodia.[38] The theory was that if Australia accepted the boat arrivals as refugees, as it had done with the Vietnamese, it would appear that Australia regarded the negotiations as untenable. Cambodian boat people detained in Australia at this time were at the mercy of Australian foreign policy and a minister's desire for a grand triumph. Australian interest in conflict resolution in this process was both political and humanitarian, to give due credit to the efforts of the Government and Gareth Evans who had a desire to see the Cambodian conflicts resolved and the resultant stoppage of refugee outflows. The humanitarian motive for peace and stability was essential, given that millions of people had been killed, and the political motive was necessary, given that regional trade and defence interests were countered by the ongoing hostilities in Cambodia. However, this contrasted to the treatment of the Cambodian boat people detained in Australia.

Cambodian boat people who arrived between 1989 and May 1992 were detained solely on the basis of their method of arrival. Until 1992 persons arriving by boat or plane, who were detained by immigration officials before having technically entered Australia, were deemed not to have entered the country and were classified as 'prohibited non-entrants' under Section 88 of the *Migration Act*.[39] Prohibited non-entrants were detained until the vessel departed, or until they were granted an entry permit, or such earlier time as the officer directed.[40]

Other classifications applied to boat people, the main items of interest being:

- *Unprocessed persons:* Under Section 54b to Section 54h of the *Migration Act*, if an officer suspects that a person, who has travelled to Australia in a boat or has disembarked at an airport, would upon entry become an illegal entrant, and that it is not possible to decide whether to grant the person an entry permit, the person becomes an 'unprocessed person'. Such a person may be kept in a processing area until granted an entry permit. If the entry permit is refused, they become a 'prohibited person', one who has been requested to leave Australia, or has been refused or has not applied for an entry permit. A prohibited person must be removed from Australia as soon as practicable.
- *Designated persons:* Under Section 54j to Section 54u, the Act refers to people who arrived in Australian territorial waters after 19 November 1989 and before 1 November 1993 without visas, who were

in Australia, and who did not present a visa or entry permit. Designated persons were kept in custody and released only for the purposes of being removed from Australia or when granted an entry permit. They were removed upon request only if they did not apply for an entry permit or if refused an entry permit. This class appears to have included boat arrivals who had not entered Australia, as well as boat arrivals who had entered undetected.

- *Illegal entrants:* Section 92 of the Act enabled an officer to detain in custody an illegal entrant. The illegal entrant was brought before a prescribed authority (magistrate) within 48 hours. The prescribed authority ordered the release or authorised a person to be detained for no more than seven days. The Minister could order the release of a person in custody at any time.[41]

The category of designated persons was the one consistently applied to boat people, as government policy at that time dictated that they should be placed in detention centres or prisons until a decision was made about their future, particularly if they had no identity papers. New South Wales, Victoria and Western Australia had, and still maintain, special detention centres, but prisons are used in other states. In South Australia one 'unprocessed person' was placed in prison in 1991/92, but most designated or unprocessed persons went to Villawood detention centre in Sydney or Port Hedland in Western Australia.[42]

Between 1989 and 1992 policy distinguished between authorised asylum-seekers (who arrived with a passport and a visitor visa or entry permit) and unauthorised asylum-seekers (with no official documentation or entry permits). The unauthorised or prohibited entrants or unprocessed persons were detained from their date of arrival until a decision was made; the authorised asylum-seeker was able to enter the country and move about freely. Detention or freedom depended solely on the method of arrival, not on the strength of claims to refugee status. The process of determining refugee status is stressful for both groups, but exacerbated when the applicant is in detention.[43]

In December 1990 the DORS Committee was replaced by the Refugee Status Review Committee, an inter-departmental advisory committee that reviewed written refugee applications from asylum-seekers.[44] The administrative process of refugee determination was maintained, with the primary decision to be made by Immigration Department officials and any appeal to be heard by the committee. This new system established, for the first time, a formal right of review for rejected applicants for refugee status, while retaining the character of the determination system as a merit-based process. A representative of the UNHCR and a community representative nominated by the Refugee Council of Australia were included in the review process.[45] However, a successful application for refugee status would result in a four-year temporary entry permit and not the permanent resident status that had applied before.

Applications from asylum-seekers soared in 1989 after Prime Minister Hawke announced refuge for students from the People's Republic of China who were in Australia during the Tiananmen Square massacre and the pro-democracy movement, since they could be liable for persecution if they returned to China. Before 1989 the annual average number of submissions for refugee determination to the DORS Committee was about 500. In 1990/91, there were 13 954 new requests for asylum and by the end of 1991 the Refugee Status Review Committee caseload stood at 23 006, of which 72 per cent were Chinese nationals. Only 672 boat people, Cambodian and Chinese nationals, were included in this figure.[46]

Boat people, and especially the Cambodians, detained at this time were confused by the granting of temporary status to the Chinese nationals. Many in the Government were also confused by this policy, which had been made by Hawke in an emotive and spontaneous manner that exemplified 'policy on the run'[47] and highlighted the flaws in an administrative system that prioritised ministerial discretion.

A total of 27 359 Chinese students who had arrived before 21 June 1989 were granted permanent residence status, as a special group, by the Hawke Government in June 1990. This response was viewed as generous, awkward, tardy, expedient and exclusive. It was at least consistent with the important principle of giving the benefit of the doubt to the asylum-seeker. The boat people were treated in a much more suspicious, controlled and inequitable manner.

Discrimination within Australia's migration policy became apparent in the lack of fairness, consistency and equity in the treatment of claims to entry for the Chinese students and for the predominantly Indochinese boat people. Discrimination was explicit in the means of entry and, as Viviani points out, in the favouring of citizens of China over citizens of Cambodia, Vietnam, and other countries.[48] An element of elitism seems to operate here: the Chinese were students and therefore intellectuals with the prospect of adding value (in employment and intellectual expertise) for the Australian community, while the Cambodian boat people were perceived as unskilled 'others' who could be hidden away in detention centres. There were unskilled persons among the boat people, but there were also highly educated doctors, engineers and business people. The characterisation of the boat people as a poor, uneducated rabble is a misrepresentation. Of the refugees arriving in 1978, 8.9 per cent came from professional backgrounds, 7.8 per cent from administrative or clerical, 17.4 per cent from retailing, 17.1 per cent from farming or fishing, and only 3.3 were classified as unskilled.[49]

The Chinese students lived freely in the community while their claims were being decided, though they were legally liable for mandatory detention. Like other illegals (such as overstayers) they were granted liberty, welfare benefits and employment. In contrast, extraordinary measures were taken to maintain control over boat people, and the majority of Cambodian boat people were detained. The Government could offer no justification for this; it was overt discrimination based on means of entry. Australia was accused of failure to honour its commitments under the UN Convention Relating to the Status of Refugees.

Ministerial discretion had been removed by amendments in 1989 to the *Migration Act 1958*, but it was still at the core of this inequity in entry processing. This was highlighted by Prime Minister Hawke's decision on the Chinese students. Accused of inequity, he responded by stating that the Cambodians were 'just economic refugees', discounting that the Chinese students were predominantly in Australia for economic reasons. Hawke's successor Prime Minister Keating, and the Immigration Ministers Hand and Bolkus, also excercised ministerial discretion, prolonging the discrimination against the boat people during this period.[50]

Conflicts and power plays between the administration and the judicial system occurred in the early 1990s. During the 1980s people could appeal against adverse decisions in the Federal Court. The court ceased to consider the broad discretion characterising the *Migration Act* before 1989 as permitting total control by the Minister over migration decision-making. Boat people, and specifically the Cambodians in detention, were subject to this power play between the government and the judicial system. Tension was created between these two highest levels of power by the method of determination applied to immigrants, especially refugees. The results were confusion in the administrative determination system and the subordination of the adjudicative system, a point discussed later in this chapter.

By mid-1993, more than 500 Cambodians and Chinese nationals were in custody with their claims for refugee status undetermined after more than three years. The workload engendered by the sudden rise of refugee applications, mainly from the Chinese students, brought the refugee determination process to crisis. This meant months of processing delays: those who entered legally had no constraint on the right to remain at large within the community, but for border applicants the breakdown of the refugee determination system had serious ramifications. There were lengthy delays in the determination process, meaning lengthy periods in detention. Detainees were kept in custody for the entire duration of processing, including any time spent waiting for administrative or judicial review of an adverse ruling.[51] In October 1991 the Government had commissioned a detention facility at a disused mining camp at Port Hedland in the isolated north-west of Western Australia. The dispatch of boat people to this remote outpost controls the political situation by keeping detainees out of the public eye and sends a message to other would-be asylum-seekers that it is not easy to enter Australia. The remoteness of the camp also restricts access by lawyers, independent advisers and community workers.[52]

The Government was criticised for its handling of detainees[53] and grew anxious that it was losing control of the situation. It responded with the *Migration Reform Act 1992*, making radical changes to the process of migration decisions and reviews. Sean Cooney, migration lawyer, argues that the change from a discretionary system to a codified scheme was a success because it subjected migration decision-making to controls such as detailed legislative provisions and external review.[54] However, while the changes codified migration law and thereby bound it to legal structures, the use of ministerial discretion remained intact. The changes to migration law intensified the conflict between the political and legal processes, with politicians increasingly frustrated by their perceived weakening of power.

In July 1993 the first independent review tribunal for refugees, the Refugee Review Tribunal (RRT), was established, with procedures emphasising informality and non-adversarial methods.[55] This gave applicants the right to an oral hearing of their claim, although they had no direct right to legal or other representation within the hearing. Response to the introduction of the tribunal was mixed. The executive director of the Refugee Council of Australia acknowledged that it speeded up refugee applications and was an improvement on the previous Refugee Status Review Committee.[56] These committees consisted mainly of government representatives, causing suspicion that deliberations might be unduly influenced by government policy. The Refugee Status Review Committee had also been criticised as too cumbersome, adding to the lengthy delays in decision-making processes.[57] The tribunal, though an improvement, is also criticised for the lack of legal representation for the claimant and the denial of the right to examine or cross-examine witnesses. Michael Clothier, lawyer and former senior member of the Immigration Review Tribunal, has likened both these tribunals to small claims tribunals, which rely on one person being both judge and interrogator; but this is quite inappropriate for a life-determining process.[58]

While the establishment of the Refugee Review Tribunal moved from the 'culture of control' to conciliation in decision-making processes, refugee determination remained an administrative process 'controlled' by the immigration bureaucracy and the Immigration Minister. Participants from non-government organisations and government departments review applications for refugee status, but it is the Minister who makes the decision. The tribunal's task is to consider the merits of each case against legislated criteria, which are derived from international law such as the 1951 Convention and the 1967 Protocol. Asylum-seekers access a faster and less formal review mechanism by which they can appeal against negative primary determinations. This allows more opportunity for asylum-seekers to present their cases and respond to adverse official findings. It is the fairest system to date and has substantially improved Australia's ability to meet its obligations under the Refugee Convention.[59]

The interpretation of the Convention definition of refugee definition and the manner in which criteria could be interpreted by individual committee members were the main disadvantages of this review system. This highlights the arbitrary values inherent in the administrative system, where the chances of success may depend just as much on which member is allocated to a refugee's file as on the merit of the refugee's case.

The *Migration Amendment Act 1992* stipulated mandatory detention for all 'designated persons' in Part 2, Div. 4B of the Act, which referred to all refugee claimants, including boat people, who arrived in Australia between 19 December 1989 and December 1992. It was an anomaly that many boat people were classified as not having arrived in Australia, but this group of designated persons was included in the Act as 'unprocessed persons'. This caused controversy between judicial and government sectors, as Section 54R of the Act states that the courts could not order the release of a designated person from detention. The Government's tactics show the extent of its concern the threat that the 600-odd refugee applicants of the time posed to the nation, and also indicate the steps it would take to control immigration and specifically refugee issues; however, the 'shackling' of the courts came as a surprise to some.[60]

Mary Crock explains this conflict as part of the 'control' mechanism of the Government, which 'feared' that the judicial system was 'usurping the policy-making role of parliament, and threatening the very fabric of immigration control . . . the courts were seen to be letting in people that the government, acting through its bureaucracy, wanted to keep out. They were threatening the legal structures erected to keep the invading hordes at bay.'[61]

The layers of fear are complex: fear of the 'other', the Asian boat people, is overplayed with government fear of losing control to the judicial system, and of electoral backlash if the public perceived it as being too soft on the boat people. Crock succinctly points out that

> virtually every change made to the *Migration Act* in and after December 1989 can be related in some way to the issue of Parliamentary/bureaucratic control of immigration. It is no co-incidence that many of the changes made have had a direct impact on the power of the courts to intervene in immigration cases.[62]

The outcome of this struggle was the ultimate supremacy of Parliament as law-maker in Australia; no one on the bench at the time was prepared to force the Government to release the detainees. The Government perceived that the judiciary had overstepped its jurisdiction. Immigration and refugee policy was to remain an administrative process where the Parliament would be supreme. Detainees were the losers, caught in the power struggle.

In a controversial move, the Government legislated for mandatory detention. It thus forestalled a Federal Court bail application by fifteen Cambodian boat arrivals who had been held in detention for almost two years awaiting a decision on their refugee claims. It was argued that the detention arrangements breached human rights requirements set down in various international treaties such as the International Covenant on Civil and Political Rights and the Convention Relating to the Status of Refugees which Australia has signed. As Crock argues, this piece of legislation, the provision of Div. 4B in the Act, was one of the most blatant examples of political interference as a direct assault on the courts in the context of a particular case. This amending Act extinguished the right of action of the Cambodians to damages for false imprisonment and set the rate of damages payable to a designated person for wrongful detention at one dollar a day, lauded as 'an attempt at damage control with total disregard for basic human rights and common law principles'.[63]

A High Court challenge was mounted in the case of *Chu Kheng Lim v Minister for Immigration, Local Government and Ethnic Affairs* (1992) 67 ALJR 125. The High Court objected to an obvious attempt to oust the courts, in the form of Section 54R of the Act which stated that the courts could not order the release of a designated person from detention, but found the Act valid in other respects. It held also that the incarceration of the plaintiffs before the passage of the amending Act had been unlawful, although there was no abuse of power because those affected were non-citizens or aliens.[64]

In June 1994 the Government introduced the Migration Legislation Amendment Bill (No. 2), which retrospectively amended the *Migration Act* so that all persons detained were deemed to be 'legally detained'. This defeated any claims before the High Court, either at that time or in the future, seeking compensation for unlawful detention.[65] The High Court reiterated that aliens have fewer human rights than citizens under Australian domestic law, and retrospective legislation ensures that any arbitrary application or mis-application of policy can be legitimated at a later date. The judges argued that Div. 4B was validated by Section 54(1) of the Act, which gave the detainees the power to end their incarceration by voluntary repatriation. However, assuming that genuine refugees cannot go home without fear of persecution, the Cambodians who had applied for refugee status were not free to end their custody by repatriation on these terms.

The charge of alienage hangs on a thin thread in upholding the validity of legislation that 'would not be accepted for a moment in a field other than immigration'.[66] The High Court revealed that the subject legislation would not be valid if it was to be applied to Australian citizens. Prisoners on remand in Australia have a right to bail or release on conditions pending their trial, but this was denied the Cambodian plaintiffs even though lengthy delays may adversely affect the processing of refugee applications. Persons charged in Australia with even the most serious offences are not treated in the manner that the detainees have been. In the criminal justice system persons are presumed innocent until proved guilty, while in the immigration detention system asylum-seekers are presumed guilty until proved innocent.[67]

The question remains in human rights terms, should there be different treatment for citizens and aliens? In respect to national sovereignty and citizenship rights, it is clear that there are differing rights conferred on citizens and aliens. However, in human rights terms, the detention of asylum-seekers for periods which exceed the required time is a violation.[68] The failure by the Government, administrative bodies and the High Court to fully recognise and consider the significance of the plaintiffs' potential status as refugees goes against the declarations in the Convention Relating to the Status of Refugees. For a genuine refugee, return in these circumstances could contravene Article 33 of the Convention, which prohibits the refoulment of a refugee 'in any manner whatsoever to the frontiers of territories where his [sic] life or freedom would be threatened' on specified grounds.[69] It is a risky situation in which the Australian Government could have contravened the Convention and the Protocol as well as putting refugees' lives at risk.

This controversy took its toll on the Cambodian detainees. By 16 December 1992, eighty-nine of those who had arrived on the *Beagle* were to be deported after their refugee applications were rejected. Most of them believed they would be killed or tortured if they returned home, and two attempted suicide on hearing of their imminent deportation. A reprieve in the form of a right to appeal before the Federal Court was granted at the end of the year, but not before two men had voluntarily returned after spending three years in detention.[70]

Public outcry over the detention crisis procured an inquiry. On 27 May 1993, the Senate passed a resolution requesting the Joint Standing Committee on Migration to inquire into immigration detention practices in Australia.[71] In February 1994 the Standing Committee reaffirmed the principle of sovereignty to determine the eligibility of non-citizens to enter and remain in the country, and the right to detain

such entrants as an appropriate means of processing refugee appli-
cations.[72] Detention policies of other countries, including the United
States and Canada, were compared and, although it was recognised that
Australia was the only country to require mandatory detention, the
Standing Committee was satisfied that applicants had sufficient oppor-
tunities to challenge adverse decisions.

Senator Christabel Chamarette gave the only dissenting report,
saying that Australia's detention policy breached several international
conventions on human rights in relation to the length of detention and
the detention of children. Of major concern to Senator Chamarette was
the practice of detaining illegal arrivals but not detaining illegal overstayers, highlighting the discriminatory practice by which detention
depended on mode of entry into Australia. This aspect of detention
policy is significant for a particular category of unauthorised persons,
who are most likely to be boat arrivals and asylum-seekers.

Senator Barney Cooney issued an Addendum detailing the role of the
judiciary and the undermining of its power to order the release of
detainees. Although it is 'right and proper for the Executive to have
power to release those it detains',[73] it should not be the exclusive right of
the authority that incarcerates people to decide the circumstances and
conditions of their release.

Senator Cooney had reservations about the Standing Committee's
recommendation that removed detainees' access to the judicial system.
Cooney recommended that a provision be made in the *Migration Act* to
give the courts power, in appropriate circumstances, to release people
held in administrative custody under the legislation.

> This power should be available to the courts from the time such
> people are first detained under the Act . . . and the courts should
> be defined to include the Immigration Review Tribunal and the
> Refugee Review Tribunal as well as those courts of record which
> deal with matters arising under the legislation.[74]

His proposals were ignored: the Standing Committee's recommendations were aimed at curtailing the litigation of migration in the courts
and providing administrative processes that would close off access to
review and appeal in the higher courts (save for the right of access to the
High Court, which is guaranteed in the Australian Constitution).[75] The

tension between administrative processes, such as refugee determination, and the judicial system is exemplified in the Standing Committee's recommendations. These tensions in immigration issues have continued. Issues of democracy and governance surface in this argument where one tier of a democratic system, the judiciary, is pinpointed by the Government for exclusion from particular issues.

The Standing Committee received 112 submissions from government departments and agencies, immigration advice organisations, legal bodies, aid agencies and ethnic community organisations. Generally these groups expressed support for the sovereign right of Australia to detain illegal entrants but were strongly critical of the length, the physical conditions and the administration of detention. Only twenty-two submissions, including fourteen from the Department of Immigration, supported the existing detention policy; fifty-eight directly opposed it.[76]

Maria Lawton analysed the submissions, excluding second submissions from the same source and supplementary submissions from the total. In her figures, the total was 96 with only 8 supporting the existing system of detention and 84 requesting alternatives. Four more—the Department of Immigration and Ethnic Affairs, the Department of Foreign Affairs and Trade, the Australian Protective Service, and the Victorian Government—had no specific comment.[77] An overwhelming majority (86.5 per cent) of the submissions called for changes to the existing system of detention.[78]

Critics identified an 'obsession with control mentality' that flavours the report, a mentality based on a fear of the judicial system overruling the administrative system, and therefore overruling the Minister.[79] Immigration Minister Gerry Hand was strongly supported by Shadow Minister Philip Ruddock and by the bureaucracy, all advocating a restriction of judicial powers and the maintenance of detention policies. The control mentality was rife.[80]

Kerry Murphy captures the power struggle between the courts and the Government in his query: 'why are the politicians afraid to let the courts review decisions of bureaucrats?'[81] The answer is that the Government's decisions would, in many cases, be found to be illegal and in contravention of human rights obligations.

Some of the actions taken by the Government at this time were highly questionable. For example, it rushed through legislation the night before the hearing in the Federal Court of *Lim v Minister for Immigration,*

*Local Government and Ethnic Affairs* (1992) 67 ALJR 125. In this case the plaintiffs, who had been detained illegally for two years, applied for release on bail. The High Court recognised their detention as illegal, but an application for compensation for unlawful imprisonment was met with legislation, as mentioned before, to limit payments to one dollar per day. As Murphy asks, 'would this be acceptable for anyone else?'

This legislative intervention in the 1992 *Lim* case exemplifies the battle between the government, the courts and the 'immigration club' over detainees. Minister Hand claimed he was misled by lawyers and refugee representatives, and that he 'had been taken for bit of a dill' and 'would crack down on refugees'. The Government blamed advocates such as the Refugee Council, church groups and human rights lawyers—the 'immigration club'—for delaying the determination process and thus increasing detention periods. The detainee advocates argued that justice was being obstructed by the administrative process and that the human rights of detainees were being violated. Both sides blamed the other for delays in refugee determination.[82]

The Standing Committee was formed as an independent, bipartisan committee. Its chairman, Labor Senator Jim McKiernan, was on record before the inquiry as favouring detention, stating: 'if the refugee assessment procedure was changed, Australia would be inundated and boats filled with people, who can afford the fare and the bribes that go with it . . . will land on our shores by the scores'.[83] After the report was released, McKiernan created headlines in regional papers by stating that Australia's generosity in accepting boat people was being abused. He cited the court battles between the detainees and the Government, indicating that the courts should back off. McKiernan encapsulated the mindset of control in his catch-phrase 'defend, deter, detain'.[84] In contrast to McKiernan's argument legal, ethical, medical, professional and political experts claimed detention is not a viable legal, economic or humanitarian option.[85] Judge Marcus Einfeld forthrightly stated: 'erring on the side of humanity for those who are *prima facie* genuine and comparatively risk-less is more consistent with Australia's legal structures, sense of justice and traditional standards of fairness than our present detention policy'.[86]

The Refugee Council of Australia responded with concern that the dissenting report of Senator Chamarette and the Addendum by Senator Cooney, which reflected the views of the majority of the submissions, was ignored by the Standing Committee:

> That it is a dissenting report and not the report of the majority which takes on board that which the informed community, the bureaucracy and international agencies are attempting to say to the government should be the cause of concern. The parliamentary committee process is called into question when a committee can be seen to have a predetermined position which it seeks to support irrespective of evidence presented. If government purports to represent the people, it must be seen to be taking into consideration that which they say . . . it is also the cause for concern when a political process exists that will give an unrepresentative report precedence simply because it is supported by the majority of a committee without regard to the fact that it may be supported by the majority of the stakeholders.[87]

In its concluding remarks the Refugee Council made the pertinent point that Australia, by adhering to the recommendations of the Standing Committee's report, was in breach of international human rights mechanisms and that disapproval would be expressed by international agencies, non-government organisations and members of the public. In the Refugee Council's opinion the report would not enhance Australia's reputation on the international arena 'as a free society where people are free before the law and it will make it that much more difficult for our government to espouse human rights issues in the international arena'.[88] However, the government legitimised the detention policy with the recommendations of the Standing Committee's report, setting a limit for detention of 273 days controlled by the administrative process.

In October 1993 the Minister for Immigration, Senator Bolkus, initiated a plan which required that the Cambodian detainees should return to Cambodia for twelve months and then reapply for entry into Australia under the sponsorship of community groups. Ironically, the Cambodians were asked to put their faith in both the Australian and Cambodian governments as a way to break the impasse of lengthy detention periods. Fewer than half the Cambodian detainees elected to take this option, with the last returning in March and April 1995.[89]

The Cambodians repatriated for twelve months were required to fund their return to Australia and the first few months' living expenses, supported by charities such as the Society of St Vincent de Paul, which also offered to support newly released detainees.[90] This exercise of ministerial discretion applied to the Cambodian detainees only and was denied to boat people from other countries. Viviani points out that boat people, and in particular the Cambodians, were singled out for 'special treatment', not always to their advantage but as an example to deter further boat arrivals.[91] Senator Bolkus released the remaining Cambodian refugees at the end of 1995, granting them humanitarian entry to Australia. This highlights the changing rules and processes of refugee determination during this period. Two Cambodian detainees, held for over five years, were released in October 1995 after winning a legal battle against the federal Government. They had been illegally detained. This decision exposed flaws in government treatment of illegal immigrants; the two refugees were in detention for over five years, a quarter of their lives (they were twenty and twenty-one years of age).[92]

The trickle of Cambodian asylum-seekers who arrived on Australia's northern shores by boat from 1989 to 1991 had produced a sustained political response of unprecedented hostility. The second wave of boat people showed up the inadequacies in Australia's refugee determination system, with power struggles between the Government and the courts reflecting the problems inherent in an inflexible administrative detention regime in respect of asylum-seekers. A mindset of 'immigration control' had besieged successive governments and immigration ministers who, under ministerial discretion, could adapt refugee law to their own political ends. This indicated a shift from refugee protection to immigration control in Australia's refugee determination process.[93]

Boat people became the scapegoats of refugee policy in this period, in contrast to overstayers and the Chinese students. The detention of the boat people was an act of discrimination based on origin and mode of entry. The second wave of boat people exposed discrepancies in Australian refugee and detention policies that were publicly exposed by David Chang and his starter's pistol. He highlighted the serious failure in Australian Government refugee policy that had inflicted harsh, inhumane and discriminatory detention on Cambodian and Asian boat people.

## The Third Wave or 'Forum Shopping': The Chinese

Against the background of this intriguing and complicated web of politics, law and personalised battles, the third wave of boat people began to arrive in Australia in late 1994.[94] Once again furore erupted, with the press sensationalising the events unfolding on Australia's northern shores. Headlines thundered, 'Boat people flood feared', 'Refugees at peak since Vietnam', 'Bolkus: We can't stop boat people' and 'Boat people slip past security'.[95] This sudden influx of asylum-seekers, labelled by the media as 'the Refugee Crisis',[96] provoked new fears of an invasion with the arrival of 431 boat people during December.

Most of these arrivals were from China, with a few boats of Vietnamese coming from Galang detention camp in Indonesia. During 1994, 953 boat people arrived out of a total of 1659 since 1989.[97] These asylum-seekers caused concern for both the government and refugee advocates because they were predominantly Vietnamese asylum-seekers resettled in southern China in the 1980s. Having been forcibly returned from Hong Kong, or from detention camps in Indonesia, to cramped conditions and displacement, in China, they had set out from Behai in southern China.

They were affected by the 'Comprehensive Plan of Action' (CPA), an international agreement on Vietnamese asylum-seekers in Asia.[98] This accord was brokered by the UNHCR to resolve the prolonged Indochinese refugee problem through resettlement programs in third countries and repatriation to Vietnam. The CPA established a process to assess asylum-seekers throughout Southeast Asia for refugee status. Those who obtained refugee status were permanently resettled in a variety of countries, including Australia. Those who were screened out were eventually returned to Vietnam. The camps were closed, and the CPA was finalised in 1997.[99]

In November 1994, the *Migration Legislation Amendment Act (No. 4)* was passed. It aimed to prevent Vietnamese asylum-seekers being considered by Australian authorities for refugee status.[1] The amendment was a response to the arrival in Australia in July 1994 of a boat code-named *Vagabond,* originating from Galang, the UNHCR camp in Indonesia. All seventeen Vietnamese on board had been rejected for refugee status by UNHCR under the CPA. They all applied for refugee status on arrival in Australia; three were accepted as refugees by the DIEA while the rest were rejected. They sought review by the Refugee Review Tribunal, but the Minister issued a conclusive certificate on the ground that it was contrary to Australia's national interest to allow the appeal.[2]

As soon as the *Migration Legislation Amendment Act (No. 4)* was enacted, fifty-seven Vietnamese asylum-seekers, who had arrived by boat during September and October 1994 from the Galang refugee camp, were forcibly repatriated. They made a sensational exit by air, bound hand and foot and carried bodily on to the aircraft by immigration staff at Port Hedland. A clear message was being sent that 'forum shopping', as the then Minister put it, 'was not on'.[3] Bolkus emphatically declared that Australia had an international obligation under the CPA to deport asylum-seekers, such as this group of people, who had been refused refugee status in another country.

The granting of refugee status to some of the early third wave asylum-seekers had made it clear that it was easy to enter Australia. Hawke's 'policy on the run', which granted Chinese nationals refugee status after the Tiananmen Square massacre, also sent messages to China that asylum-seekers would be accepted easily. The majority of the fifty-one asylum-seekers who arrived on the *Unicorn* from southern China in June 1994 had sufficient evidence of hardship and persecution to be granted refugee status.

Minister Bolkus decided that the wrong message had been sent overseas and, in order to justify immediate restrictive measures, suggested that the decision-makers in these cases had misunderstood the real situation of the refugee claimants. The Government precluded applications from any person who is either covered by the CPA or who has a right of abode in a 'safe third country'.[4]

Bolkus and the DIEA commenced talks with China, as a 'safe third country', in a bid to stem the flow of new refugees and to soften the impact of the repatriation of asylum-seekers to China. However, Bolkus was on record as saying that 'we can't stop the boat people'. Newspapers demanded that the Government 'get tough' and send a clear message to China that asylum-seekers could not 'waltz into Australia and get refugee status'.[5] Bolkus and immigration officials blamed organised human traffickers and crime gangs as the instigators of the latest influx of Chinese boat people.[6] Although this was a real issue, it was also an attempt to divert attention from detention and human rights violations.

In December 1994 Bolkus clarified that diplomatic efforts had led to the arrest of 'human traffic' entrepreneurs in China and the curtailment of boats bound for Australia.[7]

> Our two-pronged objective has been to; one, stem the flow and secondly to organise return for those who have no right to be here . . . going on to say that . . . unless you're [an asylum seeker] prepared to spend a long time in detention, unless you're prepared

to pay money you're going to waste, and unless you're prepared
to return to China after detention, it's not worth it (coming to
Australia, that is).[8]

Further events exposed the vulnerability of Australia's coastline and
border. Some boats landed in Darwin harbour and people were ashore
before being detected, alarming immigration officials and fuelling the
fear of an invasion.[9]

Some asylum-seekers cited the Chinese Government's one-child policy as a form of persecution and hence a reason for seeking refugee status
in Australia.[10] A Federal Court decision of 1994 ruled that China's one-
child policy, combined with the threat that couples with one child could
be forcibly sterilised if returned to China, could create a well-founded
fear of being persecuted.[11]

This court ruling by Justice Sackville would allow a large proportion
of China's one billion people valid claims to refugee status in Australia
and 'the effectiveness of Australia's refugee determination system would
be threatened if it were allowed to stand'.[12] In February 1995 Minister
Bolkus released legislation to overturn this ruling. The Government
was criticised for these amendments by refugee advocates including the
president of the Indochina Refugee Association, Marion Le. She said that
Canberra appeared to be sanctioning the one-child policy, which was
a gross abuse of human rights. Eve Lester, coordinator of the Victorian
Refugee Advice and Casework Service, further criticised the policy,
saying that Senator Bolkus knew that some of the third-wave arrivals
may have come under protection obligations as refugees and that is why
he proposed to change the law. Lester argued that in some Chinese pro-
vinces the one-child policy is carried out by forcible sterilisation of men
and women and forcible abortion of foetuses. This is persecution and
to ignore this, by passing legislation that the one-child policy can no
longer be the basis of a claim to refugee status, is to condone persecution
where it occurs in China. However, the Government took the view that
it would be difficult, time-consuming and costly to sanction each couple
to the degree that positive persecution was proved, thus the asylum-
seekers from southern China were sent back. Apart from refugee and
humanitarian groups who opposed the new legislation on human rights
grounds, legal groups, members of the Liberal and National Parties,
Catholic Bishops and Independent Senator Harradine, who considered
resigning over the incident, also criticised the legislation.[13]

Replying to these criticisms, Bolkus stated that it would ensure that people affected by their government's fertility-control policies, but with nothing else in common, would not be regarded as coming within the definition of a 'particular social group'.

> The Bill will not ban consideration of fertility-control policies in all circumstances . . . people who are members of groups other than the policies themselves, such as people from a particular village, would still be able to receive refugee status on the basis of a discriminatory application of fertility-control policies.[14]

Under the *Migration Amendment Act (No. 4)*, refugee applicants were rejected if their claims for asylum rested solely on the one-child policy. The Department of Immigration could deport Sino-Vietnamese (not Chinese nationals, but Vietnamese nationals who have been resettled in China but not given citizenship) without processing any claims made by them from 30 December 1994, affecting up to 700 detainees. After intense negotiations between Chinese and Australian officials, the detainees from the third wave were deported back to China at Australia's expense.[15]

Senator Bolkus sent a clear message:

> [the] doors are closed . . . you won't have a chance if you come from the southern part of China, if you're Sino-Vietnamese in background, if you've received protection from China as all these people have in cooperation with the UNHCR: then you won't be able to claim asylum status here.[16]

This message was heeded, as boat people from that region ceased leaving. Chinese officials co-operated by making it clear that Australia would not accept people unless they were genuine refugees. It was not the prospect of detention that deterred the would-be refugees, but the knowledge that they would be repatriated.

Alarm was raised by the arrival of fifty-two boat people in March 1995. However, it was ascertained that they were the end of the last wave, having departed southern China at the end of August 1994. Once it was clarified that they were Sino-Vietnamese who had resettled in southern China, these boat people were denied the right to apply for refugee status and were deported to China.[17] The deportation of the rest of the Sino-Vietnamese of the third wave did not go so smoothly. Many were detained at Port Hedland or at Curtin air force base near Derby, WA, in what has been described as 'virtual concentration camps'.[18] The harsh, isolated conditions traumatised many asylum-seekers.

In July 1995 the Sino-Vietnamese detainees who were to be deported demanded the return of their boats, which had been burned. In protest they took to the roof of the detention centre at Port Hedland. The protest went on for nearly a week, but to no avail; the protesters were deported. The Government was also criticised for the cost involved with the deportation of the Sino-Vietnamese boat people. Bolkus was accused of 'grossly underestimating' the cost to Australia of resettling the 700 boat people in China. The Australian and Chinese governments had agreed that the repatriation costs of $500 000 were to be paid to China by the federal Government. This was part of the UN Memorandum of Understanding signed in January 1995 that enabled the return of people verified to have settled as refugees more than ten years previous. The figure of $500 000 was queried by the opposition party's spokesperson Senator Short, who estimated the resettlement cost to be $1 million and total costs of repatriating the boat people in the range of $10 to 15 million. A group of 118 Sino-Vietnamese boat people had their appeal for refugee status rejected by the Federal Court in February 1996 and were deported.[19]

Chinese and Sino-Vietnamese arrivals dwindled after June 1997, effectively marking the end of the third wave. The height of the arrival of the Chinese and Sino-Vietnamese in the third wave was late 1994, early 1995. There were significant arrivals in 1996; three boats of Chinese arrived in March, April and June 1997, with a total of 253 boat people who all, bar four, were returned. The arrival of boat people of other nationalities, such as Afghani, Kurdish, Sri Lankan and Iraqi, began from mid-1995 with an increased influx in 1997. Boat arrivals have fallen since 1994/95 when there were twenty-one, compared to fourteen in 1995/96 and ten in 1996/97.[20] Most arrivals since then have originated from Iraq and Sri Lanka, with a new dilemma occurring in 1999 of boat landings of Chinese as human trafficking. The third wave raised problems as complex as any presented by the two previous waves. Solutions had to conform not only to Australian domestic policies concerning immigration control, but also with UN and regional initiatives on displaced persons. The third wave was marked by accusations of Australian violation of human rights and overt discrimination in many areas of refugee policy, especially detention of all boat people and the use of ministerial discretion.

In late 1994 legal access to detainees at Port Hedland detention centre was curtailed because boat people were not informed that they could challenge their detention in a court of law. Although this breaches human rights (under the *Human Rights and Equal Opportunity Commission Act* and the International Covenant on Civil and Political Rights 1966) the Immigration Department refuses to inform detainees of this right, providing access only if requested by the detainee. As a result of this method of control, fewer detainees requested legal assistance. Detainees in isolated camps such as Port Hedland are denied legal assistance and information about the Australian immigration system. This has resulted in higher levels of denials for refugee status in the primary stage and fewer applications to the Refugee Review Tribunal. There is no directive for asylum-seekers who arrive by boat to be advised of their right to legal advice (Section 193). It is necessary for detainees to have legal advice to lodge a sound application due to the complexity of the refugee determination process and language, cultural and education barriers. The majority of asylum-seekers are not aware that they must ask for asylum to engage Australia's protection obligations. Human Rights Commissioner Sidoti portrayed the curtailing of legal access to detainees:

> No other western country permits incommunicado detention of asylum-seekers. Already, international criticism of DIMA's practice of detention has been voiced by Amnesty International. According to international perceptions, Australian detention practices involve a breach of international, civil, political and human rights . . . It is incomprehensible that a country with such a proud record of commitment to finding durable solutions to refugee issues should resort to measures denying the basic rights of an individual. [This is] . . . the first step to place the Department of Immigration outside Australia's human rights laws.[21]

## Conclusion

The detention of boat people from 1989 exposed the confusion of Australian refugee policy. Not only are the determination system and the policy process inadequate, but the Australian parliamentary system is inexperienced and insecure in regard to immigration policy. There is no dispute that immigration policy is an expression of sovereignty of the nation-state and that Australia, in its refugee and detention policies, has every right to regulate the entry and exit of persons. However, refugee policy derives from international obligations to which Australia is a signatory, and which recognise that external factors beyond the control of the state will determine whether certain individuals can enter or remain within the state.

An international organisation, the UNHCR has a mandate for the international protection of refugees, but in practical terms the responsibility for protection is located with individual states, which have the power to control entry and residence. In Australia's case refugee policy has at times been subsumed under immigration policy, with the distinct obligations and goals of refugee protection being overridden by immigration control.

It is the last aspect, control, that has been highlighted by the practice of detention in Australian refugee policy. Australia has chosen the governmental administrative system over the adjudicative system, giving primacy to ministerial discretion. A change of government creates a shift of focus and policy according to the incumbent minister. The administrative system for determining refugee status became entwined with immigration policy, as in the treatment of the Chinese students after the Tiananmen Square massacre, and foreign policy, as in the treatment of Cambodian asylum-seekers during the Cambodian Peace Plan initiatives.

Boat people attracted sensational media attention, clearly out of proportion to their actual numbers. A total of 2988 boat people arrived between November 1989 and September 1997, and of this total, 2289 were removed from Australia. Fewer than 3000 people over eight years does not constitute an invasion. With just under 700 stayers over eight years, it cannot be argued that refugee policy is not working. On the contrary, such a small number needs investigating, especially the number of Chinese returned in 1996/97 when the percentage of returnees was higher than those granted refugee status.[22] This occurred in the period when detainees were not informed of their legal rights. Many of these returnees could have been *bona fide* refugees if they had gone through the review process, highlighting the anomalies in the administrative system and the extreme and discriminatory measures the Government will take in order to control who enters Australia.

In May 1996 the Minister for Immigration Philip Ruddock canvassed for the removal of the tribunal system which would abolish the Refugee Review Tribunal. He consistently criticises the tribunal system for being too slow and would like to streamline appeals by removing at least one of the layers in the process of immigration and refugee status applications. He argues that the existing system routinely leads to protracted litigation through the Federal Court on points of law or through the High Court on human rights questions, and this results in delays to the process with appellants remaining in detention until the matter is resolved. Removal of the tribunals would help reduce delays; however, it would strengthen the bureaucratic authority of the Department of Immigration over individual applications. This would lead to increased power for the Minister and the Minister's decision-making process in regard to individual and group applications for refugee status. The tribunal system was set up to avoid or mitigate this situation and give a broader input into the refugee application process; without it, there would be a culture of control by the Minister.[23]

Australia's mandatory detention policy breaches international human rights standards. It has been used by successive governments as a policy of control and discrimination. Alternatives to detention have been mooted by many sources. The 'Alternative Detention Model', endorsed by the Human Rights and Equal Opportunity Commission and a number of peak organisations in the *Charter of Minimum Requirements for Legislation Relating to the Detention of Asylum-seekers,* provides a more flexible and more appropriate detention model consistent with human rights requirements.[24]

# 5
# International Comparisons

Immigration, especially refugee policy, is a central issue for politics and public policy in advanced industrial democracies at the beginning of the twenty-first century. The electoral politics of Europe, North America and Australia show the level of anxiety and fear aroused by unplanned migration. Sudden influxes of asylum-seekers, often a nation's 'other,' highlight national insecurity. During the 1970s and early 1980s a policy shift occurred in international migration: low politics, with a focus on 'problems of domestic governance, especially labour market and demographic policies', was replaced by high politics, with a focus on relations between states, including questions of war and peace, boundaries and territories.[1] However, this shift was short-lived; during the late 1980s and 1990s political interest reverted to low politics and domestic governance. As the previous chapter showed, Australia followed this pattern. Boat people had easy entrance in the late 1970s, but by the 1990s they faced administrative, legal and public barriers, accentuating the tensions between domestic governance and international obligations.

This chapter presents a comparative study of refugee policies in several countries, with specific reference to asylum policy and the use of detention. Britain has historical, political and immigration links with Australia; France provides a model with its system of 'denizens'; the

European Union is developing policies in an area that is experiencing large flows of asylum-seekers. The United States and Canada are immigration nations like Australia, but they have developed different refugee policies.

All these countries have constructed an 'other', and the details of their policies and attitudes reveal how they manage their 'other'. Some, such as Canada, have taken a humanitarian approach, incorporating structures of equity and fairness; others, such as France, have allowed asylum-seekers social rights.

## United Kingdom

*Proudly they learn all men to condemn*
*and all their race are true-born Englishmen.*
*Dutch, Walloons, Flemings, Irishmen and Scots,*
*Vaudois, Valtelins and Huguenots . . .*
*Fate jumbled them together, God knows how;*
*Whate'er they were, they're true-born English now.*

Daniel Defoe[2]

Traditionally, Britain has been one of the great emigration countries of the world, with immigration having a less significant place.[3] Britain has traditionally maintained immigration control, a factor which now places it outside the aims and policies of the European Union. After World War II immigration legislation specifically targeted and controlled immigration from countries of the new Commonwealth, particularly the West Indies and the Indian subcontinent.[4] As a signatory to the 1951 Convention Relating to the Status of Refugees and its 1967 Protocol, Britain had international obligations to allow family reunion of the West Indians, Pakistanis and Indians entering Britain.

Against these international obligations the Conservative Government maintained every conceivable administrative and legislative device to restrict coloured immigration and coloured refugees, which it justified in terms of 'race relations'.[5] Anti-immigration parties and groups such as the National Front have stoked the anti-alien and anti-immigrant feelings, which influenced the Conservative Right, under Thatcher from the late 1970s, to maintain tough controls on immigration, especially 'coloured' immigration. The restrictive policies of both Thatcher and

Major, due to economic recession and high levels of unemployment, gained popularity with the British public during the 1980s and 1990s.

Numbers of asylum applications rose from 1500 in 1979 to 13 000 in 1989; most were border claimants predominantly from the former colonies of the United Kingdom.[6] The Refugee Determination Unit, part of the Home Office, is the authority for determining claims for asylum. Applicants who have been rejected can appeal to the Immigrant Advisory Service.

Initially, applications are made to an immigration officer at the port of entry, and this report is forwarded to the Home Office, where it is passed or rejected. Applicants should get temporary admission after the interview, but if the immigration officer believes the applicant will abscond, the applicant is detained, with the right to seek bail if no decision is made on their case within seven days. If both bail and temporary admission are refused, the asylum-seeker is detained pending a decision on the case, rarely in excess of twelve months. Detention is a highly contentious issue in the United Kingdom, and in 1993 a Charter for Immigration Detainees was compiled by the Joint Council for the Welfare of Immigrants and other organisations representing refugees, migrant workers, and human rights.[7]

Two Acts were introduced in the 1990s. The *Asylum and Immigration Appeals Act 1993,* including the *Asylum Appeals (Procedure) Rules 1993,* set up new procedures for asylum appeals; it also reduced asylum-seekers' access to housing, introduced fingerprinting of asylum-seekers (including children), and reduced the time-scale of appeals. In 1996 the *Asylum and Immigration Act* allowed for certain asylum applications to be certified on refusal, bringing them into the accelerated appeals system. To be certified, a refused asylum claim must meet one of the following criteria:

a) The applicant is a national of a country included in a list of Designated Countries of Origin . . . In considering an asylum claim from a national of a Designated Country regard will be given to the fact that the country has been designated as one in which it appears there is, in general, no serious risk of persecution;

b) The applicant arrived at UK immigration control without a passport and could give no reasonable explanation for so doing;

c) The applicant sought leave to enter, or gained leave to enter, using an invalid passport;

d) Five additional categories of asylum claim which may be certified: claims that do not raise a fear of persecution for a Convention reason; claims that are manifestly untrue or the basis of the application has fallen away; claims made after the initiation of enforcement action; claims which are manifestly false or where evidence submitted in support of the claim is manifestly fraudulent; claims which are either frivolous or vexatious.[8]

The asylum-seeker can seek employment six months after submitting the application, and income support is available only if they have claimed asylum at the port of entry to the United Kingdom. Temporary housing is available from local authorities only while their application and any subsequent appeal remains undecided, and only if they have no other accommodation. All unsuccessful asylum-seekers have the right to appeal to an independent adjudicator prior to removal from the United Kingdom.[9] Asylum-seekers are also entitled to medical and dental treatment, and education of school-age children is the responsibility of local education authorities. Adults on income support can get concessionary fees for adult and further education courses.[10]

Overall, the UK system is 'regarded as an effective, flexible and discretionary; one that largely protects claimants rights while placing a strong emphasis on deterrence mechanisms'.[11] However, strong criticism by Amnesty International of the arbitrary detention of asylum-seekers was followed by a hunger strike by asylum-seekers in Rochester Prison, Kent, in January 1997. Asylum-seekers from Nigeria, Somalia, Algeria and Romania sought recognition of their prolonged incarceration, without access to any court or similar review body while their applications for asylum were considered by the Home Office.

Amnesty International reports that the average length of detention has increased to eight months, and sometimes up to twelve months. Immigration officials are not obliged to give specific reasons for the detention of an applicant, and there is almost no judicial scrutiny of decisions to detain; this results in arbitrary decision-making and the wrongful and unnecessary incarceration of particularly vulnerable persons. Amnesty's criticism is valid criticism and the increase in detention facilities, particularly in prisons, illuminates the point. The number of asylum-seekers incarcerated at any one time has increased to 800, a three fold increase since 1993; approximately 300 detainees are held in prisons,[12] although their only 'offence' is to have sought asylum.

## France

France has been a country of immigration, but it no longer wishes
to be . . .
Pasqua[13]

During the twentieth century immigration was a fundamental feature in the formation of modern France.[14] However, unlike Australia, Canada and the United States, France has not endowed immigration with the status of a founding myth. Hollifield contends that the legitimacy accorded to legal immigration in France is the outcome of the republican consensus that is both nationalist and universalist.[15] This is evident in the period after World War II when French political development promoted the universalist ideals of the French Revolution, especially in human and civil rights, while at the same time promoting French nationalism. Immigration became a major aspect of the policies of economic and social reconstruction, aiming to maintain an open society. However, the synthesis between republican and nationalist ideals is fraught with tensions, which have given rise to anti-immigration groups such as Le Pen's Front National.[16]

France accepted guest-workers from the 1950s, initially from other European states; with the decolonisation of the 1960s, migration from former African colonies rose. By the 1970s the French economy relied on foreign workers, who were employed in substantial numbers in almost every sector. Employers lobbied successfully for the government to ease restrictions on immigration. Then an economic recession, beginning in 1973 with the Arab oil embargo, brought an end to this period of high and open immigration and the flexible use of foreign labour.

Immigrants were classified as guests rather than settlers, 'more as a liability than an asset . . . and the French government began to back away from official ties to former colonies in North and West Africa'.[17] Socialist governments during the 1980s, led by Mitterand, initiated liberal immigration policies with the protection of French labour. A backlash, led by the Front National and other anti-immigrant and xenophobic groups, emerged in the late 1980s, and continues today.

As refugees and asylum-seekers entered Europe in the late 1980s and early 1990s, France managed to control and limit the influx relatively well, much better than most of its European neighbours. Numbers of asylum-seekers rose from 30 000 in 1985 to 55 000 in 1990.[18] In 1993 a new right-wing government restricted immigration, naturalisation and refugee policy.

In 1993 the Minister for the Interior introduced a bill to prevent illegal immigrants, including asylum-seekers, from benefiting from French social security, especially health care. This onslaught on foreigners' social rights was resisted, and eventually the right to emergency medical care was granted. Just as disturbing was a bill to limit the civil rights of immigrants and asylum-seekers by increasing the powers of the police and the administration to detain and deport unwanted migrants.[19] These 1993 bills were restrictionist measures to stop immigration, a tall order as asylum-seekers and refugees flowed out of Eastern Europe.

France has two authorities responsible for determination of refugee applications. The Office for the Protection of Refugees and Stateless Persons (OFPRA), a public institution in the Ministry of Foreign Affairs with both budgetary and legal autonomy, was formed in 1946 as part of the National Immigration Office to manage refugee and immigration flows. The Refugee Appeals Commission is an administrative tribunal that hears appeals against negative decisions from OFPRA.

Only 1 per cent of asylum-seekers apply at the border; two-thirds of the remainder enter France illegally, mainly via Italy or Belgium, while one-third come in on legitimate visas.[20] Upon admission the asylum-seeker is granted a temporary residence permit by the Prefecture and has one month to submit a written asylum application to OFPRA. Decisions are, supposedly, to be made within four months, although the average time is six to eight months, and the applicant can be called for an interview.

Three categories of application for asylum exist:

- Clearly founded applications, where the asylum-seeker is granted a residence permit from a diplomatic office; is well known to OFPRA or to non-government organisations for their commitment; or is from a country where human rights violations are common.
- Clearly unfounded applications, where no serious human rights violation is documented in the country of origin, or changes have

occurred in that country, or the motives of the applicant bear no relation to Article 1A of the Geneva Convention. Such applications may occur when the applicant has economic motives, or presents a false identity or false information, which is the basis of the claim.

- Requests requiring further investigation. These cases have a longer procedure for determination.

An applicant can be refused a temporary stay under three circumstances:

- The asylum-seeker has a tried country in which they are effectively admissible and protected against refoulment.
- The stay of the asylum-seeker represents a serious threat to public order.
- The asylum claim is fraudulent, is an abusive use of the asylum procedures or is used only to prevent a pronounced or impending removal measure.[21]

The Refugee Appeals Commission deals with 80–90 per cent of the rejections from OFPRA. Legal aid is available to applicants through the Office of Legal Assistance, created in 1991, which deals with approximately 350 claims per month. During the procedure an applicant is granted a three-month residence permit, which is renewable, but work permits have not been granted since 1991 and social assistance is minimal and only for a maximum of one year. Detention, as mentioned before, is allowed for asylum-seekers at airports for up to thirty days in 'waiting zones'[22] while an initial assessment is made. Apart from this legislation, an asylum-seeker may be detained only in exceptional circumstances, and even then the law provides guarantees.[23]

French policies, like those of other European countries, must conform with those of the European Union.

## European Union[24]

During the 1990s dramatic political, economic, social and cultural changes in Europe—the unification of Germany, the collapse of communist regimes, conflicts in Eastern Europe—produced high instability and mass movements of people. Member states of the European Union have tightened their immigration policies, and a restrictive approach has been taken to refugees and asylum-seekers by both authorities and groups of the right.

The Treaty of European Union, or Treaty of Maastricht, had as its major goal, upon its signing in February 1992, the achievement of political union and the final stages of economic and monetary union in Europe. Immigration policy illuminates the concept of the community or union as compared to individual states. The Schengen Agreement of June 1985, between the Benelux states (Belgium, the Netherlands and Luxembourg) and France and Germany, was a precursor of this concept.[25]

Harmonisation is the basis of immigration policy implemented by the European Union, and the *Single European Act* of 1987 instigated 'an area without internal frontiers in which the free movement of goods, *persons*, services and capital is ensured'.[26] EU officials and European governments are facing the challenge of implementing a border-free Europe while providing adequate protection 'against illegal immigration, false asylum claims, drug smuggling, and terrorism . . . and while EU bureaucrats are convinced that harmonised immigration and asylum policies are needed now more than ever, national governments (not just the British) are dragging their feet.'[27]

The principal agreements set up to eventually create a border-free Europe and common visa policies are the Schengen Agreement, the Ad Hoc Immigration and Trevi groups, and the *Single European Act*, all of which have been aimed at co-ordinating refugee and asylum policies and sharing information, ultimately alleviating the illegal immigration problem which currently exists. The Trevi Group was established in 1975 to bring together officials responsible for law enforcement and which, by the late 1980s, extended to include the examination of questions connected with illegal and clandestine immigration and asylum inflows. Out of this group the Ad Hoc Group on Immigration was formed in 1986, focusing on issues pertaining to immigration. The high degree of inter-group influence and negotiation has resulted in various agreements such as the Dublin Convention, signed by all EU members, designed to prevent multiple or successive applications being submitted by an asylum-seeker in more than one state; and the problem of 'refugees in orbit', where no state accepts responsibility for particular asylum-seekers. The ratification of the Maastricht Treaty in 1993 also endorsed limited political rights, such as voting in local elections, for nationals of one member state who reside in another member state, a step towards the creation of an EU citizenship.[28]

Most European states, like Britain and France, took restrictive measures regarding asylum-seekers and immigration in general during the 1990s. Governments claim that these restrictive measures are aimed at illegal immigrants and not at refugees; but in fact the barriers, such as visas and carrier sanctions, have a deterrent effect for genuine refugees in attempting to reach Europe. Harmonisation policies find the lowest common denominator to make all EU states equally unwelcoming, and at times they tinker with the Convention definitions.[29]

The European Union has not been able to come up with a common solution to contemporary challenges of asylum issues. Nationalistic considerations have prevailed over humanitarian and human rights concerns as focus on protection of refugees has shifted to focus on protection of the receiving countries' borders. European governments have enacted a range of anti-immigrant laws, creating a 'Fortress Europe' and expelling many illegals. As far back as March 1995 the UNHCR criticised the European Union's agreement on 'minimum guarantees' for asylum procedures, which the UNHCR is concerned may erode basic asylum principles. Asylum-seekers could be barred from the processes of appeal, a basic principle of international refugee law, and not be allowed to remain in the country until a final decision is made.[30]

The UNHCR is concerned at the increasing use of detention in Europe; asylum-seekers are detained for weeks, months and even years in closed camps, prisons or airport transit zones while they await a decision on their claim or access to the asylum procedure. The European Council on Refugees and Exiles criticises local courts for basing detention orders on insufficient, and often misleading, information provided by local authorities, without investigating individual cases to the extent possible under the law. However, the council also reports that the average time of detention is ten days, arguing that the public debate and criticism relates only to a small percentage of the detainees.[31] This is a spurious argument: nothing justifies the unnecessary, and at times unlawful, detention of any individual.

Conditions of detention vary throughout Europe: in some countries detainees have gone on hunger strike, rioted and even committed suicide. Harmonisation, being worked upon by the fifteen member states of the European Union, will hopefully enable all states in the region to have consistent policy on reception conditions for asylum-seekers and refugees and will include the human rights considerations that are part of the Geneva Convention.[32]

Tensions within the nation-state and community or union debates have taken priority in the formation of the European Union. In migration policy individual member states have differed in their preferred outcomes for policy of the European Union; the plight of asylum-seekers has been overlooked or placed second to political and economic directives in the formation of EU policies.

As a political union the European Union must create a new conception of insiders, outsiders and citizenship, which is still in process and, at times, contentious. The rise of xenophobic groups such as the Front National in France and neo-Nazi groups in Germany has caused division in European states, with asylum-seekers sometimes suffering the racist backlash caused by unemployment, insecurity and economic recessions.[33]

## United States of America

> Give me your tired, your poor,
> Your huddled masses, yearning to breathe free,
> The wretched refuse of your teeming shore.
> Send these, the homeless, tempest-tost to me,
> I lift my lamp beside the golden door!
>
> Emma Lazarus[34]

America is undisputedly a nation of immigrants and by its nature will always be one. Yet for more than a decade a backlash against illegal immigrants has shaped the political discourse about immigration and refugees. The general public, as in Australia, appears to be unhappy about immigration;[35] its relationship with employment and welfare causes unease, and at times anger, towards specific groups such as the Cubans, Haitians and Mexicans. Opinion polls report that Americans would prefer to have immigration levels reduced, but taxes, crime and health care are higher priorities.[36]

Immigration policy, which includes refugee policy, has two strands: the legal 'front door' for immigrants and the 'back door' for illegal aliens. Despite attempts to keep the front door open while closing the back door, illegal immigration is high. Illegal entry into industrialised countries such as the United States has become the most important method of entry. [37]

US refugee policy has, historically, been ideologically driven, fuelled by the Cold War doctrine from the 1950s of accepting political refugees escaping from communist or leftish regimes and therefore entwined with foreign policy.[38] Of refugees entering the United States from 1946 to 1990, 96 per cent came from communist or ex-communist countries such as Cuba (628 000), Indochina (612 000), Afghanistan (14 000), and from the communist states of Eastern Europe and the former Soviet Union (729 000).[39]

Although the United States did not sign the 1951 Convention Relating to the Status of Refugees, it did ratify the 1967 Protocol. Foreign policy determined the formulation of the United States refugee definition with the inclusion, between 1953 and 1980, of 'any person fleeing a communist-dominated state', reflecting the Cold War bias. This definition remained in effect until the *Refugee Act 1980* formally removed opposition to communism from the statutory definition of a refugee, complying with the refugee definition of the Convention. The change in definition subsequently increased the number of people potentially eligible to enter the United States from 3 million to 15 million.[40]

The *Refugee Act 1980* set the guidelines for refugee legislation providing, a federal policy for admissions without the bias of ideology or geography. It superseded several *ad hoc* legal measures that had been developed under emergency conditions. The *Refugee Act* addressed three areas: '(1) establishing the right of asylum in United States statutory law; (2) instigating a federal policy of continuing refugee admissions; and (3) institutionalising resettlement assistance for refugees'.[41]

The Act also establishes a statutory basis for granting asylum in the United States consistent with the 1967 Protocol. If a request for asylum is denied by the Immigration and Naturalization Service (INS), the asylum-seeker, designated 'alien', may renew the asylum request with an immigration judge during a deportation or exclusion hearing. The *Illegal Immigration Reform and Immigrant Responsibility Act 1996* expanded the eligibility for asylum by including in the refugee definition aliens who have been subject to or have a well-founded fear of being subject to coercive population-control methods, such as forced abortion or involuntary sterilisation.[42]

The admission of refugees and granting of asylum have been subject to the pressures of foreign policy, budgetary restrictions and lobby groups, rather than adhering to Act and thus, in some regards, have violated US obligations under international treaties. Although the United States has admitted a larger number of refugees for permanent residence than most countries, it has been a major player in the root causes of refugee flows in certain areas, such as Central and South America, exemplifying that foreign policy dictates refugee policy. In

many cases the provisions of the Act for a fair asylum policy and ideologically neutral admissions were not implemented; instead, the United
States continued to favour refugees from communist or former communist countries. The United States admitted 731 647 refugees during
October 1981 to September 1990, 95 per cent were from communist
countries, while refugees from other parts of the world, such as Africa
where there was genuine persecution, were not granted entry.[43]

During 1980 the 'Mariel boatlift', in which up to 130 000 Cuban
emigrants arrived by boat on the shores of the United States, became a
benchmark for refugee policies. The Mariel boat lift started on 1 April
1980 when six Cubans applied for political asylum at the Peruvian
embassy in Havana, Cuba. President Castro withdrew the guards, allowing over 10 000 disenchanted Cubans to enter the embassy grounds,
seeking asylum. The asylum-seekers were allowed to leave to countries
that had agreed to resettle them, including the United States who agreed
to take 3500. After three days Castro terminated the exodus, leaving the
asylum-seekers stranded in the embassy grounds. In the United States
the Cuban-American community responded by assembling a small fleet
of boats, bringing supplies to the stranded asylum-seekers and returning
to the United States with the Cuban emigrants, thus beginning the
Mariel boatlift. Cuban exiles had been welcomed in the United States for
the previous two decades, admitted under the parole of the Attorney-
General as part of the immigration program. The *Refugee Act 1980* restricted the parole power to exceptional, individual cases, but the sudden
arrival of the Cuban asylum-seekers threatened to undermine the
Act.[44]

The Carter administration created a new status for the Mariel emigrants; the special entrant category negated refugee or asylum status and
prevented them from applying for reimbursement or resettlement costs;
or for permanent resident status, which is the first step towards citizenship. Between 20 April and 20 June 1980, over 125 000 Cubans arrived
in the United States by boat. This included criminals and people suffering from mental illness. Most of the Mariel Cubans were technically
inadmissible under US immigration law as they lacked a valid passport
or visa.[45] As was the case with the sudden arrival of the Cambodian boat
people in Australia during 1989 and early 1990, government agencies
responsible for determining asylum claims were overwhelmed. The
immigration service had too few staff to evaluate individual applicants;

the asylum system became overloaded and the public perceived the Government as being unable to control its borders. A similar scenario happened in Australia where public opinion, fuelled by the media, perceived a lack of control of Australian borders and an invasion. However, the number of asylum-seekers who arrived in the United States in one year alone (1980) was 150 000 to 160 000; in Australia only 3000 boat people arrived over eight years, from 1989 to 1997.[46]

Following smaller groups during 1980, a large influx of Haitians arrived during 1981, escaping the Duvalier regime of political persecution and human rights abuse. Again the classification of these groups of migrants was based on US foreign policy directives. Haitian boat people were not recognised as Convention refugees but as economic migrants escaping poverty; therefore asylum could be refused. The Reagan administration had previously given priority, in terms of development aid generally allocated for the Caribbean and Central American region, to the Duvalier regime, which President Reagan recognised as an anti-communist ally.

A new category was devised, 'Cuban and Haitian Entrants Status Pending', which allowed those who had arrived before 1980 to be paroled but not to be legally defined as refugees,[47] a political move to dissipate criticism of the treatment of the Haitian boat people. The enacting of the special entrant status undermined the provisions of the *Refugee Act 1980* and presaged the future politicisation of admissions.

The influence of US foreign policy led to the instigation of an 'Interdiction Program' in September 1981 to stop the flow of Haitians, based on three objectives: to keep a friendly relationship with the non-communist Duvalier regime; to promote economic development of Haiti; and to prevent all undocumented and illegal migration from Haiti to the United States. The Interdiction Program allowed the US Coast Guard to board Haitian vessels on the high seas and return those whom the US officials deemed unsuitable for asylum application. There was no concern for human rights or democratic reform in Reagan's foreign policy goals in this instance.[48] Of the 1981 influx of 23 000 Haitians who were given asylum hearings aboard a US ship, only eight were allowed to enter the United States to pursue their claims. Of the 24 600 Haitians intercepted between 1981 and 1991, only twenty-eight were allowed to enter. This was a successful method to reduce asylum claims on-shore. Haitians who evaded the Coastguard and landed in the United

States were detained, while most other undocumented aliens were allowed to remain free, a system of discrimination against the Haitians. This parallels Australian practice.[49]

In 1994, after a sudden large influx of boat people, the United States reverted to interdiction and safe-haven policies. It was the goal of the INS to control the entry of persons into the United States by intercepting boat people from Haiti and Cuba and diverting them to safe havens that would provide protection to those who required it.[50] However, in contrast to the previous interdiction program, the Clinton administration put immigration control and humanitarian concerns ahead of foreign policy and ideological concerns. The safe haven procedure was a means of screening asylum-seekers, allocating refugee status for those who qualified, and repatriating those who did not and were in no fear of persecution.

While the Interdiction Program was an alternative to lengthy processing of on-shore asylum claims and detention of those who arrived by boat, it was also a method of deterring prospective boat people. Interdiction programs appeal to governments of destination, alleviating on-shore resources and stopping asylum-seekers entering the country.[51] The moral costs of interdiction are compelling if genuine refugees are deterred and therefore placed at risk within their country of origin. The fairness and accuracy of the determinations depend on the adjudication procedures and whether denials are reviewable. The interdiction process does not protect the rights of asylum-seekers unless the interdictor adheres to international obligations and humanitarian concerns. In the US case the Interdiction Program effectively became a border control program for boat people, successfully deterring and repatriating Haitians, but it violated the human rights of genuine refugees. Australia did not employ the interdiction process, although the UN Comprehensive Plan of Action (CPA) had similarities whereby asylum-seekers were processed off-shore rather than allowed to enter the on-shore programs.[52]

Detention as a deterrent was revived in response to the influx of Cuban and Haitian asylum-seekers. In 1954, the abandonment of the policy of detention by the INS was characterised as 'one more step forward toward humane administration of the immigration laws'.[53] Previously refugees, asylum-seekers and immigrants were screened and held, if necessary, at the Ellis Island immigration inspection and control centre in New York Harbor. After the 1954 policy change the vast number of aliens entering the United States were released on conditional 'parole'; 'sometimes required to post bonds or placed under supervision'.[54]

The liberal parole policy was explicated by the US Supreme Court in a 1958 case, setting out that

> the parole of aliens seeking admission is simply a device through which needless confinement is avoided while administrative proceedings are conducted . . . physical detention of aliens is now the exception, not the rule, and is generally employed only as to security risks or those likely to abscond . . . *Certainly this policy reflects the humane qualities of an enlightened civilization.*[55]

Only a tiny number of aliens were detained from 1954 until the policy changes of 1980. The INS suspended the policy of release and detained aliens on an *ad hoc* basis during the unanticipated arrival of 130 000 Cubans by boat. The Cubans were either released immediately or detained for a period at INS detention centres, while the Haitians who arrived during this period were incarcerated to prevent them from seeking refuge in the United States.[56]

Haitian refugees were initially treated as illegal immigrants and then as economic refugees. Under the latter category they were classified as fleeing dire economic conditions rather than political repression, and thus had no rights to aid and were not given the public support provided to groups such as the Cubans, Vietnamese, Hungarians or Soviet Jews. Cubans had emigrated to the United States in greater numbers than the Haitians. The Cuban exiles exercised considerable political power while the Haitians were neither politically or economically powerful. This gave the Cubans influence and power as a domestic pressure group with the result that they could influence domestic policy and so, were treated differently from the Haitians. The Vietnamese were treated very differently from the Haitians. The United States perceived the Vietnamese as political allies whom they were morally obliged to assist. In contrast, the Haitians were detained for years and after release got no support in finding jobs and housing, or otherwise adapting to life in the United States.

By 1984 the INS had apprehended 1.3 million undocumented aliens, with an estimated two to three times as many slipping through. In this crisis detention was seen as a method that would deter prospective 'illegals'. The newly arrived immigrants, especially the illegals, were blamed for the social problems that were undermining US society, with the effect of renewing concerns about illegal immigration and the 'alien' crisis.[57]

Paradoxically it is because immigrants, and especially illegals, supplied cheap labour that the back-door entry of guest-workers into the workforce was tolerated. After World War II the Bracero program was instituted, allowing US employers to import workers from Mexico on a temporary basis. This continued legally until 1964 and illegally after that. It became commonplace, post-Bracero, to employ illegals for low-paid manual work. Within this context of contradictory economic and political factors the US Congress enacted the *Immigration Reform and Control Act 1986,* allowing illegal immigrants who had been in the United States since 1982 to apply for legal status. Only a small number were anticipated, but 3 million applied with an approval rating of 96 per cent.[58]

The 1986 Act made it illegal for US citizens to knowingly employ aliens not authorised to work in the United States. Monetary penalties ranged from $250 to $10 000. Kitty Calavita argues that, although the 1986 Act legalised millions of undocumented immigrants, it did not ease employer sanctions or solve the problem of illegal immigration.[59] However, public backlash against immigration was fuelled by concern, in the 1980s, that the United States had lost control of its borders and immigration restrictionism intensified.[60] Detention became an alternative that was used to deter the flow of illegal immigration.

The detention policy applied to all aliens who entered the United States without valid entry documents under the Act. Without documentation entrants can be detained and precluded from release, even if they pose no security risk or no risk of absconding. Also, 'aliens may be held pending final determination of their admissibility and may also be held indefinitely after a final order of exclusion has been issued until the US finds a country willing to accept them'. Helton points out that the automatic detention of aliens infringes basic obligations under the Convention and Protocol Relating to the Status of Refugees and, although detention as a deterrent measure may be politically and publicly popular, it is of uncertain effect.[61]

Economic issues were still at the centre of the debate when Congress passed the *Immigration Act 1990.* Three principal factors were integral to this reform. Firstly, the US economy and the workplace were transformed by globalisation, that is, employment shifted from manufacturing to service. Secondly, employment fell in the intensely populated areas where manufacturing once took place and where illegal immigrants had settled. Thirdly, fertility rates declined so that immigration was still required to supply population growth and a skilled workforce. Family reunion was a priority and the proportion of 'economic visas' issued rose considerably, from 54 000 before the Act to 140 000 after. This Act liberalised immigration policy while targeting illegal aliens; in other words, 'closing the back door while keeping the front door open'.[62]

The *Immigration Act 1990* revised all grounds for exclusion and deportation, 'significantly rewriting the political and ideological grounds', limiting the exclusion of aliens on foreign policy grounds, and repealing the bar against the admission of communists as non-immigrants. While asylum policy is regulated by the *Refugee Act 1980* as well as refugee policy, in 1991 new regulations established a corps of asylum officers within the INS. Authority for decision-making shifted from district directors to the Asylum Officer Corps, and a resource documentation centre was set up to provide information on human rights conditions throughout the world. While 73 637 asylum applications were filed in 1990, only 62 000 were filed in 1991.[63] By the end of 1993/94 a backlog of 420 794 asylum cases resulted from administrative shortcomings, such as a shortage of asylum officers and the class action by Salvadoreans and Guatemalans on grounds of discrimination against them in the 1980s. INS asylum officers refer cases that are not granted asylum directly to immigration judges, who consider the asylum claim in the context of deportation hearings.[64]

Persons who enter legally or without inspection may affirmatively apply for status with the INS. Approximately 65 per cent of affirmative asylum-seekers have been in the United States an average of six months before they apply. Documents are filed with the INS or an immigration judge. Applicants are interviewed and given a list of providers of legal aid; attorneys or personal representatives may attend asylum interviews. Asylum officers make the final determination, although an immigration judge will examine a claim regardless of whether an asylum officer has already made a determination. Asylum officers interview applicants who are in detention to identify those who might be eligible for asylum and whose parole might be in the public interest. Applicants must establish they have a 'credible fear' of persecution.

Appeals from immigration judges go to the Board of Immigration Appeals, part of the Executive Office for Immigration Review, and, depending on the nature of the proceedings, appeals can then be taken to the federal judicial system. If a claim for asylum or withholding is denied by the board and the applicant is undergoing deportation proceedings, it is possible to seek review in the US Court of Appeals,[65] similar to the process of review in Australia.

New asylum applications that are scheduled for interview are finalised, in 35 per cent of cases, within 120–150 days. An average case before an immigration judge can take more than twelve months and the Board of Immigration Appeals may take up to two years to decide an asylum appeal. However, while the determination status is being processed, the applicant has permitted to work, unless they are in detention, and relief for social assistance, in limited circumstances, is available from federal, state and local governments. Applicants are eligible to live in federal or state housing and their children may attend state schools. There are also private relief programs that supply services such as language education and legal representation.[66]

Detention remained within the 1990 Act but lost credibility on grounds of cost, space and increasing recognition that detention of genuine refugees is a violation of international law. Helton captures the nature of detention, as has often been applied by US procedures:

> Detention as a migration deterrence device applied on a categorical basis can violate both treaty and customary international law prohibitions against prolonged arbitrary detention. For example, the Universal Declaration, the cornerstone to any argument in support of protecting the 'inalienable rights of all members of the human family' (Preamble), declares, 'No one shall be subjected to arbitrary arrest, detention or exile'.[67]

Under international law the only permissible grounds for detention of aliens are that the individual might abscond, or for reasons of public safety. Refugees have the same protection as aliens under international law and, legally, may not be detained unnecessarily.

In 1990 an INS Pilot Parole Project was established to determine whether refugees were unnecessarily detained. The INS produced a set of requirements to be agreed upon by all aliens requesting release under the pilot program. The main requirements, after they had been cleared, were that they report to the local INS office monthly, appear for all immigration hearings, and appear for deportation if ultimately ordered excluded.[68]

Community involvement was considered crucial for the project as well as legal representation; where both were provided, there were high levels of compliance with the reporting requirements. The Pilot Parole Project, which concluded in October 1991, demonstrated the value of a durable release authority, since it provided 95 per cent compliance regarding appearances while on parole.

This carefully administered program, working with community and government agencies, was shown to be a successful alternative to detention. It prevents the unnecessary detention of refugees and the resulting human rights violations, and it is also cost-effective; it is much cheaper than maintaining detention facilities. In his conclusion Helton sums up the program:

> the experience of the US immigration authorities with a pilot release program demonstrates that *interests of immigration control can be reconciled in a workable fashion with the human rights of refugees*. The INS detention policy can be put into better alignment with an articulated mission of humane treatment for deserving aliens and targeted enforcement in respect of others. The experience could usefully guide policy making elsewhere.[69]

Despite the end of the Cold War, foreign policy and ideological pressures still dictate US refugee policy. Detention only became an issue in the 1980s, as with Australia, due to sudden increases in asylum-seekers. The US authorities have approached the issue of detention in a systematic manner, trying alternatives such as the Parole Project. However, the majority of Haitian boat people were, from 1981, detained and treated in a similar manner to the Cambodian boat people in Australia. Both of these groups were subject to detention as a deterrent, and both groups had their human rights violated by their detention.

The Parole Project alleviated the human rights concerns and, for the authorities, the high costs of detention and the lack of facilities. The major emphasis for the United States has been on controlling 'back door' illegal immigrants who arrive on the borders of the US in millions,[70] a factor with which Australia does not have to contend.

In most industrialised countries barriers are going up against migrants and refugees alike, and the United States is no exception. Although still accepting high numbers of migrants, the United States is placing restrictions on them. The *Immigration Reform and Nationality Act 1996* proposed harsh measures for immigrants, which limited welfare benefits, medical and educational facilities or access to them. The *Illegal Immigration Reform and Immigrant Responsibility Act 1996* also had a substantial impact on the asylum and refugee process when the definition of a refugee was expanded to include aliens who have been subject to, or have a well-founded fear of being subject to, coercive population-control methods such as forced abortion or involuntary sterilisation, as in the case of the Chinese one-child policy. This is a reflection of the pragmatic approach to policy-making of the time.[71]

## Canada

*They are too near to be great*
*But our children*
*Shall understand*
*When and how our*
*Fate was changed*
*And by whose hand.*[72]

Canada, like the United States and Australia, is a country of high levels of immigration. Canada and Australia have taken a similar stance on immigration, incorporating 'white policies' for similar periods before embracing multicultural policies. Most Western countries experienced increases in refugee and asylum applications during the 1980s; Canada and Australia both reduced their intake of immigrants in response to a world economic recession and the impact on their economies and levels of unemployment.

Australia and Canada share a common public law tradition, but have diverged in their regulation and control of refugee claims and illegal immigration. While Australia adopted, principally, the discretionary administrative model, Canada transferred from the administrative model to an adjudicative model in 1967. No person can be refrained from entering or be removed by a simple executive order, and a claim must be adjudicated unless the entrant has departed voluntarily. This model does not emphasise initial entry; it uses a non-universal and relatively simple visa system, submitting all claims for entry to an adjudicative process, which implies a right to entry for purposes of determination. This process 'extends constitutional procedural guarantees and legislation to refugee claimants, whose claims are submitted to a distinct adjudicatory agency; and makes extensive use of legal professionals in the decision-making process, leaving considerable room as well for resort to the courts'.[73]

A weakness of the adjudicative model is that determination is slow and expensive. Its main problem, however is in establishing the most appropriate procedure for adjudication of refugee claims.[74] The Canadian model relies on the concept that the state is not dominant; Australia emphasises the state and deploys more power in the administrative process. Under the adjudicative model the administrative system can be challenged; the Canadian system allows for this, giving more power to the judicial process. The adjudicative model contains a procedural administrative process, unlike the Australia model, which is discretionary. Refugee claims are presented to the Convention Refugee Determination Division of the Immigration and Refugee Board, an independent administrative tribunal performing quasi-judicial functions. If the claim is unsuccessful at this primary stage it enters the review system of the Adjudicative Division where adjudicators assess it; if it is unsuccessful, there is access to review and appeal in the court system.

Both models aim for regulation and control, but the adjudicative model is more effective than the administrative model. The adjudicative model is impartial and therefore fairer, and the treatment of asylum-seekers in Canada generally exemplifies this. Canada has recognised that illegal entrants and asylum-seekers have rights, especially the right to be heard and, if their claim can be justified, the right to be granted 'landed immigrant status'. This allows access to welfare benefits and freedom in the community while awaiting determination,[75] rights which have been denied in Australia.

Consequently it is possible to be granted refugee status on humanitarian grounds in Canada through the courts. The treatment of refugee claimants is consistent with the underlying assumptions of Canadian law:

> that some measure of international mobility is inevitable; that no rigid distinction can be drawn between early and late arrivals; that constitutional guarantees cannot therefore be preserved uniquely for one group; and that refugees should be treated no worse, in procedural terms, than other entry claimants.[76]

We have seen that refugee claimants in Australia are not entitled to welfare benefits, employment permits or medical care, a strategy designed to discourage applications for refugee status.

The Canadian *Immigration Act 1976* is the cornerstone of immigration and refugee policy, laying down the principles and objectives.[77] The Act defined three categories of individuals eligible for landed immigrant status:

- Family class.
- Humanitarian class, which includes Convention refugees and also persecuted and displaced persons who do not qualify as refugees under the rigid UN definition but who are members of a specially designated class created by the Canadian cabinet for humanitarian reasons.
- Independent class.[78]

The Act recognised a class for refugees, selected and admitted separately from immigrants. This complies explicitly recognition with Canada's legal obligations under the UN Convention and Protocol Relating to the Status of Refugees to protect foreign nationals against involuntary repatriation to countries where there is justifiable fear of persecution. The Act lays down criteria for the determination of refugee status and provides a legal process, at times complicated, with many levels of decision-making and at least two levels of appeal,[79] in contrast to the free rein for ministerial discretion in Australia. The Canadian Act's emphasis on humanitarian values highlights the difference between Canadian and Australian refugee policy. Australia's rhetoric of humanitarian values is undercut by administrative and foreign policy processes.

The Immigration and Refugee Board, responsible for refugee determination, has three divisions: the Convention Refugee Determination Division, the Immigration Appeal Division, and the Adjudication Division. The board is an administrative tribunal that operates independently of the political process and reports to Parliament through the Minister responsible for the *Immigration Act 1976*. The Refugee Division determines refugee claims in a manner, which is both flexible and informal in accordance with the Act, the Canadian Charter of Rights and Freedoms, and the Convention Relating to the Status of Refugees.[80]

'Fairness, compassion and openness' are the foundation of Canada's refugee determination. The three goals of this system are:

1. To hear and determine refugee claims as quickly as possible, in accordance with the law and in a manner which reflects Canada's *humanitarian traditions;*
2. To ensure that individuals and groups cannot use refugee claims or 'the refugee status determination process' as a means to circumvent our national immigration policies; and
3. To reassure the world community that Canada has an effective and *humanitarian* determination process that is consistent with our international commitments.[81]

The Convention Refugee Determination Division hears and determines all refugee claims made in Canada fairly and expeditiously and offers protection to those who genuinely need it, while discouraging abuse or misuse of the system. In this way, it is claimed, the Immigration and Refugee Board reflects 'the humanitarian values of Canadian society'.[82] At the hearing, every effort is made to ensure that claimants can put forward their cases as thoroughly and completely as possible. Claimants have the right to participate fully in the process, to be represented by counsel, and to engage the services of an interpreter. The presentation and acceptance of evidence at hearings is not restricted by technical or legal rules of evidence; the process is designed to elicit all the relevant information pertaining to a claim. A Refugee Hearing Officer assists the panel by ensuring that all available and relevant evidence is presented.[83]

In the case of a negative decision, claimants may apply for judicial review by the Federal Court Trial Division, but they must obtain leave of a Federal Court judge to do so. If the Federal Court agrees to hear the application, it will deal with questions of law, jurisdiction, alleged capricious findings of fact, or alleged failure to observe a principle of natural justice. If the Federal Court allows the application, it sends the claim back to the Refugee Division for rehearing.[84]

An Australian critique, in the National Population Council's *Refugee Review,* points out that the Canadian system is costly and results in long delays. The complex, multi-stage process, structured to give the applicant every chance to prove refugee status, does produce delays in review and adjudication, but it is thorough, with acceptance rates among the highest in the world. The Australian critique also claims that the Canadian process, while admirable in social justice terms and humanitarian intent, results in a growing number of claimants.[85]

Canada has a system that is bound by justice to give asylum-seekers 'a fair go', to be thorough in the determination process; Australia, steeped in the myth of 'a fair go', is prepared to cut corners for either economical or political reasons, leaving some asylum-seekers without full justice or recognition of their status, as in the case of the Cambodian boat people.

During the 1980s, refugee flows and asylum applications increased dramatically in Canada and refugee issues dominated the immigration scene. Two dramatic events brought asylum-seekers to public attention in the late 1980s. The first of these, in 1986, was the landing of the 'Tamil boat people' who, as it was ascertained later, had set out from West Germany. The second event occurred in 1987 when a group of Sikhs made an equally dramatic and newsworthy landing, by boat, on the shores of Canada.

Minister's permits were granted to the Tamils enabling them to stay in Canada and they were welcomed by the Minister for Immigration, Gerry Weiner, who vowed 'that boatloads of refugees would never be turned back as they once were'.[86] However, the Sikhs were treated differently, with the government recalling Parliament for an emergency session to amend the *Immigration Act*, introducing Bill C-84, the Refugee Deterrents and Detention Bill. This Bill gave the government authority to detain refugees for seven days without review, to keep undocumented refugees in detention indefinitely, to turn back boatloads of refugees in Canadian waters, and to conduct forcible searches for evidence that a person in the country of departure planned to help refugees to come to Canada. Clearly the Canadian Government feared the arrival of an overwhelming number of undocumented refugees.[87]

The Bill was watered down with deletion of the provision to turn back ships in Canadian waters and the non-reviewable seven-day detention. It was ironic that Bill C-84, enshrining Canada's harsh new attitude towards asylum-seekers, was introduced soon after Canada was awarded the prestigious UN Nansen Medal for 'recognition of their major and sustained contribution to the cause of refugees'.[88] The arrival of the Sikh asylum-seekers evoked discriminatory practice in an otherwise fair refugee policy and showed how one event can change the policy towards a particular group.

Canadians began to question the sudden influx of asylum-seekers and the genuineness of their plight, asking if they were leapfrogging the immigration queue and moving ahead of genuine refugees. Some Canadians saw the sudden influx of asylum-seekers as an invasion. Adding to this alarm was the controversy over what was to become known as the Singh Decision: claimants were awarded the right to judicial hearing, in which their credibility could be determined by a full oral hearing. Refugee claimants were guaranteed virtually the same social and legal protection accorded to Canadian citizens under the Charter of Rights and Freedoms. The resulting backlog of refugee determinations was at the expense of the Canadian taxpayer.[89]

In 1992 the *Refugee Reform Act* was modified by Bill C-86, deleting a number of the screening hearings held during the refugee determination process. Agreement of both panelists was required for the claim to succeed to the next stage, whereas previously only one of the two votes was required to proceed.[90] These changes aimed at expediency and cost efficiency. Bill C-86 also strengthened provisions that had been adopted, but not implemented, regarding the return of asylum-seekers to 'safe third countries', countries in which asylum-seekers had sojourned or traversed en route to Canada.[91] This was intended to break the process of 'asylum shopping', a strategy that Australia had experienced. However, the notion of a safe country is amorphous and this method can be interpreted as passing the buck.

Asylum-seekers enter Canada by two methods; either by boats from Europe or overland from the United States. Canada has been at the forefront in negotiations with other Western states in bilateral agreements on the removal of previously denied applicants and in the prevention of asylum seeking, and asylum shopping.[92] Half of Canada's refugees in the 1990s and into the 2000s are expected to be inland asylum-seekers, the majority coming from Central America via the United States. These agreements are important for Canada to stop the flow of asylum-seekers or to divert the flow back to other countries of 'first asylum', which the claimants have tried already.

Canada is not alone in this policy. As mentioned before, Australia is part of this group, and the CPA was a strategy in which both Australia and Canada participated (Chapter 4). This is one method which liberal democratic states are utilising to 'manage' immigration: they justify it in terms of their need to exercise control. However, these initiatives depart from the liberal principles, such as open policies and humanitarian concerns, which these states espouse.

Refugees are accepted by Canada through one of four programs in the refugee and humanitarian class: government-assisted; private group sponsorship; joint assistance; family class. Detention of asylum-seekers is strictly limited and preventive detention is regarded, by Canadian law, as an exceptional measure. However, arrivals may be detained if the immigration officer has a reasonable belief that the asylum-seeker: is an unconfirmed identity; is a danger to the public; is likely to abscond; is working without a valid work permit; or has overstayed their visitor's permit. If the purpose of detention, inquiry, examination or removal has not been enacted within 48 hours, the detainee is presented before an adjudicator for review of the reasons of detention. A follow-up review is required within the next seven days and at least once during every subsequent thirty days.[93]

Detention reviews, as with all immigration inquiries, are conducted by adjudicators who, as independent decision-makers, can order the detention or removal of persons deemed to pose a threat to the public. Adjudicators can order the continued detention of a person or the release of a person from detention, and set the terms and conditions of release, including the payment of a security deposit or the posting of a performance bond.

Detention reviews are conducted in public in the presence of the detainee and the adjudicator under the principles of natural justice as set out in the *Adjudication Division Rules.* Hearings must be recorded and the reasons for decisions must be given. Adjudicators have a primary role in the determination and review process, deciding if a person can obtain release from detention and reside in the community while awaiting their decision. Parliament has conferred broad discretionary powers upon adjudicators in that they may order the release of a person pursuant to the *Immigration Act* 'subject to such terms and conditions as they deem appropriate, including the payment of a security deposit or the posting of a performance bond'.[94] Adjudicators have power over the Minister to order the release of a detainee, even if the Minister has decided against release. In Australia the Minister makes the final decision. The strength of the adjudicative system is with the ability of the adjudicator to give an informed and impartial decision, which is separate from the political system.[95]

Under Canadian law detainees have rights to counsel, medical treatment, outdoor exercise and fresh air, indoor leisure and recreational activities. Legal aid lawyers are available, with legal representation being a right under the Act. Refugee applicants are not entitled to work until they have had a full board hearing and are determined as Convention refugees, but they are entitled to apply for welfare, including free prescription drugs and dental care. Education is available for children while their parents' claims are being assessed, and housing assistance is available on request. The provincial governments provide this social assistance, with eligibility based on need. The UNHCR has no role in the determination process and no right to intervene. In 1994, 70 per cent of claims were approved, with the main groups originating from Sri Lanka, Somalia, Iran, and the former Soviet Union.[96]

Immigration in Canada remains contentious, and, as in the United States, illegal migration looms large in the debate and the making of policy. Economic and social returns to Canada from immigrants are still positive,[97] although not as substantial as in earlier periods. The Canadian system of immigration regulation, within the jurisdiction of the *Immigration Act*, is more vulnerable to pressure from both public and private interest groups than in either Australia or the United States, but less susceptible to foreign policy than in the United States.

As in most liberal democracies, the trend in Canadian immigration policy has been away from the humanitarian to the economic, with an emphasis on business immigration. The percentage of business immigrants increased from 31 per cent in 1994 to 36.4 per cent in 1996, while the percentage of refugees entering Canada decreased from 25 per cent in 1991 to below 10 per cent in 1994. However, Canada has continued to admit more refugees per capita than any other country in the world. The 64 per cent of asylum-seekers who were granted refugee status in 1991 reflect a Canadian admittance rate, on a per capita basis, five times the rate of the United States.[98] Detention, while not mandatory as in Australia, does exist for undocumented arrivals. However, the adjudicative process, with its series of reviews along with release on parole, provides a humane, flexible and non-discriminatory process.

## Conclusion

After a liberal approach to immigration and refugee intakes during the 1970s, all these countries embarked on a more restrictionist approach to asylum-seekers and refugee determination during the 1980s and 1990s. It was an era of mass movements of people due to internal national conflicts and economic downturns throughout the world, which provoked a backlash against immigration. US refugee policy, like Australian refugee policy, was variable during the 1990s, and the admission of refugees and granting of asylum has continued to be determined by ideological and foreign policy concerns. Asylum-seekers escaping communist regimes have been granted access to the United States and, in most cases, escaped detention, while other groups (such as the Haitian boat people) have been detained as economic immigrants for, at times, lengthy periods. They appear to be the exception in an otherwise relatively fair detention policy. Although illegal immigration is a major problem for the United States, detention has been applied systematically; the parole system alleviates the need for expensive detention centres and the accompanying controversies.

Of these countries, Canada is the most liberal with its immigration policy, including the refugee determination process. Canada has adopted a sound process in the adjudicative system, and has a co-operative relationship between the administrative and judicial systems. Canada's *Immigration Act* enshrines a humanitarian approach. In the 1990s Canada, like most liberal democracies, put economic or business immigration ahead of humanitarian immigration, but the humanitarian aspect remains at the core of Canadian refugee determination.

The Canadian model, despite lengthy delays in determination and high costs, appears to be the most effective, most humane and fairest of the models we have looked at. The experience of the Sikh boat people in Canada in 1987 and the early 1990s resembles that of Cambodian boat people in Australia in 1989 and the early 1990s, and of Haitian boat people in the United States in 1981 and again in 1994. Other groups, such as the Tamils in Canada, the Vietnamese in Australia, and the Cubans in America, were not treated so harshly. Specific groups were targeted in a discriminatory manner for political purposes, such as deterrence for other would-be asylum-seekers, and to allay growing public discontent and fear. This was part of the worldwide backlash against asylum-seekers and refugees during the 1980s and 1990s, in which states used detention for deterrence.

European countries also increased the use of detention to counter the large increase of asylum-seekers in Europe during the 1980s and 1990s, in such numbers that Australia's influx of boat people looks minute in comparison. A backlash against migrants and the perceived threats of their increased numbers created a volatile climate in which refugee and detention policies were being established. The United Kingdom, France and the European Union have increased the use of detention, either in prisons, as in the case of the United Kingdom, or in airport transit zones, as in France, as a reaction to the increase in asylum-seekers. The asylum dilemma is one of the greatest challenges facing the European Union, and the harmonisation process will need to focus on international conventions for humane treatment for asylum-seekers to persist.

This comparative study exposes Australia's mandatory detention system as draconian and extreme for the total number of asylum-seekers who present at Australian borders. It is also more discriminatory towards boat people—that is, a particular mode of entry—than the other countries. The number of asylum-seekers in Australia is tiny in relation to the countries studied in this chapter, and there is little prospect of increased influxes to Australia resembling the numbers faced in Europe and the United States. Of the models studied, the Canadian adjudicative system appears to provide an impartial, fair and humane system, which Australia could well follow to avoid the human rights violations incurred by the current detention regime and discriminatory practices.

# 6
# The Politics of Race

I believe we are in danger of being swamped by Asians . . .

Pauline Hanson, 1996[1]

With her maiden speech in the federal Parliament in September 1996, Pauline Hanson reopened the immigration debate begun by Geoffrey Blainey and John Howard a decade before. It is contestable whether this is a debate or a moral panic about invasion by 'the hordes from the north'. This fear, grounded in racism in the Australian psyche, can be traced to the attitudes of white colonists towards Chinese immigrants during the nineteenth century.

Immigration debates have existed since immigration began in Australian settler society. The Chinese labour debate of the nineteenth century, the White Australia policy, multicultural policies, the immigration debates and finally the Hanson factor disclose the submerged features of Australian identity and explain why Australia has treated strangers, and particularly Asians, in the manner it has.[2]

## Colonisation and the First Boat People

The earliest known inhabitants of Australia were migrants. The Bradshaw Rock paintings of the Kimberley, dated at least 30 000 years ago, depict 'boats'.[3] The first white settlers were certainly boat people, having set out, albeit unwillingly, from England to a new land. Two hundred years later refugees from Asia, known as the boat people, set out on a similar journey that demanded immense courage. The expectation of a new life and new identity links the early white settlers with the Asian boat people, highlighting their hope, faith, courage.[4]

Racism was integral to the early settlers' attitudes towards the Indigenous peoples, who were treated as either noble savages or conquered natives relegated to the periphery of white society. Within a century the majority of Indigenous peoples were dehumanised and detribalised, with numbers vastly reduced in a virtual genocide.[5] Indigenous peoples were colonised and subjugated until they were not perceived as a threat to the white settlers. British imperial policy dictated that from first settlement Australia was to remain exclusively British with no foreign—that is, non-British—settlement tolerated. The isolated, thinly peopled colonies felt insecure and defenceless, and their fear of invasion by outsiders, especially those from the north, developed into the myth that Australia was to be invaded and overrun by Asians.[6]

The superior attitude of the colonists was inflicted upon non-whites, such as the Chinese, whose numbers had increased in the gold rushes of the mid-nineteenth century. The fear of the Chinese as a threat to the cultural and economic well-being of the Anglo-Australian is exemplified by an 1903 editorial in the *Inverell Times*: 'we are opposed to Chinese and other coloured aliens in every shape and form. As believers in the policy of protection, we contend that foreign goods should be excluded; and with them, foreign labor of the cheap and undesirable class.'[7]

This view was consistent in its signifying of strangers, specifically Chinese and by inference all other Asians, as inferior and unwelcome. In contrast to the harsh treatment of the Indigenous peoples, some official protection was offered to the Chinese groups; for example, Victoria established a Chinese Protectorate which helped reinstate mining claims that had been appropriated by aggressive white miners to their rightful Chinese owners. While the dominant white culture defined and regarded most non-British as 'outsiders' and inferior, it did not sanction the use of extreme violence towards the Chinese that it had permitted in relation to Indigenous and Melanesian peoples.[8]

Chinese 'coolies' were introduced into Australia as indentured labour in 1848 and 3000 were here by 1851, when gold was found. The resulting demand for labour encouraged Chinese entrants: by 1858 the colony of Victoria had an estimated Chinese population of 40 000, and in New South Wales the Chinese population peaked at 15 000 in 1861. Chinese migrants were classed as 'alien' and deemed to be in need of control. In 1855 the Victorian Government passed the *Chinese Restriction Act* to restrict Chinese entering Australia. This limited the number of Chinese arriving by ship to one for every ten tons of shipping, plus a poll tax of ten pounds. Shipmasters evaded the Act by landing their Chinese passengers in New South Wales and South Australia. This changed when South Australia passed an Act almost identical to the Victorian Act in 1857 and New South Wales passed a similar Act in 1861.[9]

A Chinese quarter was established on all the large goldfields, separating Chinese immigrants from European settlers, who equated the Chinese to 'a swarm of locusts'.[10] Fear of Chinese competition for jobs reached xenophobic heights. By 1861 the mining population on the Lambing Flat goldfields in New South Wales was 60 per cent Chinese, while on the Buckland River in Victoria the proportion was 25 per cent.[11] These Chinese populations, especially in New South Wales, caused alarm among the European settlers, partly due to the relatively high earnings of the Chinese, most of which were sent out of the country.

Riots on the Buckland River in 1857, at Lambing Flat in 1861, and Palmer River, Queensland, in 1877 were the culmination of extreme competition and racial hostility. Chinese civilisation and labour were widely seen as inferior from the 1850s throughout the eastern states. In Queensland a fierce anti-Chinese movement influenced the 1883 election campaign, which was dominated by the 'Chinese Question'.[12]

Contemporary rhetoric depicted the 'swamping' of the 'handful' of white people by 'swarming' Asians, 'the hordes from the north'. The Chinese, who were almost all male, were despised on the whole. There were only eleven Chinese women recorded in eastern Australia at 1861. The high proportion of Chinese males posed a sexual and economic threat, as well as an imagined racial threat. During this era the desire among the white colonists to keep Chinese immigration in check resulted in the belief that the only feasible policy was one of exclusion.[13]

In 1888 Henry Parkes, the Premier of New South Wales, used the anti-Chinese feeling to win an election on the exclusion issue. He prevented the *Afghan*, carrying Chinese immigrants, from docking and passed an Act 'intended to amount to practical prohibition'. This incident and the subsequent Acts of that year were overwhelmingly approved, allowing Parkes to 'override the subsequent protests from both the Imperial and Chinese governments as well as an unfavourable verdict in the courts'.[14] Eventually all non-Europeans were excluded by the Commonwealth *Immigration Restriction Act 1901* that effectively implemented the White Australia policy.

Early white colonists were concerned that white civilisation would be 'swamped' by Chinese who would work for lower wages than Anglo-Australians. Bereson and Matheson argue that federation was a result of the anxiety felt by the British colonists that their culture was being overwhelmed by Chinese. Political parties of the time agreed that all non-Europeans should be excluded and it was considered imperative, for the interests of 'white civilisation', that the separate colonies had a uniform migration policy to prevent the entry of Chinese and other non-whites.

A white Australia was central to the federation identity, having strong overtones of exclusiveness. The term 'white Australia' dates from 1898. However, the concept existed in the 1840s when it was understood to mean the safeguard of social (white) purity and protection against cheap (coloured) labour, with the racist component constituting an Australian ideal. White Australia became the unifying theme underlying Australian federation, nationalism and identity. This was captured by leading politicians of the time such as Prime Minister Edmund Barton in 1901: 'I do not think that the doctrine of the equality of man was ever really intended to include racial equality'. Labor Party leader Billy Hughes stated: 'our chief plank is, of course, a white Australia. There's no compromise about that! The industrious coloured brother has to go: and remain away.'[15] One of the strongest racial slurs came from J. C. Watson (Labor Party leader 1901–07): 'the objection I have to mixing of coloured people with the white people of Australia . . . lies in the main in the possibility and probability of racial contamination'. This was the prevailing ideology, and it was to remain in the Australian psyche for decades.[16]

By 1901 and the advent of federation, any move to import Asian or Pacific Islander labour was totally rejected. Chinese numbers declined rapidly due to growing state restrictions against 'Asians' and to return migration to China, with the number of Chinese falling from 29 907 in 1901 to 15 224 in 1921. Melanesians from various Pacific Islands were imported as labourers, mainly to Queensland, during the 1860s. With the rise of the Australian labour movement in the 1890s and the emergence of a 'virulent racist nationalism', most of the islanders were returned by 1908. The move by the new federation to exclude foreign immigrants coincides with the development of official 'protection' policies, which similarly excluded Indigenous peoples from white society. Both groups were classed as racially inferior and therefore unable to merge into colonial society, feelings found a rationale in the ideas of Herbert Spencer and the Social Darwinists.[17]

Henry Parkes used Social Darwinism to justify prohibition of Chinese migration, which he saw, 'like education or public health, as touching the deepest interests of society which government would neglect only at its peril'.[18] Clearly he, like other influential colonists of the time, perceived all groups except the British as inferior and a threat to the purity of the Australian (British) race and identity. Premier Fysh of Tasmania, Victorian conservative H. G. Turner, and H. K. Rusden wrote of the danger of protecting weak races, in the *Melbourne Review* of 1876: 'The survival of the fittest means that might—wisely used—is right. And thus we invoke and remorselessly fulfil the inexorable law of natural selection ... when exterminating the inferior Australian and Maori races ...'. This statement is meant to cover other groups such as the Chinese or 'Asians'. Racial, as well as economic, attitudes towards the Chinese were summed up in the *Bulletin,* on 17 June 1893: 'Australia for the Australians: the cheap Chinaman, the cheap nigger, and the cheap European pauper to be absolutely excluded.'[19]

Henry Parkes' speech on 16 May 1888, celebrating a century of white colonisation, also set the agenda for a white Australia:

> I contend that if this young nation is to maintain the fabric of its liberties unassailed and unimpaired, it cannot admit into its population any element that of necessity must be of an inferior nature and character ... we should not encourage or admit amongst us any class of persons whatever whom we are not prepared to advance to all our franchises, to all our privileges as citizens, and all our social rights, including the right of marriage.[20]

Inherent in this speech is the racial superiority of the white person, including the fear of miscegenation, a sexual threat to white men. This is obvious in the case of the Chinese where the majority were male, seen as a threat to white women, and thus to white men. Pre-federation racism was steeped in the imperial Social Darwinism prevalent at this period, which continues to resurface.

At the end of the nineteenth century migrants captured the restless spirit of the vast, expansive continent of Australia. Migrants were to exist, as Richard Nile so eloquently posits, in

> a kind of spiritual exile, of unbelonging, and for whom Australia has been not only the last great region of the world to come under the influence of the Europeans . . . but the least endowed of the continents. Australia enters the imagination as a place of forced necessity and last resort where displaced souls have had to travel first and work hard to remake their lives.[21]

The isolated location of the Australian continent, combined with the arduous and lengthy journey for migrants, especially in early colonial times but also later for the boat people, demanded fortitude, courage and determination to enter an unknown space. To the Irish the Antipodes were a 'limbo: the most diabolical of all spiritual conditions . . . the land of the living dead',[22] a position in which the boat people, as detainees, would find themselves during the 1980s and 1990s.

## The White Australia policy

Immigration is commonly considered to be one of the major factors in federation.[23] Underpinning the construct of the Australian nation was the imagined nation, and during the latter years of the nineteenth century Australia was increasingly imagined as a white nation. In creating the Australian nation and amalgamating separate units, it was politically and culturally helpful to identify a common enemy. Non-whites— the Indigenous peoples, and particularly the Chinese—became the 'other'. A Conference of Premiers in 1888 on the Chinese Question passed resolutions for a uniform policy severely restricting Chinese immigration.

Federation and the formation of a new nation involved the modernisation of frontier colonies, and the Chinese, more than any other 'coloured' people, were seen as a threat to this process. The Chinese were regarded as 'polluted' and impure. One strategy employed to restrict Chinese immigration was the imposition of quarantine controls.[24] Total exclusion was never practicable: 30 000 Chinese, as well as some 17 000 other non-Europeans, were living in Australia before the *Immigration Restriction Act* became law. Some of these residents had been naturalised under the laws of the colonies and so were permitted to bring their wives and children to Australia.

These loopholes in the *Immigration Restriction Act* permitting wives and children to enter were removed by proclamation in 1902 and again in 1905 on the premise that the Chinese had taken advantage of these concessions. In 1905, the words 'European language' were changed to 'prescribed language', and students, tourists and businessmen were permitted to enter and stay in Australia for a maximum of five years. This concession was extended to the Chinese in 1912. During the next fifty years the Act was amended on a number of occasions (in 1905, 1910, 1912, 1920, 1935, 1940 and 1949), mainly to incorporate the concessions related to specific events and to strengthen its provisions in relation to illegal entry.[25]

Inherent in this new 'imagined community', to use Benedict Anderson's term, was the identification of the Chinese as, culturally, the type of community or nation the future Australia would not embrace. The 'Chinese' presented the starkest example of what 'Australians' were not. Whites, including French, Germans and Scandinavians, were embraced and metaphorically became 'British' together, establishing non-whites as outsiders and the 'problem'. The imagined community of a white Australia was based on the myth of the cultural and biological superiority of the white European race.[26]

The birth of a new nation with federation in 1901 provided the opportunity to reserve Australia for white emigrants. The imagined community became a legal reality with the restrictive and exclusionist policy of the *Immigration Restriction Act 1901,* passed on the 23 December 1901. It was one of the first acts to be passed by the new government, denoting the importance of the White Australia policy.[27] A constitutional issue of the time was the power to restrict the entry of 'aliens' and indeed to determine who were 'aliens' of the nation. It became apparent that any non-white was to be categorised as an 'alien'. This policy became one of the principles guiding the new nation, and the foundation of the new Australian identity as predominantly white. It was designed to safeguard the country from the surrounding 'coloured races' who were disposed to invade its shores.[28]

The White Australia policy separated Australia from its neighbours for nearly one hundred years, from 1880 to 1973, and fears of 'Asianisation' surfaced repeatedly, fracturing national unity.[29] These fears are so irrational as to suggest that collective insecurity is central to the Australian sense of identity and has been since nineteenth-century Australians accepted the myth of 'invasion from the north'.

With the White Australia policy came a new sense of identity, a signifier of difference from other peoples in the region, and this became a major force in the generation of Australian nationalism. Yarwood and Knowling contend that racial questions were not lively political issues in the colonies in the lead-up to federation. They argue that historians exaggerated the importance of immigration and the 'race/Chinese Question' in generating the federation movement itself.[30] Ronald Norris, in his research on the official convention debates of the 1890s, concludes that the idea of white Australia acting as the 'compelling force for federation is a gross exaggeration if not entirely incorrect'.[31] This account, along with other histories of the federation period,[32] is frighteningly silent on immigration control and racial matters and the resonance here parallels the silence on Indigenous people in Australian (white) histories.

Racial tensions and the Social Darwinist thought of the time underpinned the racial policy that influenced the formation of federation. The early and rapid implementation of the *Immigration Restriction Act* illuminates the importance of immigration control for politicians of the time. Silence on immigration control does not indicate that it was absent from political and public thought. Silence often surrounds racial issues in the manufacture and control of a history that silences and marginalises particular groups.

Yuan Chung-Ming, in his account of this period, disagrees with Norris: he says that if it were not for the Chinese in Australia and the perceived threat of large numbers to come, the inauguration of the Commonwealth might not have happened at that time. He argues that the Chinese, under the rubric of 'coloureds', were set as the 'other', as oppositional foes, in the formation of the Australian identity.[33] This highlights race, and especially anti-Asian feeling, as the basis for Australian identity formation around federation. The Chinese became the scapegoats: 'if they were poor they were seen as forming a servile class, undermining the social homogeneity of Australia; if they were more successful than whites because of their expertise, hard work and frugal ways they were seen as attacking employment and wage standards'.[34]

Central to the *Immigration Restriction Act* was a dictation test, which operated throughout the long life of the Act. As a means of exclusion, the dictation test followed the practice of the Government of Natal. The Act provided that 'any person who, when asked to do so by an officer, fails to write out at dictation and sign in the presence of the officer a passage of fifty words in length in any European language directed by the officer is [a prohibited immigrant]'.[35]

There were objections that the dictation test would discourage 'qualified European immigrants', but in practice the test was not applied to them. Although the test was not explicitly racist, it was structured to exclude poor and uneducated European and Asian immigrants.[36] This was an example of implicit racial control rather than an explicit colour bar, which would have caused tension with neighbours and with Britain. British authorities were concerned by the tone of the *Immigration Restriction Act,* and argued that immigration was a British jurisdiction, under the auspices of foreign affairs.

The virtual complicity of all potential parties in the Act's principles set the tone of a distinct racial policy. The dictation test remained the most powerful weapon against perceived undesirables, used until 1958. Without any mention of race or colour it enforced racist principles of exclusion, and as Yuan Chung-Ming argues, 'must be deemed as one of the most perfect camouflages that ever existed'.[37]

Politicians promoting white Australia at the time were proclaiming that Australia was ethnically homogeneous, and 'that Australia was 98 per cent British or British stock', a figure which was first produced in a official census shortly after federation and continued to be used for the next fifty years. This deceit, Brian Fitzpatrick argues, was 'an amiable, self-satisfying fantasy, the most important consequence of which was to help Australia see itself as a central player in the British Empire'.[38] Minorities were not recognised and the promotion of the Australian racially homogenous white identity demanded the silencing of existing non-white inhabitants, especially Indigenous and Chinese peoples.

Elaine Thompson proposes that Australian 'egalitarianism', emerging from these roots, is paradoxically based on a xenophobic notion of Australian identity. White Australia was the direct product of Australian egalitarianism focusing on *sameness,*[39] but the sameness excluded Chinese at that time, and any Asians that followed. By 1901 there were four classes of people with different rights and status in Australia: British subjects of European origin, born within the British Empire; non-British aliens of European origin including white Americans; non-Europeans; and Aboriginal peoples.[40] Two criteria of racial or ethnic origin and legal nationality were used to determine these classes and ultimately who was accepted or excluded as an 'Australian'.

Trade unions were major supporters of the White Australia policy, perceiving immigrant labour, and especially Chinese labour, as a threat to working conditions. At the turn of the century the labour movement argued that increases in numbers of Chinese labourers, who would work for lower rates, would result in loss of jobs for Australian labourers. In fact, increases in the labour force at the time resulted in increased pro-duction and effective demand, culminating in a higher standard of living for both Australians and Chinese migrants. Ministers and officials of the time would have preferred to break all ties and contacts with the 'coloured' world, but vessels delivering necessary goods to Australian ports were crewed by Chinese, Japanese and Indians. Customs officials imposed specific, discriminatory controls on Chinese crews, who were required to be photographed and have handprints taken.[41]

The *Immigration Restriction Act* set up discriminatory legislation against resident 'coloureds', including Aboriginal peoples, who were dis-qualified from obtaining old age and invalid pensions, and South Sea Islanders, who were deported. Legislation confirmed the status of the resi-dent Asia-born population as 'unwanted visitors'. There was a dialectic link with the strategy to keep the 'coloured inferior races'[42] out and the emerging sense of an imagined Australian community and identity, which signified 'whiteness' as a sign of superiority and inclusion, basic tenets of racism.

Representations of the 'other' during this time were summed up by the Melbourne *Age* in 1896:

> the problem of Negro citizenship in the United States is given up by the philosopher as unsolvable . . . in Australia, fortunately, we are free from this race problem. The aboriginals were of too low a stamp of intelligence and too few in number to be seriously con-sidered. If there had been difficulty, it would have been obviated by the gradual dying out of the native race. What we have to be afraid of is that, from our geographic position, *we shall be overrun by hordes of Asiatics*.[43]

The myth of 'the hordes from the north' was established in the psyche of the new 'Australian citizen'. As the century progressed, the rise of Japan as a major power in the Pacific region reinforced the need for the exclusionist principle in immigration policy, as well as creating general unease among politicians and the Australian population. This continued throughout the twentieth century, characterised during World War I by the intense anxiety of Prime Minister Hughes over peace negotiations exemplifying concerns of national security in the face of the 'yellow peril'.

Immigration was largely restricted to British migrants for the next four decades, the Department of External Affairs administering laws aimed at preventing the entry of Asian and other non-European people. Between 1901 and 1905 Section 5 of the Act was amended four times to strengthen the Department's control over persons suspected of having entered the country illegally. This pattern continued, and eight decades later the Hawke and Keating Labor Governments several times amended the *Immigration Act* to suit their perceived need for control.[44]

In a report by the Commonwealth Statistician in 1921, the policy of Asian exclusion or the White Australia policy was proclaimed an overall success.[45] As Andrew Markus says, within white Australian society there was an increasing 'racial arrogance, a ready acceptance of widening discriminatory practises, and an intolerance of diversity'.[46] Racial discrimination within the Australian community, in general, was unstated and uncontested until the 1960s, when it began to be questioned and challenged. By the end of the 1930s immigration policies remained unchanged. While white Australia was intact, concessions were made to the passport system allowing merchants and students specific, but limited, entry. A separate category of persons eligible for entry, Chinese chefs, was instituted in 1939 but strictly controlled.

With the outbreak of war in the Pacific in 1941 the entry of persons under the passport system ceased; as might be expected, there was hostility towards Japanese in particular, and by extension to other Asians. Restrictions were renewed for Asian immigration, but it was Australia's response to the European refugee dilemma that was viewed as restrictive. Australia was defensive about accepting any large intake of war refugees, including Jewish refugee children.[47] Although an undertaking to receive 15 000 refugees over three years was made, only about 3000 were accepted. Parliament was reluctant to admit large numbers of refugees; as the Minister for the Interior, John McEwen, explained, permits for entry would be 'granted strictly in accordance with the Government's general *white alien immigration policy*'.[48]

After World War II federal policy boosted immigration and relaxed immigration restrictions, but not for Asians. Initially British migrants were targeted, and this was later extended to previously excluded, or restricted, European categories. The establishment of a large-scale immigration program, captured by the slogan 'Populate or Perish', was a reaction to the near invasion of Australia by Japanese forces during the war. This program was implemented by the Chifley Labor Government (1945–49) to increase the population by 2 per cent per annum, with 1 per cent coming from immigration while retaining strict adherence to White Australia policy guidelines. The 1 per cent became the recognised figure for population increase by immigration up until the present, fluctuating occasionally, but overall fairly consistent.[49]

Following the revelations of Nazi atrocities committed against the Jews, racial discrimination was disavowed by most Western nations. Instead, communism became the political threat, with the ideological battle against communism taking priority over tensions of race. Balances of power shifted and ideological battles between the major power blocs of Russian communism and American capitalism took precedence, with both blocs vying for friendships with the 'coloured races of the Orient',[50] thus undermining the intellectual justifications for racism.

After World War II official Australian attitudes to groups previously considered undesirable changed, and an era of assimilation began. The 'Australian way' was pursued, with new migrants encouraged to become like the 'old' Australians. Essentially the shift in policy regulating immigration from Europe was based on pragmatism, 'populate or perish', and the provision of labour for economic development.[51] However, Asians, were not considered assimilable. Arthur Calwell, the minister in charge of immigration in the post-war Labor Government, was very effusive in his new expansive immigration policy. However, he was equally effusive in his determination to maintain a white Australia. This was linked to the historical foundations of the White Australia policy and the desire to exclude competitive cheap labour. He cautiously portrayed the increases in immigration as 'the subject of measured controls and planning, from selection of people "with a view to meeting our known labour requirements" to their placement in suitable employment'.[52] Calwell, as the first Immigration Minister and a strong proponent of racial exclusivity, was also the last to present racism as publicly acceptable. He fervently administered the White Australia policy on the basis that if there were exceptions to the rule, if any Asians were allowed entry, then this would open the floodgates on Asian immigration.

The *Migration Act 1958* regulated the migration of non-Europeans. This Act did not mention race; it facilitated a gradual modification of policy without, in most cases, the need for legislative change. It did, however, abolish the dictation test introduced in 1901. These domestic changes coincided with the Declaration of Human Rights, issued by the United Nations, which institutionalised the principal of racial equality internationally. UN agencies such as UNESCO campaigned against racial discrimination, making overt discrimination unacceptable, which in turn had an effect on Australian attitudes. However, changes were remarkably slow, with few substantial reforms in the 1950s, reflecting the hold of racism on Australian society.[53] UNESCO sponsored meetings in Europe, between 1949 and 1951, of academic experts aimed at producing authoritative statements on race as part of an educative program to counter racism. The findings from the first meeting were published in 1950, saying:

> there is no proof that the groups of mankind differ in their innate mental characteristics . . . scientific evidence indicates that the range of mental characteristics in all ethnic groups is much the same . . . all normal [*sic*] human beings are capable of learning to share a common life . . . such biological differences that exist between members of different ethnic groups have no relevance to problems of social and political organisation, moral life and communication between human beings.[54]

Despite changing attitudes on the international scene, in Australia the 'bring out a Briton' campaign took priority in immigration. Prejudice against immigrants from Southern European countries continued, based on the notion of superior Anglo-Australian institutions and values. Assimilation was not a two-way process. Immigrants were expected to become 'Australian', taking on the Anglo-Australian cultural and social values prevalent between 1945 and 1965. Language was a prime focus, with new immigrants required to speak English in order to 'blend in'.[55]

During the immediate post-war period the restrictive interpretation of the immigration policy resulted in instances where Chinese were denied facilities accorded them in the policy. Asian migrants—including Indians, Ceylonese and Persians, but particularly Chinese—were discriminated against. The main protagonists were the Returned Servicemen's League (RSL), patriotic societies such as the Australian Natives Association, and many of the trade unions including the largest, the Australian Workers Union. The Australian Natives Association, with origins in the anti-Chinese gold rush days of the nineteenth century, maintained that Australian racial purity must be safeguarded at all costs.[56]

By the early 1960s policies of integration had replaced policies of assimilation. James Jupp defines three major phases of immigration settlement policy after 1947: assimilation from 1947 until 1964; integration from 1964 until 1973; and multiculturalism from 1973. The integration policies of the 1960s were a softer approach to immigration, and recognised that immigrants enrich the culture as well as the economy. Assimilation was based on cultural conformity, but integration envisaged a community based on diverse cultural patterns, relying on pluralist principles. The Immigration Department replaced the Assimilation Section with the Integration Division in 1964, a move that reflected the changing nature of the immigration debate. There was competition for potential migrants as the world economy experienced an upturn and Western democracies needed labour, so Australia accepted migrants from Yugoslavia, Turkey and Lebanon, a move towards the east and Asia. The eastward shift continued: in 1966 Canberra sanctioned the intake of small numbers of non-Europeans from areas previously excluded under the White Australia policy, and in particular Asians; also provisions to the Act relaxed eligibility for citizenship from fifteen years to five years, removing a discrimination against non-Europeans.[57]

As Australian economic interests in Asia increased and criticism of the White Australia policy became more widespread, a 'whites-only Australia' became a 'dangerous anachronism'. Opposition to the White Australia policy within Australia was increasing, censure coming from the public as well as political parties. The most effective was the Immigration Reform Group, formed at the University of Melbourne in 1959 to protest against the restrictive nature of Australian immigration, particularly in relation to Asians. They exposed the prohibition on non-white immigration and produced recommendations for a more liberal immigration policy.[58]

In 1965 a unanimous vote by the Labor Party at its federal conference deleted all references to White Australia from the party's platform. These trends culminated in the passage of the *Racial Discrimination Act 1975* by the Whitlam Labor Government. While the White Australia policy had been officially abolished in 1973, the *Racial Discrimination Act* made it illegal

> for a person to do any act involving a distinction, exclusion, restriction or preference based on race, colour, descent or national or ethnic origin which has the purpose or effect of nullifying or impairing the recognition, enjoyment or exercise, on an equal footing, of any human right or fundamental freedom in the political, economic, social, cultural or any other field of public life.[59]

It thereby renounced discrimination between prospective migrants on any ground of race, colour or nationality.

Between 1965 and 1975 Australia's participation in the Vietnam War had created a major shift in immigration policy and attitude towards Asian immigration, especially Vietnamese refugees. Coinciding with the reunification of North and South Vietnam in 1975 was a liberalisation of Australia's immigration policy towards Asian-born people as well as increasing involvement with the Asian region. Refugees, and especially boat people, fleeing the communist regime of the reunified Vietnam captured the attention of Australians and indeed the world.[60] The Fraser Liberal–Country Party Coalition accepted these refugees on political and humanitarian grounds, and in conformity with the Cold War doctrine of accepting anyone fleeing a communist regime.

At the close of the Vietnam War in 1975 there were approximately 1000 Vietnamese in Australia. During 1975/76 Australia accepted 539 Vietnamese refugees, soaring to a peak of 12 915 in 1979/80. After 1980 there were fewer refugees from Vietnam, but the number of Vietnamese joining family members steadily increased.[61] The Vietnamese refugees represented a turning point in immigration policy, the outcome of which was the introduction of Australia's first refugee policy in 1978 (Chapter 4). This sought to reconcile domestic, economic and social issues with the increasing pressures from the international community to play a humanitarian role in settling refugees. Six years after the White Australia policy was officially dismantled there had been a small, but noticeable, influx of Asians.

Not only were legal and bureaucratic attitudes changing, but a shift from exclusiveness, based on the polarity of superiority/inferiority and dominance/suppression in terms of race, to principles of cultural pluralism and inclusion was taking place.[62] This shift, noticeable from the late 1960s, introduced new meanings to history and to Australian identity. However, between 1947 and 1972 tolerance to diversity was only just beginning.

## Multiculturalism

In the decade 1972 to 1982 multiculturalism as a concept and as a government policy emerged in Australia.[63] During a visit to Singapore in 1971 John Gorton, as Prime Minister, made a statement highlighting the acceptance of a multi-racial Australia, and warned against the prevalence of racism in the world. Australian policy was

> to abolish governmental discrimination on grounds of race within Australia . . . the course we are following holds great chances of achieving real racial tolerance . . . if we build up gradually inside Australia a proportion of people who are not of white skin, then as that is gradually done, so there will be a complete lack of consciousness of difference between the races . . . then that may provide the world with the first multi-racial society with no tensions of any kind possible between any of the races within it . . .[64]

In a show of bipartisan support the Labor Party, at its 1971 conference, added to its platform the requirement that immigration policy be based 'on the avoidance of discrimination on any grounds of race or colour of skin or nationality'.[65] Gough Whitlam, Leader of the Opposition, promised that a Labor government would admit more Asian immigrants, using a points system similar to the Canadian scheme.

Multiculturalism was a term used by the Canadians in the 1970s to denote cultural pluralism and the increasing receptivity to ideas of cultural diversity. The Canadian Government defined multiculturalism as: 'recognition of the diverse cultures of a plural society based on three principles: we all have ethnic origin (equality); all our cultures deserve respect (dignity); and cultural pluralism needs official support'.[66] This definition corresponded closely with Australian interpretations of the term. Australia made efforts to clearly define multiculturalism for the Australian public, both in policy implications and identity building. Advisory councils were established, such as the Australian Ethnic Affairs Council, which produced a submission entitled *Australia as a Multicultural Society,* and joined with a like-minded body, the Australian Population and Immigration Council, to produce a discussion paper entitled *Multiculturalism and its Implications.* Both papers gave insights to the process known as multiculturalism, and what the process would mean for Australians. Generally the word multiculturalism was used to represent a society consisting of a variety of ethnic groups, and held few political implications. However, it also meant the guarantee of equal representation and opportunity regardless of racial or ethnic background, which, as Ian McAllister says, 'has distinct policy implications for government activity across a wide range of areas'.[67] Multiculturalism was criticised for its focus on ethnic origins and, in some cases, the perceived over-recognition of minority groups in a liberal democracy.

After the election victory of the Whitlam Labor Government in December 1972, changes were much more rapid; race was resolutely disregarded when applications were considered from prospective immigrants. Al Grassby, the Immigration Minister and a strong advocate of multiculturalism, installed a migrant assessment system similar to the Canadian one that made no reference to race or religion. He also produced the first comprehensive statement of government policy towards immigrants, *A Multicultural Society for the Future*, in 1973. Grassby was also instrumental in obtaining a more equitable stand on naturalisation and citizenship, introducing legislation in 1973 that reduced the required length of residence from five to three years and encouraged immigrants to become Australian citizens. Ceremonies did not include the requirement to renounce previous allegiances, implying that immigrants could become 'good Australians' while still retaining an association with their past interests. Grassby institutionalised pluralist principles.[68]

From this time interest groups and government organisations popularised the concept of a multicultural society and introduced a range of policy initiatives to promote it. Groups such as the Ethnic Affairs Council adopted formal statements recognising and advocating a multicultural society based on a diversity of ethnic groups and cultural identities. They also produced recommendations on how to ensure 'equality of opportunity in the labour market, and equal access to government services and resources'.[69] The Government established agencies in response to the increasing demand for multicultural inclusion. For example, the Australian Institute of Multicultural Affairs was formed in 1979 with the mandate to improve community relations as well as conduct research on aspects of immigration and ethnicity.

The reconstituted Department of Immigration and Ethnic Affairs (DIEA) acknowledged new claims from ethnic communities. Multiculturalism dominated discussions about migrants in Australian society during the 1970s. A submission by the Ethnic Affairs Council to the government in 1977 stated:

> our goal in Australia is to create a society in which people of non Anglo-Australian origin are given the opportunity, as individuals, to choose to preserve and develop their culture, their languages, traditions and arts; so that these can become living elements in the diverse culture of the total society, while at the same time they enjoy effective and respected places within one Australian society.[70]

Under the Fraser Government the 1978 Galbally Report, *Australia: Review of Post-Arrival Programs and Services to Migrants*, tabled in Parliament in ten languages, instituted policy on migrant services and multiculturalism. It was a benchmark in the development of services and resources for migrants such as improved language-training facilities, funding for migrant organisations to assist service delivery, and welfare services. Consultation took place between ethnic community groups and government agencies. Such organisations as the Special Broadcasting Service (SBS) and the Australia Council were formed in order to foster multiculturalism in media and the arts.

Migrant Resource Centres were established throughout Australia as focal points for individuals and organisations to obtain information about resources and services. Galbally also recommended the Telephone Interpreter Service, enabling non-English speakers to summon emergency help.[71] The Galbally Report became a point of reference for procedures in dealing with groups of varying ethnic background and, to its credit, its initiatives remained unchanged throughout the 1980s and into the 1990s.

Assimilation policies had been founded on a false notion of Australian society and identity, an idealised view of Australian life based in the past and connected to the British 'motherland'. While assimilation policies were a 'mismatch between policy and the realities of Aboriginal and migrant life',[72] multicultural policies brought to the fore Australia's internal divisions, bigotry, discrimination and racism, and highlighted the obstacles faced by outsiders, especially Asian migrants. Proponents of multiculturalism, such as Malcolm Fraser and Galbally, recognised this as a process to 'heal' these divisions and exclusions. Multiculturalism advocated processes of inclusion and recognition of difference that confronted the insecurities of Australian identity.

As we have seen, the insecurity based on fear of Asianisation erupted in the late 1970s with the arrival of the boat people. Although the numbers were small, the public outcry and media coverage illuminated the underlying fear that Australia was about to be overrun by 'the hordes from the north'. Along with the demands from the international community and Asia-Pacific countries, the arrival of the Vietnamese boat people put pressure on the Fraser Government to re-evaluate migration from Asian countries. Markus argues that the rise in immigration, especially from Asia, was a result of these external pressures rather than of humanitarian concern; more likely it was a combination, with the external pressures, such as the arrival of the boat people, triggering the humanitarian concern.[73]

Humanitarian concern was particularly evident in the policy initiatives and management of Minister for Immigration MacKellar in the Fraser Government of the late 1970s, as we saw in Chapter 4. Nancy Viviani argues, 'Australia had managed this small but significant challenge to its sovereignty successfully',[74] and the control of borders, deterring of further boat people and humanitarian obligations played a prime and successful role in the political agenda.

Multiculturalism and the controversies over it shattered the stereotyped myths of the white Australian identity for the increasingly educated, urban society. However, multiculturalism, like the notion of Australian identity, meant different things to different people, an aspect of plural society, but one that involves tensions.

## The Immigration Debates: 1984–1988

Under the rubric of multiculturalism, initiatives were introduced to ensure access, equity and participation for all Australians irrespective of their origins. On the surface there appeared to be a consensus on Australian immigration policies by both major parties during the late 1970s and early 1980s. Fraser emphasised multiculturalism as a process of constructing an Australian national identity based on ethnic diversity in a socially cohesive society. However, many Australians perceived the increasing numbers of non-European migrants, particularly Asians, and the services and 'ethnic rights' afforded them as a threat to the Australian identity and economy.

At the beginning of the 1980s multiculturalism was a new and confusing concept to many Australians, and the rapid changes, including increased Asian immigration, opened fault lines in Australian society. Viviani argues that the backlash against multiculturalism arose from the emphasis placed on cultural diversity at the expense of concern with equality. Multiculturalism emphasised the rights of ethnic groups and the benefits and services available to them, but many Australians, including those born overseas, saw this as inequitable, especially in regions and groups with high unemployment.[75]

The backlash against multiculturalism focused on Asians, or more precisely the Indochinese (the Vietnamese in the late 1970s and the Cambodians in the 1980s). The Indochinese arriving under humanitarian and refugee programs represented invasion by 'the hordes from the north'. As Betts describes, 'the alien poor of the racist nightmares of the past were made real on the television screens of the present'. The boat people triggered exaggerated fears, activating 'our deepest collective neurosis—the Asian invasion', grossly out of proportion to the actual number of boat people who arrived over the next two decades.[76]

Professor Geoffrey Blainey's attack on Asian immigration in 1984 was the most public and widely recorded expression of this increasing dismay about levels of Asian immigration. The term 'Asian' is a contentious one, as outlined earlier in this book, and particularly Orientalist; to Blainey's credit, he acknowledged the diversity of peoples in the Asian area. However, he attacked the rising numbers of Asian immigrants and the falling numbers of British immigrants, implying a threat of Asianisation and a loss of the traditional Anglo-Australian identity. The term 'Asianisation' created controversy and it was assumed, mainly by the media, that Blainey was the first to use it. Blainey argues that the then Immigration Minister, Stewart West, first used the term.[77]

The 1984 Immigration Debate, as it became known, was sparked by a lecture given by Professor Blainey at a Rotarians' Conference in Warrnambool in March. He argued that the policy of such heavy Asian immigration could explode the bipartisan consensus, thereby undermining the benefits of multiculturalism. He called for 'mono-cultural values as well as multi-cultural values', a contradiction in itself, demonstrating his confusion over multiculturalism. He called for 'shared values as well as different values',[78] which was, ironically, much the same concept that had been advocated by both Fraser and Hawke Governments.

Blainey claimed that the White Australia policy had been 'turned inside out' and that organisations such as the ethnic lobby groups had hijacked government policy, producing advantages for minority groups, especially Asians. Blainey called for restrictions on immigration and warned against 'massive increases in immigration from Asia'.[79] More than a decade later similar statements and arguments signified that the 'debate' still simmered.

During the early 1980s the Hawke Labor Government increased the Family Reunion Program, enabling larger numbers of Asian immigrants to join their families, and fuelling fears of certain groups and individuals. Blainey perceived multiculturalism as undermining social cohesion. He argued that the promotion and encouragement of cultural identification had been taken too far, especially in the case of Asian migrants whose cultural traditions and practices are markedly different from those of the 'dominant Anglo-Saxon culture of Australia'. Blainey argued that intense cultural identification would splinter society, resulting in cultural groups congregating together in ghettoes, forming a 'nation of tribes and presenting a threat to social harmony'.[80]

Blainey evoked the early colonial settlers as the historical representation of Australian identity. This distinct white-Anglo identity was linked to the nation-building of the early settlers and their descendants who, Blainey saw, developed the country 'politically, socially and economically'.[81] Contemporary Australian identity flowed from this early settler identity, excluding the non-British. This casts doubt on European migrants' claim to Australian identity. Blainey appears to exclude all non-British, but closer scrutiny of his arguments and media releases reveals that it is Asians who are his target.[82]

In an Orientalist argument Blainey contends that Asians are less likely to assimilate than immigrants from European countries, thus explicitly exposing Asians as his 'other'. Initially Blainey argued that high unemployment in Australia was the major factor in his call for cutbacks in immigration. He claimed that, in the early 1980s, Australia was in a depression and that, historically, immigration had been cut and even halted during economic downturns.[83] According to him this depression and the high levels of unemployment were adequate reasons for stopping immigration. However, counter to Blainey's argument, there was no depression in Australia in 1984 and immigrants do not necessarily take jobs from Australians. Indeed, other researchers have argued that immigration in fact *creates* employment.[84]

Blainey had taken the lid off the melting pot (to draw an analogy with American multiculturalism) setting loose fears of overwhelming Asian immigration. This, as Rasmussen and Tang elucidate, unleashed Australia's own group of Don Quixotes who set out to protect their country from the danger of the Asian immigration program. Don Quixote had been a 'quaint harmless figure who generally hurt no-one but himself, . . . [but] Australia's Don Quixotes, among them Geoffrey Blainey, Bruce Ruxton, Ron Casey and John Stone, may not be so innocent'.[85] The media sensationalised the so-called debate as proponents of the far right voiced Australians' fears and insecurities surrounding Asian immigration. It rekindled the underlying racism towards Asians and the perceived fear of invasion from the north.

Blainey's nationalistic version of Australian history, exemplifying the Orientalist position, perpetuated an idyllic account of the Australian way of life and identity, and blamed immigrants, particularly Asians, for social instability.[86] It legitimised racist taunts from extremist minority groups, which would re-emerge a decade later in the rhetoric of Pauline Hanson. Radio personalities, particularly talkback hosts such as Derryn Hinch, espoused anti-immigration views that stirred the underlying racial tensions and insecurities. Some media reports were biased. For example, the *Sun Herald* claimed that 62 per cent of Australians were against Asian immigration, but failed to mention that 64 per cent of those interviewed had also expressed disapproval of the overall number of immigrants coming to Australia. This silence shows how Asian immigration was misrepresented in relation to immigration in general. The Hawke Government was accused by the opposition spokesperson on immigration, Michael Hodgman, of pursuing an anti-British and anti-European immigration policy.[87]

A month after his speech to the Rotarians, Blainey introduced a new argument, claiming that Australian democracy was under threat from Asians who come from countries without democratic traditions.[88] He implied that Asian migrants would automatically assume those political ideologies from which many were escaping, and that they did not have the ability or intelligence to adapt to a new political system. Blainey ignored the central fact that many Asian migrants coveted the freedoms of liberal democracies.

Supporters of Blainey also espoused democratic traditions in the form of freedom of speech, defending Blainey's right to express his views. Blainey was cast as the victim of social intolerance because of the vigorous critique of his outspoken views. However, his critics, mindful of the difficulties of a full frontal attack on democratic rights, presented more subtle variations on the argument. Kathy Laster in an article in *Migration Action* argues that, while Blainey was considered to be wrong, 'his game strategy was better and his opposition weak'.[89] Blainey retaliated by suggesting that they were advocating a 'surrender Australia policy'.[90]

Blainey's attacks on immigration and multiculturalism were directly related to his fear of Asianisation and loss of the British identity but, as Merle Ricklefs asks, 'why Asians?'[91] Was it the insecurity of the historian who saw the traditional ties with Britain diminishing and a new future being forged for Australia, or was it a racist attack on a particular group of people? It is puzzling: he had not previously taken a strong stand on immigration, and to people who knew him well he was not a racist figure.[92] He was Chair of the Australia-China Council at the time of his speech, although he resigned soon after. His attacks were aimed at the Minister for Foreign Affairs, Bill Hayden, for his alleged plan for the 'Asianisation of Australia', and the Minister for Immigration, Stewart West, for perceived bias against British migrants. When questioned about his views, Blainey was clear that Asian migration was not of benefit to Australia. In one instance he revealed his fears that Asian migration was 'bringing in people who look different and from a very different culture and this is creating tension'.[93] This can also be said about Turkish or Jewish immigrants; Blainey was specific about Asians, his 'other'. Ricklefs' analysis of Blainey's arguments concludes that he was engaged in racist rhetoric and motives.[94] Blainey has taken on the Orientalist mantle, seeing 'Asians' and their children as inferior and unsuitable to become Australians. The controversy inflamed the assaults on Asian immigration and on multicultural policies. During the second half of 1984 the debate lost momentum but seeds had been laid for later and similar attacks.

Four years later, John Howard reopened the so-called debate in a radio interview when replying to questions about the level of Asian immigration. Like Blainey, Howard claimed that he would not 'like to see it [the level of Asian immigration] greater . . . it is in the eyes of some of the community . . . too great, it would be in our immediate term interest and supportive of *social cohesion* if it were slowed down'.[95] The link between social cohesion and cuts in Asian immigration mirrored Blainey's views. But Blainey was an academic and non-political figure, whereas Howard was Leader of the Opposition, with his views representing party policy. In fact, the party position was at odds with Howard's, and many from the Opposition, including the Shadow Minister for Immigration, Alan Cadman, distanced themselves from Howard's claims. Howard's anti-Asian stance would haunt him when he became Prime Minister in 1996.

The release of the Report of the Committee to Advise on Australia's Immigration Policies, generally called the Fitzgerald Report, in June 1988, reignited the so-called immigration debate. Although this report was 'Australian nationalist' in tone and unconcerned about a continuing refugee and migrant intake from Asia,[96] it portrayed dissension on multiculturalism: 'many people, from a variety of occupational and cultural backgrounds, perceived it as divisive'. The public perceived multiculturalism as driving immigration policy, and community attitudes to immigration 'reflect confusion, anxiety, criticism and scepticism . . . public support in some quarters is faltering and community consensus in favour of immigration is at risk'.[97] Multiculturalism, with the original informing ideals of justice, equality and esteem, had become obscured by a multiplicity of meanings that had rendered the term a liability.

The report provoked an outcry particularly in conservative sections of the community, which seized its critique of multiculturalism as an extension of the 1984 Blainey debate. As we saw in Chapter 3, Opposition Leader John Howard saw the report as 'a stick with which to beat the Hawke Government'[98] and publicly announced his support of Fitzgerald's critique. Howard released the 'One Australia' document that proposed a review of Asian migration and a tempering of multicultural policies in the interests of 'social cohesion'. Uproar ensued among the two main political parties, the media and sections of the public, while prominent Liberals distanced themselves from Howard. Prime Minister Hawke accused Howard of 'opportunistically abandoning Liberal support for racially non-discriminatory immigrant selection, and multiculturalism'.[99] Howard was at odds with the bipartisan support for humanitarian intakes and multicultural policy, which the Liberals, under Fraser, had implemented. Howard's mishandling of the immigration and multiculturalism issues contributed to his downfall and replacement as Liberal leader by Andrew Peacock in May 1989.

Along with Howard, anti-multicultural and anti-Asian groups seized the Fitzgerald Report with enthusiasm. They hailed it as an indictment of Labor policy, and criticised the management of numbers, reporting community doubt about the selection program and the policy of multiculturalism. In hindsight, the report attempted to be non-partisan and to reflect attitudes found in the community, but its naive presentation of its findings ignored political reality. The report was easily misrepresented and used in a sensational way to inflame and distort a situation that had polarised the Australian public. Its main failing was its undue emphasis on economic considerations: 'the sharper economic focus . . . is the most central issue in immigration reform'.[1] Freeman and Jupp categorise the report as defending the status quo, written in an ideological framework where the majority of politicians and bureaucrats were of Anglo descent, a combination that frequently works to the disadvantage of non-English-speaking migrants.[2] The Fitzgerald Report exemplified both the white Anglo-Australian status quo, and the underlying fear of Asian migration.

Blainey and Howard found support in diverse quarters—anti-immigration racist groups as well as Australians concerned with employment and loss of jobs. As the controversies created by these public figures fuelled racist attitudes and specifically the fear of Asians, the structural response was to enshrine the principle of a racially non-discriminatory policy. Ironically, this was the opposite of what Blainey and Howard intended.

Blainey lost profile after a short period, although the ripples caused by his remarks are still evident. Howard remained, tempered by the reaction to his views, and the so-called debates on Asian immigration went underground. They resurfaced in 1996 after the Liberal–National Party Coalition, led by Howard, won the election. From the late 1980s, the arrival of boat people, initially from Cambodia, then East Timor and China, highlighted the fear of invasion from the north. Mackie claims these issues were relatively minor but the detention of boat people, while ignored by most Australians, did incur reprimands from the international community for human rights violations.[3]

The media sensationalised the boat people, especially the length of detention incurred by the Cambodians and the ensuing legal battles. Headlines portrayed the boat landings as 'invasions' and 'floods', warning that there are 'more set to come',[4] once again stirring up fears and insecurities about Australia being overrun by Asians and the resultant challenge to the white Australian identity. Yet Asian immigration continued to have a place in the overall immigration program, with non-discriminatory selection procedures and a relatively high ratio of Asians within the overall migrant intake.

During the early 1990s signs started to appear at both ends of the political spectrum that Asian immigration was about to resurface as a contentious issue. Groups on the far right such as the League of Rights, National Action and Australians Against Further Immigration put forward essentially racist arguments for a reduction in the intake of Asians. On the left there were similar arguments from the Labor member for Kalgoorlie, Graeme Campbell, who castigated the high levels of Asian immigration as a threat to Australian employment.[5] However, the most controversial views came from a relative unknown: the Independent member for Oxley, Pauline Hanson.

## The Hanson Factor

Wake up Australia before it is too late!

Pauline Hanson, 1996[6]

The implication of Pauline Hanson's call was that Australia needed to wake up and stop Asian immigration before Australia became Asian. In the run-up to the 1996 election, she was a godsend to the right, articulating in the language of the battlers what politicians would not say. In doing this, Hanson 'created a space for those who preface their xenophobic statements with "I'm not racist but . . ." while Liberal Party politicians and candidates needed only to remain silent to indicate their assent to their views, thus benefiting from the huge electoral swings to their side of politics'.[7]

While this set the racist tone of political and social discourse, it also guided the politics of the new Liberal–National Party Coalition Government. John Howard, as Prime Minister, created a space for 'free speech', which he claimed had been stifled under the political correctness regime of the previous Labor Government. Howard's re-imagined Australia was a nostalgic vision of the 1950s, a period of assimilationist policies, white Australia and the settler identity.[8]

This political space was seized by Pauline Hanson in a coup that was to open the immigration debate, giving free rein to the vitriolic and uninformed rhetoric of race politics. She gained support from many sections of Australian society by inflaming old fears and insecurities that had been dissipating by the processes of multiculturalism. Freedom of speech became a rallying point for many commentators who might not have agreed with Hanson's views but advocated space or rights for her to voice them. However, most opponents of Hanson did not advocate silencing her but called for balanced reporting rather than the sensationalised accounts that were inflaming and inciting fears, insecurities and hatreds. Ironically the Hanson phenomenon, as it has been called, created the opposite effect from what Hanson hoped to do; that is, the ensuing discussions united a major proportion of Australians against her.[9]

In her maiden speech to federal Parliament Hanson emphasised that her vision was of a single society, which rejects racial emphases and addresses social issues. Her solutions included halting immigration, especially from Asia because Asians 'don't assimilate and they form ghettoes', and the abolition of multiculturalism, among others. Hanson argued that these 'solutions' would bring about social harmony, recreating a white Australia and an Australian identity based on the settler identity, just as Blainey had projected in the 1980s.

In the Hanson scenario the politics of race are interwoven with the politics of blame; the Indigenous and ethnic, specifically Asian, groups are the scapegoats. Matthew Cook says:

> Hanson's appeal is explicable only because the identification of
> scapegoats appears pernicious, emotional reaction to which we are
> all susceptible . . . having these reactions reflected by someone in
> a position of power is a simple but unsatisfying form of reassur-
> ance . . . . the enthusiasm for her reflects the fragility of our
> culture.[10]

For the Pauline Hanson One Nation Party, 'even an enemy invasion
would have been kinder than the death of a thousand cuts that mainstream Australia is now experiencing in this cowardly battle of psycho-
political warfare'.[11] The suggestion that Australia was being 'swamped
by Asians' was a sensationalist claim that incited fear and xenophobia,
exemplified by the supporters of Hanson. The claim 'swamped by
Europeans' would not have incited the same response. Statistics from the
Immigration Department show that people from European countries are
still our major migration source, with 6.6 per cent from the United
Kingdom, 6.4 per cent from Europe and 4 per cent from East Asia.
Clearly Australia is not being swamped by Asians; New Zealanders are
settling, especially in Queensland, in higher numbers than any other
group of migrants. In fact Queensland is more likely to be swamped by
New Zealanders than by Asians![12]

Howard's response to Hanson was silence; he let her fill the spaces
and articulate the views he had expressed in 1988. He resisted calls to
denounce Hanson and her views until 8 May 1997 when, at a meeting of
the AustralAsia Centre of the Asia Society, he distanced his government
from Hanson. He described her 'as wrong and some of her supporters as
racist'. This belated repudiation was an attempt to restore Australia's
reputation in Asia. Howard had finally conceded that a racist reputation
could affect business.[13]

Although Howard was happy to trade with Asia, he argued that
Australia's Asian connection could be 'quarantined from social and community change at home'.[14] A major flaw in Howard's framework was
revealed in this notion that Australia could resist cultural and social connection with Asia while engaging in the economic sphere. Howard
feared the loss of white Anglo culture and British heritage. In their need
to retain the past and to isolate and exclude all those deemed different,
Hanson and Howard were one.

The combination of Hanson and Howard on the public and political scene raised questions overseas about Australia's direction regarding race and its internal social cohesion.[15] Ironically, both Howard and Hanson feared that high levels of Asian immigration would break down social cohesion, and yet by reopening the immigration debate (so-called) they allowed racist rhetoric and fears to fracture social cohesion. Uncertainty and insecurity produced in part by the processes of globalisation found scapegoats in Asians and immigrants, as well as Indigenous and dis-advantaged peoples.

Marcia Langton presents an imaginative analogy between Eva Peron and Pauline Hanson, where Eva Peron reinvents 'herself as the sartorially resplendent patroness of the poor to distract the attention of the strug-gling masses from their country's downward spiralling economy and con-ditions under the repressive Junta'. Similarly Hanson's effect is 'to distract the attention of battlers from the difficulty of stretching their paypackets to meet basic needs by the use of simplistic, white supremacist ideology, and to concentrate their anger on the wrong, but soft, targets'.[16]

Hanson filled a political void presented by Howard, whose leader-ship was inadequate to deal with the wider implications of this space. Australian society fractured into a 'them' and 'us' binary divide that was reminiscent of the late-nineteenth-century debates over 'coloureds' and 'whites'. A volatile and damaging situation evolved in which both Indigenous peoples and Asian peoples experienced greater discrimination and some violence. Howard's inaction over Hanson and the One Nation Party damaged Australia's credibility within the Asian region as well as among other Western liberal democracies. For example an article in the Thai paper *The Nation*, titled 'Where do the real problems lie in Aus-tralia?', reported that Hanson's dire warnings about Australia's future needed to be dismissed, and that unless the race debate 'matures' Aus-tralia faces the prospect of evolving into a 'small backward-looking land' influenced by those who distrust foreigners. An article in the Indonesian *Observer*, an English-language paper, titled 'Hanson will haunt Australia', stated:

> there are still people in Australia nurtured on the discarded racist theories that held that some people[s] are superior to others . . . these views have been blamed for a rising number of racial attacks

on Asians in that country . . . we would like to call on the large majority of understanding Australians to do something about this before fears rise in Asia that Australia remains a racist country despite its promotion of multiculturalism that followed the dismantling of the policy of accepting only European immigrants. This was only about 25 years ago.[17]

Although Hanson has faded into the background somewhat, the divide she represented and fuelled, remains particularly evident in the support for her views in rural areas compared to opposition of her views in urban areas.

## Identity Politics

Australian identity and the politics surrounding it have always been contentious and complex. Immigration debates (so-called) have denoted times of change in Australian settler society. Late-nineteenth-century rhetoric and arguments against Chinese immigration resemble those Blainey, Howard and Hanson against Asian immigration in the late twentieth century. Australia, as a nation, is lacking confidence in its place in the world, still coming to terms with an adolescent identity crisis, as well as racist attitudes.[18]

Immigration debates represent Australian views of how strangers are accepted and the security of Australian identity. How a nation treats strangers, in this case those with marked differences, is a sign of the maturity and security of the nation. Australian identity is in an adolescent phase, and the maturing process is analogous to the period of 'multiculturalism'. Its adolescent insecurities have not yet been resolved (in this case, the insecurity of being overrun by 'Asians').

During the multicultural period (which might be defined as running from the early 1970s to March 1996 and the election of the Howard Coalition Government[19]) social attitudes and fears towards Asians and the 'other' changed. Australia began to accept Asia, initially through trade and tourism, then through cultural ties, realising that Asians were not so different and not to be feared. While this acceptance increased and the barriers fell, some resistance remained as the reaction to boat people from Asia attests. The detention of boat people, although not universally contested by the Australian public, gained sympathy with an increasing number. The violation of the boat people's human rights by detention forced the recognition that asylum-seekers, even Asians, had rights, and certainly the right to be treated humanely.

In the culturally plural society of Australia at the end of the twentieth century, there were two main ideological groups concerned with identity: the conservatives and the liberals. Both groups contain many shades of opinion and neither group is unanimous; however, they can be categorised broadly.

The conservatives are still fighting for an exclusive Australia, based on a settler identity that was forged by the early British colonial settlers who massacred the Indigenous peoples and excluded Asians. White Australia was, and still is in many cases, the priority of this group, expressed in the establishment of the White Australia policy. The genealogy of this group consists of Sir Henry Parkes, through to Arthur Calwell, Robert Menzies, Geoffrey Blainey, and Pauline Hanson. The conservatives fear being overrun by Asians, who, in their Orientalist view, are inferior to the white Anglo-Australian. Camilleri contends that this fear of the Asian, captured in the term 'yellow peril', was fashioned, whether consciously or unconsciously, in order to accommodate Australia's links with Britain.[20] Significantly, 'overrunning' or 'swamping' was the method by which the early colonists settled Australia and overcame the Indigenous peoples. It is ironic that the conservatives fear the very method their forebears and exemplars used. Conservatives advocate the Anglo-Australian heritage as the basis for Australian identity; they identify multiculturalism as a threat to this identity and support exclusion and discrimination by racial categories.

The second group is a coalition of small-*l* liberals who do not discriminate along racial lines and who perceive immigration irrespective of ethnic origin as permissible and advantageous to Australia and the building of a new Australian identity. The influence of this group and their ideologies built the multicultural policies and practices evident from the early 1970s onwards. Katherine Betts argues that this group is based on 'liberal cosmopolitanism', which grew during the 1970s and 1980s, drawing on the 1960s background of opposition to the White Australia policy and Australia's involvement in the Vietnam War, support for women's liberation and other social movements.[21] This became a dominant force in intellectual circles, which often denigrated Australian popular culture, criticising it for its ethnocentrism, racism, and indifference to the needs of immigrant communities.

A guiding principle of this group is inclusivity, the acceptance of people on humane grounds under strict immigration policies but with no barriers on race or ethnicity. This group is secure about Asians; its view is not Orientalist, but perceives Asians with archetypical egalitarian Australian values. The liberal group does not fear 'the hordes from the north' and encourages mixing of the cultures, an inevitability as the processes of globalisation and hybridisation have shown.

This binary grouping is common, as we saw in Chapter 5. However, complexities and diversities among both conservatives and liberals complicate the polarity. Ultra-conservative groups and parties surfaced in the 1990s in many countries. Factors such as increasing cultural diversities, economic downturns and rising unemployment have created a 'politics of blame'; immigrants, refugees and migrant workers are easy targets. Difference provides an object for blame, as the Turks in Germany, the Algerians in France and the 'Asians' in Australia have learnt to their cost.[22]

Identity, and especially national identity, continues to be an issue in almost every part of the contemporary world. The push for a republic is an Australian manifestation of this preoccupation with identity. Australian notions of national identity arise from two interrelated sources: from history, incorporating the myths as well as the facts; and from a set of legal and political institutions.[23] This is the collective notion of identity, that is, membership of a community. In this sense Australian national identity consists of an Indigenous inheritance, a history of European colonisation that was primarily shaped by Britain, a common law tradition, and liberal-democratic political institutions. Immigration built on this foundation, especially after World War II, and the influx of cultures from various parts of Europe and later from Asia produced a culturally plural society that transformed the settler concept of Australian identity.

Opponents of this change, such as Blainey and Hanson, have called for a return to the settler identity, the Australian nationalism that fears the 'other', based on exclusiveness and assimilation.[24] This exclusive nationalism poses a threat to the identities of minority communities, especially Asian communities and refugees, and is founded on racism. A secure Australian identity would include the historical contexts and institutions while recognising Australia's ethnic, linguistic and religious diversity.

The recognition of Asia as our neighbour, in trade as well as in culture, is a measure of an increasingly confident society, one that does not need to fear our neighbours because they are different, but has an identity secure enough to cohabit with them.[25] Multicultural policies over the last two decades have provided that framework to accept the 'other' within the Australian identity. The challenge for Australia and its evolving identity is to sustain this base of multiculturalism while accepting its historical other, the Asian.

## Conclusion

The Asian, in Orientalist terms, has been constructed as Australia's 'other'. This was explicit in the early stages of white settler society when the Chinese were discriminated against and excluded. Australian identity coalesced from these beginnings, shaped by the white colonial attitude that culminated in the exclusionary White Australia policy.

Social Darwinism was influential, as in other parts of the world. It was 'coloureds'—in Australia's case the Indigenous peoples, Pacific Islanders and the Chinese—who were deemed inferior to the white British settler society. The White Australia policy was expressed in the *Immigration Restriction Act 1901,* one of the first Acts passed by the new Australian federation.

The evolution of Australian identity was directed by this Act that prevented most Asians from entering Australia until the 1970s. This restriction of Asian immigration, initially a response to the fear of Chinese taking employment from Australians, evolved into a fear of invasion by 'the hordes from the north'; it was exemplified in the White Australia policy, the immigration debates and the Hanson episode. The fear of invasion by Asians has been a recurrent theme that created a method to maintain an 'other', the Asian, and has been present throughout Australian settler history.[26]

White Australia was the cornerstone of Australian immigration, attitudes and identity until the 1970s, modified to accommodate the arrival of immigrants from Southern Europe. A gradual easing of restrictions on Asian immigration occurred from the 1950s with the introduction of small numbers of students from selected Asian countries. However, it was not until the Vietnam War, and the resultant introduction of refugees from Indochina in the 1970s, that there was a clear move away from the White Australia policy.

This ideological shift was associated with the Cold War politics of accepting immigrants from communist or former communist countries (as happened when Australia accepted refugees and migrants from European countries after World War II). It was the basis for a shift in policy and attitude to accept Asians into Australia. The formal demise of the White Australia policy in 1973 was a product of a more liberal attitude towards Asians and the beginning of 'multicultural' Australia. In this period Australia faced its insecurities and fears with the gradual acceptance of its other, signifying a mature approach and a secure identity. It was followed by a backlash in the 1980s: the Blainey controversies of 1984, Howard's comments in 1988, and the rise of Pauline Hanson in 1996.

The detention of boat people, predominantly from Asia, was a political and structural reaction to the perceived threat of Asians. This discriminatory act arose from fear, with detention used as the method of defence against the 'other'. The demise of the White Australia policy provided silences and spaces that were filled by the proponents of anti-immigration, anti-multicultural and racist rhetoric. However, it also highlighted the polarities in Australian society and the attitudes towards an evolving identity. On one hand the conservatives, exemplified by Blainey, Howard and Hanson, saw Asianisation as a threat to Anglo-Australian purity. On the other hand the liberals espoused multiculturalism, ties to Asia, and a broadening of Australian identity as fear receded. These so-called debates exposed the underlying tensions of a changing Australian identity and society in which immigration has a primary position.

# 7
# The Politics of Belonging

Citizenship is now like being a fan, who votes favourably for
media products by purchasing them, extolling their virtues, or
wearing their iconic packaging on one's bill cap or tee shirt.

T. Luke[1]

Citizenship signifies legal, political and national identity,[2] thereby determining who is included in, and who is excluded from, a nation. Loaded
with complex meanings about democracy, the nation-state, exclusion
and identity, it generally connotes the promise of 'community well-
being, personal engagement and democratic fulfilment'.[3] However, for
non-citizens, or aliens, the term denotes exclusion, not belonging and
non-identity. The valuing of citizenship entails a devaluing of aliens,
creating an area where discrimination of a nation's 'other' can occur.

Chapter 6 showed two main strands: the white settler or Australian
nationalist identity exemplified by the White Australia policy, and the
cosmopolitan identity produced in the last thirty years of the twentieth
century from a multicultural Australian nation. The original exclusionary ideology was modified from the 1970s, when multicultural policies
produced a form of citizenship 'deemed appropriate for a diverse, plural,
well-educated, independent yet inclusive, modern nation: the citizen

as cosmopolitan Australian'.[4] This cosmopolitan Australian identity retained a nationalist component but attempted to 'reconcile a recognition and affirmation of difference with an inclusive and still, in a sense, singular national identity'.[5] To create this kind of citizenship, the government had to abandon legislative and administrative discrimination on the basis of race, gender, ethnicity and disability, and substitute a conception of Australian citizenship based on equality and social justice. Nevertheless, as we have seen, discrimination still occurs at an official level.

While the White Australia policy clearly marked the Asian as Australia's other, the *Nationality and Citizenship Act 1948* defined, until 1987, an alien as 'a person who does not have the status of a British subject and is not an Irish citizen or a protected person'.[6] This clearly signified the image of the Australian, in citizenship legislation, as British (and Irish), excluding all others as aliens and requiring specific requirements for them to obtain citizenship. The *Nationality and Citizenship Act 1948* came into operation on 26 January 1949. Until then, people living in Australia were designated 'British subjects' or 'aliens'. When the Act was implemented, all British subjects were automatically granted Australian citizenship. In 1973 the *Nationality and Citizenship Act 1948* was renamed the *Australian Citizenship Act 1948*. After 1987 all migrants, apart from New Zealanders, were categorised as alien and were required to apply for citizenship. British citizens were legally categorised as 'alien' too, although culturally they remained in the dominant group. To be alien or different is to be categorised as the other, a significant and familiar cultural metaphor that marks the boundaries and limits of social identity.[7]

The politics of citizenship determines inclusion and exclusion, signifying who belongs and who does not, membership of the nation-state being the determining factor. Refugees, particularly asylum-seekers who do not have or cannot obtain citizenship, are regularly classified as aliens; they have no legal, political or social identity. While refugees are often perceived as global citizens, most do not fulfil the requirements for citizenship as determined by nation-states.

Australia's response to strangers has been ambiguous. Despite an exemplary record on immigration (as discussed in Chapters 3 and 6), it has committed human rights violations by excluding long-term detainees from social rights.[8] While ideas, resources and sometimes people move freely in the processes of globalisation, identity in the legal terms of 'citizenship' is not fluid. Identity is confined by the boundaries and territories with which belonging, as a citizen, is associated. Refugees and asylum-seekers reside in shadowlands where the abstract construct of citizenship is changing but the legal-political constructs are not.

The prescribed limits of legal citizenship diminish the extent of citizenship. Social citizenship as part of the welfare state is rapidly dissipating.[9] This is problematic for asylum-seekers, who require aspects of social citizenship when they are in limbo between legal processes, which fail to recognise their legal status or even basic human rights.

## Histories and Theories of Citizenship

In contemporary times the term citizenship is paradoxical. On one hand it is perceived as archaic, while on the other hand it is being reworked to fit with societies of the global postmodern world.[10] A notion originating from Ancient Greece, citizenship in modern times has two features: it is bound to the existence of a state and therefore to the principle of public sovereignty; and it is bound to the acknowledged exercise of an individual capacity to participate in political decisions. All persons have rights as humans, as discussed in Chapter 2; but human rights are, for the most part, citizens' rights—rights found in, and lived in, nation-states where legal and political identity is bound to citizenship.

The word citizen is Latin in origin, derived from *civitas*, but the idea of citizenship, understood as 'active membership of and participation in a body politic',[11] originated in Greece around 600–700 BC. Citizenship in Ancient Greece was available to only the privileged, the included, and was overtly discriminatory. Greek life distinguished sharply between citizens and non-citizens, a distinction which prevails in contemporary times as aliens and asylum-seekers can testify. In ancient Greek society, to be a citizen was to be a political being, to be among men, while to be a non-citizen was to face life as not fully human, to be 'subject' to an exclusive group of citizens. This meant to be literally among men, and only specific men: women, children and slaves were not included. Aristotle saw citizenship as 'participation' (but only of adult males) rather than the rights of political association and parliamentary representation found in modern democratic states.[12] Underlying this early the notion of citizenship are the concepts of equality, freedom, exclusion, discrimination and the 'other'.

The French and American Revolutions of the eighteenth century ushered in a new form of citizenship identified with democracy. Both forms have incorporated privilege, exclusion and discrimination, and provide the means by which states can discriminate against non-citizens. The first version of citizenship was small-scale, culturally monolithic, hierarchical and discriminatory: citizens constituted a minority of the population and citizenship was partial. The second form of citizenship is based in territorial and political prescriptions.[13]

The second category of citizenship has generally evolved into a state that establishes the principles and mechanisms for the distribution of civil, political and social justice. However, citizenship maintains the power to create privilege, and to exclude or include in the determination of who does or does not belong. In Australia, as in most nation-states, while it is the cultural and historical evolution of the nation that determines its 'other', it is the political and legal aspects of citizenship that enable exclusion of the 'other'. This is the power of discrimination, determined by the legal structures of the nation-state.

In contemporary times citizenship is discussed across the political spectrum as something that can define the needs of the future. In political terms, the right speaks of active citizenship, emphasising obligations; the left attempts to combine solidarity with welfare rights to develop a notion of communitarian citizenship. The centre turns the concept of citizenship into 'an almost vacuous label'[14] for anything not regarded as left or right.

In his key text, *Citizenship and Social Class, and Other Essays of 1949*, T. H. Marshall defines citizenship as the body of rights and duties, *the status*, which goes with full membership of a community or society.[15] Citizenship, as the status, is not connected to the market or the economic realm; it is a non-economic concept, defining people's position independent of the relative value attached to their contribution to the economic process. Marshall perceives the rise of modern political citizenship as coinciding with the advent of capitalism. He demonstrates that it is also an essential component of the Enlightenment, and is thus entrenched in the project of modernity. Citizenship marks a shift from the local feudal systems to nation-building projects. Identity, that is, legal identification and association tied to the nation-state, moved from the community and communal confine of religion and church to the nation territory and bondages of the state. Nevertheless, the justification remained for the exclusion of particular people on the grounds that they did not 'belong' and could not be expected to uphold their obligations as citizens.[16]

The three elements of Marshall's theory are the civil, the political, and the social. The civil element is composed of the rights necessary for individual freedom; that is, liberty of the individual, freedom of thought, speech and religion, the right to own property and to conduct valid contracts, and the right to justice. The political element is the right to participate in the exercise of political power. The social elements 'range from the right to a modicum of economic welfare and security to the right to share, to the full, in the social heritage and to live the life of a civilised being according to the standards prevailing in the society'.[17] Civil elements are connected to the institutions of the courts of justice, the political elements to the parliament and local government, and the social elements to the educational system and social services.

The principle of equality is central to Marshall's theory in which all people are free and, in theory, capable of enjoying rights. In these terms, citizenship grows by enriching the body of rights that people can enjoy. If people are not free, as in the case of aliens, prisoners and asylum-seekers, their rights of citizenship are withdrawn or non-existent.[18] This is a powerful sanction, one that can be justified in the case of hardened criminals and obvious law-breakers, but it raises the question of how far this power of institutions should go. The system of detaining asylum-seekers in Australia is a prime example of exclusionary politics where asylum-seekers are excluded from citizenship, placed in limbo without rights or identity. When viewed in this context, denial of citizenship and therefore identity is a denial of access to the basic human rights of social citizenship, namely, access to freedom and social benefits, identity and belonging.

Although citizenship has not eliminated inequality, through the social institutions of the welfare state it has provided a path for social justice policies and politics of access and equity in major areas of social and economic life. The connection of citizenship to the welfare state is crucial for Marshall's project to succeed and, as the welfare state is dismantled throughout the Western world, Marshall's concept of citizenship, especially social citizenship, is thrown into disarray.[19] However, citizenship remains a fruitful notion for analysing the problems of our time and interpreting how migration and refugee issues fit in.

Marshall's three elements are connected to specific historical moments. Civil citizenship became established prior to and during the eighteenth century, centring on the rights necessary for individual freedom. Political citizenship, the right to political participation, was primarily established in the nineteenth century. Social citizenship, emphasising the citizens' rights of economic and social security, was implemented after World War II.[20]

Marshall was the first to conceptualise and defend social citizenship as the pinnacle in the historical development of modern citizenship. Social citizenship was the final stage, the ultimate ideal where the full participation of the individual in the community could be realised. Marshall perceived the gaining of full social citizenship as not only the final stage but the 'end of history' or at least 'the end of the history of social citizenship'. There is a fundamental difference between the principles of a liberal and democratic society, based on civil and political rights, on the one hand, and the social rights as expressed in the welfare state on the other hand. Liberal principles are generally expressed in a negative manner, in terms of freedom 'from' (mostly from state intervention), whereas social rights are expressed in a positive way, implying an active and even interventionist state. Thus social rights are meant to give the formal status of citizenship a *material* basis. A certain level of material well-being is guaranteed, enabling citizens to exercise their rights to full participation in the community.[21]

Marshall envisaged a state that would overcome the inequalities of class society, one in which universal education and health services would eventually dissipate divisive class cultures into a unified civilisation.[22] This is a utopian notion of citizenship, and indeed society, but one that is based on an analysis of the contradictions among the three evolving categories of citizenship as well as tensions among the citizens. Marshall acknowledges that some individuals are excluded, and that citizenship itself is a player in the field of social inequality, as exemplified by asylum-seekers. Refugees, particularly asylum-seekers, are denied rights until citizenship has been confirmed, and in some cases this is a violation of their human rights. The long-term detention of asylum-seekers in camps throughout the world, including Australia, is an act of exclusionary politics based on notions of citizenship, identity and belonging, or in this case 'not belonging'.

Nancy Fraser and Linda Gordon argue that, although Marshall's essay is 'tonic reading in this period of widespread pessimism about public life'[23] and the dissipating welfare state, his views are problematic. Marshall's theory initially focused on Britain, but it ignores other cultures within Britain or for that matter beyond Britain, and gives too much priority to the welfare state. Marshall fails to notice gendered and family meanings of civil citizenship that set back social citizenship. The rise of civil citizenship helped create the norm of the family wage. Men's citizen entitlement as family head with prime citizenship status leaves the family, the wife and children, with dependent citizenship status. Marshall, while acknowledging individuals excluded from citizenship, still maintains a system that produced 'others'; women's status as secondary citizens exemplifies this. Michael Mann also criticises the ethnocentric specificity and evolutionism of Marshall's perspective, arguing that while Marshall's scheme may fit the British example, it is historically and comparatively inappropriate for other societies.[24]

To be fully inclusive, analysis of citizenship should include not only the specific histories of democratic politics in Western societies with the legacy of Greek and Roman traditions, but should also compare non-Western traditions.[25] Marshall pays little attention to race, gender or culture, and his assumption that the primary aim of social citizenship is erosion of class inequality and protection from market forces understates other key axes of inequality and other mechanisms and arenas of domination.[26] Marshall did not take into account the possibility of setbacks to his plan; he could not foresee the developments that would take place four decades later as social citizenship comes under fire from new right and economic rationalist politics.

## Citizenship and Human Rights

Marshall characterises the post-World War II debates about citizenship in terms of a shift from the 'active' political definitions to a more 'passive' sociological definition, in which the citizen is viewed as a consumer rather than a creator of rights.[27] Marshall's definition and interpretation of citizenship was founded on the high point of post-war British social-democracy, which he saw as the culmination of citizenship, the 'final stage' that would eliminate inequalities. This highlights the problems for any definition of citizenship that displaces the centrality of active political rights; these are obscured once the focus moves to what a person 'gets' rather than 'what they do'. However, this definition only works when citizens are free to pursue those political rights; for aliens or individuals who cannot pursue active citizenship rights, the avenue to social citizenship is crucial for the maintenance of basic human rights.[28]

This is illuminated by Pranger in his 1968 book, which defines citizenship as literally meaning official identity: 'as basic and important as one's personal name: in fact, a good deal more important, for having a name without citizenship deprives a person of that identity by which most of the world judges him'.[29]

National citizenship thus provides an official identity; without it, an individual is less, if at all, recognised by the nation and is therefore less human, certainly with fewer rights. (This resonates with the construct of the citizen in Ancient Greece.) Although set in national identity terms, citizenship then becomes universalised as long as the nation-state remains legitimate and intact. Citizenship is thus a universalist definition applying to all specific categories, and it relies on the recognition of universal human rights. Habermas confirms this when he recognises that citizenship rights guarantee liberty because they contain a core composed of universal human rights.[30] In practice, of course, they also need to be set within the guidelines of national jurisdictions and universal human rights declarations. Habermas acknowledges that the European asylum problem brings to light the latent tensions between citizenship and national identity, a factor that also applies in the Australian context.

Citizenship is legitimate only within a particular state, and while this is a major requirement of citizenship, it is not the only one. Marshall's definition of citizenship encapsulates most aspects of society. Contemporary situations focus on differentiation in determining citizenship, along with redefining identity, and now demand some reconceptualising of citizenship[31] at different levels: the local, the national, and the global.

## Globalisation and Global Citizens

As globalisation transforms societies throughout the world, notions of identity become multiple, which in turn affects citizenship. Borders between nation-states are breaking down, shifting and, in some cases appearing or disappearing altogether, with repercussions for the traditional constructs of citizenship and identity. Refugees epitomise this;

in many cases they do not reside in their 'country' of birth, but neither are they citizens of their new country or place of residence. Before they are granted legal citizenship of their new country, they are 'non-citizens', not belonging, legally non-existent. They are caught in the proverbial no man's land, in the borderlands of existence, marginalised, without power or access to the institutions within the country of residence; they are in the shadowlands of citizenship.

While identity is becoming multiple through the processes of globalisation, the construct of citizenship, which is still tied to the nation-state, is not. Globalisation is diminishing the power of the nation-state. Paul James argues that the nation-state is changing rather than dying. He argues that we are currently witnessing a reconstitution of the nation-state in which the institutions and practices of modernity, including citizenship, are being re-framed by the pressures of globalising postmodern capitalism. Where does this place citizens and refugees? As Bryan Turner states: 'the ultimate definition of citizenship is itself vague and uncertain. To become a citizen involves a successful definition of the self as a bona fide member of society and thus as a legitimate recipient of social rights.'[32]

Turner takes Marshall's notion of social citizenship and argues that entry into citizenship involves processes of social conflict and negotiation: 'since citizenship is defined by various forms of social closure which *exclude* outsiders and preserve the rights of insiders to the full enjoyment of welfare and other social benefits'.[33]

Asylum-seekers, such as the boat people who have been detained, are effectively excluded from society, recognised as the 'other', and positioned as outsiders. They are targeted as not wanted, not belonging, marginalised, with rights determined by the nation-state and universal organisations, that is, human rights as defined by the United Nations. The nation-state's jurisdiction on who belongs and how non-citizens are treated has been challenged and recognised as a violation of human rights.[34] The detention of asylum-seekers is an act of social closure, which meets the legal norms and constructs of Australian citizenship, but does not fit human rights constructs that the Australian government has signed and pledged to uphold. Asylum-seekers are denied access to the human and social rights that constitute both Marshall's and Turner's notion of citizenship. As 'outsiders', they are denied citizenship rights until they complete the process of 'social conflict and negotiation' that Turner expounds as a requirement for obtaining citizenship (see below).

Until this process is finalised and citizenship is achieved, asylum-seekers and refugees are treated as outsiders, the 'other', in a most inhumane manner. Incarcerating people for escaping oppression, trauma and, in many cases, torture is not the practice of a civilised society. Detention of asylum-seekers is an act of non-recognition or mis-recognition, which inflicts harm upon detainees; 'imprisoning someone in a false, distorted, and reduced mode of being' is a form of oppression. C. Taylor portrays *recognition* of people as a vital need; non-recognition and mis-recognition is a 'grievous wound' that has devastating and long-lasting effects upon the human psyche. Michael Walzer also acknowledges recognition as a component for belonging and acceptance into a community and state, arguing that non-recognition is 'not a reason for expulsion'.[35]

Globalisation challenges the autonomy and sovereignty of nation-states, relativising traditional conceptions and processes of citizenship participation and motivation. This is exemplified by the emergence of human rights concerns and institutions over the last fifty years. Citizenship loyalties may be undermined, and at times fractured, by the process of globalisation which unsettles the stability of the nation-state, but the existence of human rights instrumentalities and legislation as a global legal process oblige governments and other agencies to respect the individual.[36]

Benedict Anderson's oft-quoted concept of imagined communities illuminated the peculiarly modern sensibilities and ideologies framed by the constitutive mode of communication and production that he called 'print-capitalism'.[37] The imagined community is being exposed, subsumed by a global community fed by the new technologies of tele-media and cyber-communications along with consumer capitalism and production. The modern nation was imagined as 'being bound in time and space and embodiment, that is, within a particular territory, history and race',[38] and, I would add, culture.

Globalisation, in a positive sense, has created new levels of multi-culturalism, which challenge the traditional dominant culture of nation-states such as Australia. Turner perceives that:

> with globalisation and the emergence of multicultural politics
> as a prominent dimension of all political systems, the sense of
> strangeness of the outside world is difficult to sustain since the

*other* has been, as it were, imported into all societies as a consequence of human mobility, migration and tourism. Otherness has been domesticated.[39]

Turner implies that otherness is now accepted or diminished by a globalised culture. However, we have seen that the other is not always accepted and included in the dominant culture. While globalised cultures and multiculturalism are becoming the norm in many societies, the 'other' is more openly discussed, seen and acknowledged but not always accepted, as the anti-Asian feeling in Australia shows. Refugees are, at times, an indicator of exclusions in society and detainees an extreme example of this; groups seen as the 'other' are not accepted.

Globalisation interposes a variety of traditions on communities, thus increasing the diversification and complexity of cultures, exposing otherness to communities and individuals otherwise non-receptive to diversity, but it does not meet with the degree of acceptance and tolerance that Turner assumes. Racial conflicts, the backlash of nationalism and xenophobic actions are indicators of non-acceptance of strangers. The rise of neo-Nazi groups in Germany, for example, marks a backlash against Turkish migrants and refugees.[40] Anti-Asian groups in Australia also demonstrate rising intolerance caused, in part, by processes of globalisation.

Turner's argument is credible to a point: generally, globalisation is producing a completely new level of multiculturalism and cultural diversity. This cannot be ignored and, as Turner argues: 'globalisation requires a new cultural reflexivity',[41] which involves a rethinking and reworking of citizenship. The argument shifts: instead of 'alien cultures' as a persistent form of the binary system of the nation-state and national identity versus aliens, we are developing a new cultural reflexivity that raises the possibility that all cultural systems are local cultures: 'reflexivity and cultural propinquity in a global context also produces a new focus on the *self* in postmodernity, because the relation between individual and national identity becomes highly unstable and uncertain'. Turner is drawing attention to the role of globalisation in the social production of postmodernity, where all local culture can also become global culture.[42]

Central to cultural globalisation are the processes of democracy and postmodernism that have rendered much of the traditional literature on citizenship inadequate. Postmodernism is an increasing differentiation and fragmentation of culture as a consequence of plurality of lifestyles and differentiation of social structure. It may offer both the 'dehier-archarisation of cultural systems while also permitting the differen-tiation of culture as an outcome of the differentiation of social systems'. Globalisation of culture is associated with the growing interconnected-ness of the world economy and the development of a world market in cultural goods while also incorporating societies as 'part of a world sys-tem of societies, as part of a global order'. Turner portrays traditional and modern culture to continue alongside postmodernism, there is no need to present modernity and postmodernity as mutually exclusive develop-ments: these elements will and can exist conterminously, even if in an uneven balance. He expresses a hope that these processes will prevent current tendencies towards new forms of exclusion that are expressed in the rise of ultra-conservative and racist movements in many parts of the world which portray the exclusion of migrants and refugees as a just cause. [43]

Globalisation is in reality 'Western globalisation',[44] a combination of trends. Firstly, as mentioned before, political, social and economic activity is becoming global in scope; secondly, there is more interaction among the states and societies that make up the global community. With this increase in interconnectedness, politics unfolds against a back-ground of a world 'permeated and transcended by the flow of goods and capital, the passage of people, communication through airways, airborne traffic and space satellites'.[45] Authority over an integrated world econ-omy and information order, the interconnectedness between states, is shaped by extra-territorial forces such as transnational companies, trading blocs and multinational economic institutions.

Cultural globalisation is altering the notion of citizenship to accom-modate the broader contexts that now envelop it and, increasingly, citizenship demands will be satisfied at a global level as well as at a governmental level. However, sovereignty of nation-states is still supreme, which presents dilemmas for Turner and other international-ists. In Western societies the idea of citizenship is undergoing trans-formations relative to specific areas; seen together they all add up to a global transposition in notions of citizenship. During the 1980s and 1990s Britain and, to a smaller extent, the United States implemented changes to the Keynesian consensus that was the foundation of the welfare state after World War II. The British emphasise social rights for public education and health care, while the Americans emphasise civil rights of freedom of speech and religion and focus on civil citizenship to the detriment of social citizenship, where the market takes precedence over welfare. This highlights the different focus of their respective political and social systems; however, both countries increased their focus on the market to the detriment of their social and welfare systems. These changes set in motion the dismantling of the welfare state, the very structure that underpins Marshall's notion of social citizenship and social equality.[46] At the same time conflicts between ethnic groups throughout Europe and the former Soviet Union, and the establishment and re-establishment of ethnic and national identities, along with the movement, displacement and dispossession of peoples, unleashed underlying conflicts and hatreds. Neo-conservative groups like National Action[47] and Pauline Hanson's One Nation Party are Australian versions of a growing trend.

The implications of these conflicts for citizenship are immense. The nation-state is under question as the most appropriate political context for citizenship rights; socio-political and cultural changes challenge the state as the most suitable structure to express citizenship. Human rights discourse is presented as the superior example of political loyalty, thus undermining the notion of nation-state citizenship and national loyalties. Commitment to membership of the nation-state is being challenged by the processes of globalisation as social groups become rootless through labour migration and imported cultural influences that modify concepts of national identity. The political sovereignty and cultural hegemony of the state are eroded, at the same time that 'localism' contests the state from below. The state is squeezed between these two pressures: external challenges to its hegemony over the emotive commitments of its citizens, and local, regional and ethnic challenges to its authority.[48]

Donati argues that the time of modern continuity is over, at least in regard to linear progress in the modern concept of citizenship. He sees the emergence of a postmodern citizenship that transgresses the 'nation-state symbolic code' to embrace a 'societal symbolic code of citizenship'.[49] Citizenship becomes an expression of a society rather than of a state, combining identities and solidarities in different ways from the modern traditions. Here Donati connects with Turner's alternative discourse of human rights and humanity as the superior paradigm of political loyalty, thus giving citizenship the universal dimension of the global society. However, without the demise of the nation-state this cannot be a reality.

Turner encapsulates the contemporary situation for citizenship in what he calls cultural citizenship. This can be defined in general terms as 'a set of practices which constitute individuals as competent members of a community'. This more general, sociological definition avoids the emphasis on juridical or political definitions of citizenship. Turner's version of citizenship identifies 'a set of practices which are political, social, legal and cultural; which constitute rather than merely define the citizen; which over time become institutionalised as normative social arrangements and which determine membership of a community'. The defining of culture is a problem for Turner's argument. A universal notion of culture would make his definition of cultural citizenship possible but with such a hybridising of identity (and therefore culture) this definition of the cultural citizen presents a formidable and challenging task. Democratising citizenship, with all it entails, helps and gives position to all aspects of a culture, but it would be easy for a cultural elite to use power for their own advantage. It is here that Turner's postmodern theory comes into play, whereby hierarchical structures and high culture are deconstructed.[50]

Thus citizenship becomes the new fellowship of the modern state, and cultural citizenship 'consists of those practices which enable a competent citizen to participate fully in the national culture'.[51] Turner's redefinition of citizenship extends Marshall's notion of cultural citizenship. He perceives at least two ways citizenship can develop: either from a subaltern position, from the bottom up, as a consequence of social struggle and taking an active and radical form; or imposed from above as a hegemonic strategy of incorporation, resulting in a passive form.[52]

Clearly Turner considers the passive type of citizenship to be sustained primarily by the project of modernity. He prefers the active type of citizenship, evolving from social struggle. Social struggle and social movements are the sites for contesting and negotiating citizenship rights that will extend or defend definitions of social membership regarding who is included or excluded. Turner perceives social movements as the fourth wave of expanding citizenship rights. The first wave demoted the formal role of property in the defining of citizen; the second wave, the suffragette movement by which women won political citizenship, demoted gender as a definition of citizenship. The third wave redefined the significance of age and kinship ties within the family in the legal definition of citizenship rights. The fourth wave, brought about by social movements, has the consequence of ascribing rights to nature and the environment.[53]

Turner's generalisation is skewed. Some contemporary social movements and groups ascribe to nature and the environment as a position equal to that of human life in a scenario of global survival, but it is not the primary focus of all social movements. However, social struggle in the form of social movements and lobby groups is the entrance point for citizenship, especially for groups deemed to be outsiders excluded from citizenship rights, such as refugees and other marginalised groups. In this process of social struggle the prospective citizen contests and negotiates citizenship within democratic principles that incorporate access, equity and equal opportunity. These aspects are emphasised in Marshall's plan of social citizenship, but Turner introduces broader frameworks to include the cultural and global aspects of contemporary societies. This involves a state apparatus to control and administer these new guidelines, raising questions of acknowledgement of local and global attributes of individuals, state territories and a global or universal claim on citizenship.

Turner's cultural citizenship is planned to include cultural democratisation. In postmodern culture, this involves contesting and deconstructing the traditional hierarchy of high and low cultures where 'postmodernism mixes, conflates and confuses such divisions'.[54] Turner is vague about specific outcomes for cultural citizenship, asking what form it can take if postmodernism has fragmented culture and challenged the authority of elite culture. This affirms his argument that globalisation and postmodernism have changed social structures as well as hybridising identity, creating a new global culture, which, although Western and imperialist, can and does affect notions of citizenship and belonging.

Turner highlights tensions between modern citizenship and postmodern culture. He points out that the postmodern recognition of incommensurable difference may only be an extreme version of the conventional problematic of liberalism and the celebration of the individual. A postmodern cultural aesthetic is

> [the] recognition and acceptance of extreme cultural fragmentation, the promotion of feminist recognition of the significance of emotional commitments to different cultural preferences, and the attempt to recognise rather than to incorporate various ethnic, regional and sub-national cultures. Thus the postmodern critique of grand narratives would prohibit the imposition of national standardisation by a higher culture. The de-hierarchisation of culture would be compatible with the democratic thrust of modern citizenship norms.[55]

The defining and implementing of a new citizenship exposes tensions between citizen rights and human rights. The asylum-seeker in detention is a prime example. Displaced people throughout the world are denied citizens' rights and, in the case of detainees, human rights as well. Turner foresees the eventual demise of the concept of citizenship, since it applies only in an epoch in which the nation-state is dominant. Its demise is a condition of the postmodern celebration of difference and the resultant fragmentation of identities and groups. He perceives a convergence of global human rights, which are not bound to any specific nation-state framework, and postmodern cultural complexity, 'which recognises the incommensurability of world views, the fragmentation of political discourse and the contingency of social science perspectives'.[56] This idealistic view overlooks the strength and enduring nature of the nation-state, and ignores the problems faced by any worldwide organisation or structure such as the United Nations.

In the context of social movements both Habermas and Stuart Hall cite feminism, nationalism, environmentalism, multiculturalism and the struggle against Western hegemony as related phenomena that should not be confused with one another. They are connected in that women, cultural and ethnic minorities, gays and lesbians, environmentalists, nations and cultures defend themselves against oppression, marginalisation and disrespect, and 'thereby struggle for the recognition of collective identities, whether in the context of a majority culture or within the community of peoples'.[57] What is prominent here are social movements (and refugee lobby groups can be included) whose collective political goals are defined primarily in cultural terms, although obviously political dependencies and social and economic inequalities cannot be overlooked. The granting or withholding of citizenship and the rights it entails is an illegitimate division that social justice movements seek to overcome.

Turner argues that citizenship 'is a consequence of real and popular struggles against various forms of hierarchy, patriarchy, class exploitation and political oppression; the achievements of these struggles should not be dismissed as mere mystifications of capitalism or illusory forms of democracy'.[58] The development of citizenship is a consequence of a series of particular conflicts among social groups, lobby groups and social movements for rights and civil liberties. As changes in citizenship are brought about by social movements achieving real rights, particular criteria that define the person become less relevant in the public sphere.

Questions arise as to whether there will be real persons behind the multiple layers of particularity:

> That is, to be a person is always to be a particular person; one is defined by unique ascriptive, local, accidental and personal features. To be a citizen is to be defined by general, abstract, bureaucratic and public criteria relevant to such issues as taxation, political control and education.

A paradox exists in that individuals require particularity while citizens require generality, but it is the growth of individualism that relates to the development of modern citizenship. The development of citizenship has equally created the site for the development of individuality for educated, self-conscious, reflexive agents.[59]

The struggle for the social membership and participation that citizenship offers is important in the emancipatory process. For migrants and refugees it is a process of recognition and belonging in an environment that recognises difference, rather than attempting to assimilate them in a process of political cooptation through acculturation. Assimilation neutralises protest and contestation in social struggles to retain cultural and personal identity. Assimilation when fully applied requires the surrender of cultural, ethnic and personal identity. Since cultural and ethnic identity and genealogy can never be entirely eradicated, as diasporas of migrants and refugees exemplify, the result is usually a hybridisation.

Access to the rights connected to citizenship generally requires that one be a citizen,[60] so where do individuals apply when they are not citizens, as in the case of millions of stateless people? To whom do they put their claims, whether for human rights or citizenship? Walzer maintains that 'naturalisation . . . is entirely constrained, every new immigrant, every refugee taken in, every resident and worker must be offered the opportunities of citizenship'.[61] He is advocating citizenship upon entry under discretionary policy guidelines, but insists it should occur at the time of entry. This seemingly ideal situation would be unfair in practice, for at times decisions would be made too quickly and on insufficient information. The Rwandan crisis of the 1990s is an example of a situation where this would not work. With over a million people displaced and crossing borders, in purely practical terms, how could these people be processed and awarded citizenship? The reality was horrific with displaced refugees crowded into makeshift camps, not only in the shadowlands of citizenship but also in the borderlands of existence.[62]

Through the process of globalisation the contents and imagination of the citizen's mind are composed increasingly of elements not exclusive to a country, ethnic group or religion: 'thus no firm separation within the internal cultural world of an individual is objectively possible, or viable, in a real sense in today's world'.[63] Globalisation is thus a culturally hybridising process, whether in physical reality or in imagination, infiltrating cultural purity and therefore national identity. However, groups such as the Serbians and Croatians, the Palestinians and Israelis are more concerned with the modernist preoccupation of national territory and national identity based on cultural purity. Refugees, exiles and migrants are the obverse; while not giving over notions of identity based on historical constructs of culture, religion, and ethnicity, they are willing to expand their identities. They desire citizenship and the legal and social status this entails, without the cultural purity of the separatist and modernist preoccupation of national identity. They are, on the whole, willing and eager to enter into the hybridising postmodern condition of a multiple identity to achieve the sense of belonging that comes with being a citizen.

Citizenship in traditional political and legal terms fits well with the separatist, national identity mode, but it does not cater for the refugee who does not fit into territorial categories. Universal schemes for citizenship have foundered on the necessarily local character of citizenship, a character that has historically been bound by time, place and culture,[64] a resource that is maintained while specific boundaries exist. The price here has been inequality between citizens and non-citizens; while maintaining effective standing and equality among citizens, there is an emphasis on the inequalities between insiders and outsiders.

Turner perceives that social movements are the escape valve in late-twentieth-century societies for the contestation and recognition of inequalities. In Turner's notion of social movements and social struggle, the development of citizenship 'is not an evolutionary unfolding of the spirit but rather the consequence of a whole series of particular conflicts between social groups and the development of social movements for rights and civil liberties'.[65] The results of these struggles can be either a growth of citizenship, or a withering of established rights. Marshall's trajectory of citizenship growth—the development of citizenship rights from the civil, political and social—exemplifies the gradual inclusion of previously excluded groups. This has occurred where social movements since the 1960s have provided an example for other social groups. Turner cites the anti-Vietnam protesters during the 1960s and 1970s as providing a model for civil-libertarian groups such as the American black, gay and lesbian, and women's movements. This has worked well in liberal democracies and particularly in culturally plural societies such as America and Australia, where social groups like the Indigenous peoples have won recognition and been given access to mainstream structures such as citizenship. Asylum-seekers in Australia continue to struggle for this, having been denied citizenship rights to participate in civic and social citizenship for periods up to five years. They are hampered by their minority status and face legal and political barriers in obtaining even temporary rights to social citizenship.

Dominant groups resist the demands of other social groups in order to maintain their advantages of power and authority within the existing status quo. The growth of rights for one social group may involve a contraction of rights for others. The realisation of citizenship as an abstract right is thus the consequence of quite specific and concrete social struggles associated with modern social movements to achieve greater participation within society.[66] Citizenship rights are the outcome of attempts either to defend or to expand the definition of social membership. Over the last two centuries social movements, special-interest groups and lobby groups have elaborated and universalised the notion of citizenship to include greater numbers of persons, so that now citizenship is seen in a different light.[67] The postmodernising of culture and the globalisation of economics and politics have narrowed the focus and practice of traditional notions of citizenship.

Cultural citizenship, as previously mentioned, is Turner's method for expanding citizenship in the modern state, and would allow recognition of those in limbo such as asylum-seekers. This recognition incorporates the social citizenship aspects of Marshall's plan and global human rights concerns. Turner's cultural citizenship provides asylum-seekers, such as the boat people, with social rights and freedoms until their refugee status and identity is determined. This process involves cultural democratisation so that in divided societies (divided by class or any discriminatory system) the cultural and political elite cannot impose (further) exclusion or marginalisation on subordinate classes or 'others'. Cultural citizenship, incorporating cultural democratisation, can, and does, perform in culturally plural liberal democracies. However, problems arise where states are controlled by a cultural and political elite.

## Semiotic[68] and Consumer Citizenship

Wexler acknowledges that identity dynamics are overlapping rather than isomorphic, and individuals are treated differently within the context of the 'postmodern socially structured space' in which they exist.[69] He categorises two classes in society: the first class, or so-called middle class, which is engaged primarily in the identity work of 'ego bolstering'; and the second class comprising the youth, unemployed, the poor, women (and now increasingly men) labouring in the domestic sphere, the aged and minorities, all of whom are engaged in 'ego binding'. Wexler places these categories in his concept of 'semiotic society', that is, a society that has been overtaken by the language of culture where, 'semiosis, the structural law of value, the free play of signifiers without references'[70] has become dominant.

Luke points out that consumer citizenship has a place, even priority over national citizenship, especially in nations like the United States where citizens are not obliged to vote. A high proportion of citizens choose not to vote but are linked as a community by consumer citizenship, a unifying act that positions them as belonging to a global culture. A common critique of cultural democratisation maintains that the cultural divisions between classes are illimitable and irreducible. This is valid and still relevant to most societies, but as the category of class diminishes in importance, the distinctions between high and low culture blur. Education plays an important part in this: although education has not brought social democratisation and equality (class divisions still exist between schooling systems), this divide is crumbling, resulting in the rise of a large middle class.[71]

A new culture, a new person, a new society has replaced the old modernist system, and this incorporates a replacement of language systems or meanings and constituent practices, social organisation and the values that made citizenship such an important sign. Thus the notion of the semiotic citizen and its connection to postmodern forms of culture, which include globalising processes, are the signs and values that Wexler sees as constituting identity, and therefore citizenship, in contemporary society. 'Society' has been sublimated to culture: where society is not being produced but only simulated. Social organisation is in a post-industrialist or informationalist phase, in which the major changes are in organisational forms and modes of communication as well as in distribution and production.

In this new system the product or artifact is rapidly coded as a sign or image that gives it distributional value;[72] for example Coca-Cola as a commodity has a strong sign and consumer power in a global context, whereas the refugee as stranger, foreigner or the 'other' has a sign that is unsaleable and unwanted. Consumer citizenship is globalised in this instance, but nationalised when applied to people crossing borders. Wexler emphasises the integration of institutional spheres in a semiotic society, for example the placing of electoral politics within a system of a society based on sign-circulation, the widely recognised items of consumer society. This relates to Luke's claim that elections are now 'commodified and packaged modes of democracy; the exclusive signifier of democratic practice'.[73]

Elections are the manifestation of the public political process in which citizens are located by claiming democratic rights. But as a sign, elections are closely monitored by the media, signifying the democratic process as the culmination of citizenship. This manifests in its strongest sense within national or local elections, but on the global scene the media coverage of distant elections is brought into living-rooms throughout the world, resulting in a 'mind-imaginative' connection to elections.[74]

However, the signs are not the same for refugees and displaced people throughout the world; in some instances there is a humanitarian concern for the plight of refugees, but the connection to related citizenry is not considered. Two strata operate, the 'good' signs that pose no global threat for sovereign nations, and the 'bad' signs where there is a perceived threat to the sovereignty of a nation and its citizens (whether or not it is real). In this instance the 'significant other' is marked out with the 'bad sign', to be feared and excluded. In Australia bad signs have been constructed in rhetoric such as 'yellow peril', 'the hordes from the north'; and the term 'boat people' signifies invasion and threat. This tool of social control and social construction has been, and is still, used to discriminate against specific groups of people.[75]

Falk, in his essay 'The Making of Global Citizenship', differentiates traditional citizenship as operating spatially and global citizenship as operating temporally: 'reaching out to a future to-be-created, and making of such a person a "citizen pilgrim", that is, someone on a journey to "a country" to be established in the future in accordance with more idealistic and normatively rich conceptions of political community'. Falk sees composites of global citizenship depending on the interaction between the personality of individuals and their specific situations. He calls for a recovery of a dynamic and positive sense of citizenship 'responsive to the varieties of human situation and diversity of cultural values', which presupposes a reconstituting of the dominant political powers.[76]

This idealistic notion calls for a renegotiating of the globalisation process, promoting a much stronger transnational agenda and sense of community at the grassroots level. There are similarities with Turner's belief that social movements will provide change, but Turner is more realistic; Falk's plan is based on utopian notions of the universal global citizen. The connection between Falk's grassroots level and Turner's social movements is the requirement for citizen participation in evolving structures of democracy and politics. Both perceive an increased involvement and renegotiating of the political within social, and increasingly cultural, terms and priorities. Falk relies on a sense of belonging in a global community and the accompanying social responsibility.

Environmental and green movements are examples of this, but how do refugees fit in? In the ideal world of Falk's global citizenship, refugees would be accepted within the political confines of nation-state sovereignty. The state would take greater social responsibility for accepting 'strangers' across borders where territorial, statist identities and loyalties are given over to more temporal, global patterns of association. Identity, in this instance, is seen in a global context, with people as global citizens having global rights. Falk's highly idealistic proposal is based on long-term plans with a rosy picture of human nature, politics and economics. Globalisation in its present form is conducted along economic and cultural lines with economics taking priority in market economies that employ economic language about level playing fields, restructuring and economic rationalism. This language and ideology, and hence practices, come from the neo-conservatives and do not fit well with Falk's utopic vision of citizenship and belonging.[77]

Both Falk's notion of grassroots changes and Turner's change developing from social movements through social struggle do operate, as the women's, gay and lesbian, black and environmental movements have shown. They are continuing to make inroads into traditional structures of citizenship and the rights associated with their particular causes. Cultural diversity and the politics of multiculturalism have played, and continue to play, an important part in building identity. For example, it is no longer expected, in liberal democracies such as Australia, that migrants or refugees will assimilate; they can maintain multicultural difference. This recognition and support of hybrid identity is the prevalent condition of postmodern identities. We live in a totally different world with changed foundations: a global capitalist economy and cultural consumerism are connected to rapidly changing notions of citizenship and identity.[78]

In this changed world the exclusive homeland is not the norm for a growing number of people, as demonstrated in mass migration and movements of people. Reference to an ethnic, national and cultural tradition remains, but territorial connections are less important. This holds true for the voluntary migration of people such as transnational executives and migrant workers who move localities depending on work and business opportunities. But do the majority of refugees who move involuntarily feel contented in their new existence? Most reports indicate not; refugees, on the whole, would prefer to return to their homeland.[79] The decades-long endurance of the Palestinians and their quest for a homeland is an example. Refugees who have been displaced from their home and have entered Australia show a longing to return to their own country as a first choice.

Voluntary migration is on the increase, expanding the cultural notion of citizenship and the global citizen, but continuing to rely on the legal manifestation of citizenship. Migrants and accepted refugees are legal citizens of their new country, and many hold two or more passports. They have citizens' rights allowing them access to the legal, political, and social rights of their adopted country. However, this still does not hold true for asylum-seekers or refugees who have moved involuntarily and are waiting for citizenship in their adopted country. They remain without official or legal identity until accepted by the host country or repatriated. Identity is now in the confines of the political, where refugees and asylum-seekers are looking for a home. Home here signifies a place in the world, 'insofar as such a place makes acting in the world possible; that is, makes action meaningful through shared understandings and a shared interpretation of action'.[80]

Hannah Arendt, herself a refugee, understands what it means to be homeless. It is not the loss of a particular place but the impossibility of being at home anywhere: 'what is unprecedented is not the loss of a home but the impossibility of finding a new one'.[81] Refugees can only make new homes and this requires citizenship, as Nick Xenos recognises: 'refugees thus represent the contemporary political identity crisis'.[82]

However, citizenship is limited to nation-state sovereignty, as refugees and asylum-seekers well know. While the concepts of citizenship are changing, any moves towards the Kantian notion of universal citizenship have been thwarted. The universal citizenship foreseen in human rights has not manifested as a true universal. On the contrary, the fragmenting of universal structures such as the United Nations has seen a dissipating of universal notions of citizenship. The nation-state remains supreme in matters of citizenship and belonging, and it appears this will continue. The strongest sense of universality of citizenship lies within globalising processes, and Wexler's semiotic citizenship exemplifies this.

Globalisation has tended to imbue routine day-to-day social interaction with patterns that are, to an increasing extent, shared across the globe. This consumer-oriented relationship connects participants in a global capitalist and consumer society with its icons of Coca-Cola, Nike and Bart Simpson, conveyed by modern telecommunications to citizens all over the globe. Supermarkets carry the goods, the global range of provisions, all year round, and so make the produce of the global environment the norm for our subsistence.

As Spybey points out: 'the nation-state and the nation-state system have rendered citizenship a universal requirement for the legal sanction of human existence; a stateless person does not exist in legal terms'.[83] But stateless persons do exist, and their numbers are rising as a result of events in Rwanda, Somalia and Bosnia. Citizenship as a legal national identity requirement has become a universal, but this does not construct universal citizenship.

## Conclusion

Citizenship of the nation-state is taken for granted by citizens, but it is much sought after by aliens such as asylum-seekers. Boat people detained in Australia have no citizenship, no legal identity and in many cases diminished rights. Citizenship in this case is not universal; instead citizenship has failed in the case of the boat people where it has been used as a method of exclusion and discrimination.

Nancy Fraser and Linda Gordon argue for a reclaiming of social citizenship,[84] using T. H. Marshall's theory of citizenship, which presents a fuller and more humane understanding of membership and belonging. People are not just civil and political citizens but social citizens as well, with rights to guarantees of help in forms that give them status as full members of society, entitled to equal respect. They share in a common set of institutions and services designed for all citizens, 'the use of which constitutes the *practice* of social citizenship'.[85] This includes access to public health services, public schools, public parks and spaces, and the right to work. Australia has denied all this to asylum-seekers and boat people in detention.

Citizenship in liberal democracies is based on two distinct ideas: the right to vote, and the right to work (which is a component of social citizenship). To extend social citizenship to include refugees and people awaiting full citizenship, the right to work is necessary. The citizen rights and entitlements awarded to foreigners and denizens in some EU countries are an example where this occurs.[86] The inclusion of European citizenship in the Treaty of Maastricht is considered a major innovation and reflects the member states' intention of strengthening the feeling of *belonging* by giving the Union a political dimension. However, citizenship of the Union concerns only persons having the nationality of a member state, thus establishing a direct equivalence between citizenship and nationality. Immigrants who had resided in European states for many years previously had free movement between states; this is now overturned without reference to the European Convention on the protection of human rights and fundamental liberties. The impact on migrant workers and refugees is profound. Those most often classified as denizens, that is, residents with civil and social rights of citizenship but not political rights, now experience harsher restrictions on freedom of movement and freedom of opinion. However, the basic rights of residency and associated civil and social rights remain, placing the migrant workers and refugees out in the community with an identity that is recognisable by the state. The situation of refugees and asylum-seekers in Australia can be compared with denizens' and foreigners' rights. Rea examines the social dimension—the relationship between work and citizenship—rather than the political dimension.[87] Rea echoes my call to open the social and civil dimensions of citizenship to refugees, specifically boat people, while they await refugee determination in Australia. Such rights would alleviate the discriminatory practice of mandatory detention of all asylum-seekers.

Denizens and foreigners in the European Union context are classified as guests. They are predominantly guest or migrant workers, some refugees, who are allowed to remain in the country for employment reasons and acquire a legitimate social position relating to their status as employees. Although they have civil and social rights allowing them to reside within the community in conditions similar to citizens, they are denied political participation. They have access to health, education and employment, but limited political identity. The denizen is a second-rate citizen without political identity, but it is a more humane system than the detention of asylum-seekers that operates in Australia (with no citizenship rating and no recognised identity).

Fraser and Gordon argue that civil citizenship has undermined social citizenship. Contract-based societies have supplied the images and interpretations that have formed cultural understandings of civil citizenship, which in turn affects the standing of social citizenship. Social citizenship has been, and still is, subordinated to civil citizenship. In Turner's argument, social citizenship is becoming subordinated—or, as I argue, subsumed—into cultural citizenship. The question arises as to whether cultural citizenship, and thus social citizenship and rights, is being reduced to consumer citizenship. This chapter has shown that two levels of citizenship exist in contemporary times, an imagined citizenship based on consumer and semiotic notions, and a legal-political citizenship based on belonging to a nation-state.

Wexler's interpretation of the semiotic citizen locates citizenship in the confines of consumerism and the semiotic fields, placing priority on economics. Turner's construct of cultural citizenship is more optimistic and diverse; he emphasises the social, albeit subsumed in culture, and offers a system that could alleviate discriminatory practices towards a nation's 'other'.

Mary Kalantzis, in a speech given to the Third National Immigration and Population Outlook Conference in Adelaide in February 1995, also takes an optimistic approach, calling for civic pluralism: 'that negotiating diversity is now the only way to produce social cohesion; that pluralistic citizenship is the most effective way of holding things together; and that an outward-looking approach to the world is the way to maintain national interest'.[88] Kalantzis explains how the universal processes of globalisation accentuate and deploy diversity as a means of product differentiation, using local diversity as the basis for making global connections. Global integration, including movements of people, often interfaces with local fragmentation, producing a landscape in which difference and diversity are more critical and obvious than ever before.

Who is excluded from the share of a society's wealth depends on definitions of inclusion: citizenship is a priority because it provides access to power, wealth, employment, social services and symbols. This last is important, because 'the symbols of belonging and identity interface with who gets the job, who gets a voice, who gets decent medical services and education'[89] and who gets recognised. Kalantzis stresses the ethnic diversity and multiculturalism of Australian identity and influences on governmental policy, recognising that Australia, in dealing with its own diversity, is playing the main global game of our times. The state's challenge is to redistribute its resources in ways that facilitate civic pluralism. The dominant group(s) must learn the ways of the so-called minorities. There is no longer a call to assimilate, to be like the dominant group; rather, there is a need to be multi-lingual and multicultural citizens, which 'requires the development of very different sensibilities. The new citizen of this new state will be a person with multiple citizenship and multiple identities.'[90] Refugees fit well into this picture, but one may ask how the dominant group(s) will learn the ways, or more correctly understand the plight, of the refugee, the asylum-seeker and the 'other'.

To do this, in Kalantzis' view, would require remaking the nation-state (along the lines, perhaps, of James' reconstituting of the nation-state),[91] and rethinking the social to include local diversity and global connectedness. This questions the relationship of the citizen to the state, in which negotiating differences takes on new and important meanings. The new type of nation is thus founded upon a post-national sense of common purpose, which is a 'creative and productive life of boundary crossing, multiple identities, difficult dialogues, and the continuous hybrid reconstruction of our selves'.[92]

This, as Kalantzis recognises,[93] is already happening in Australia, despite the exception of asylum-seekers who do not have the voice they need to obtain their rights. Kalantzis is calling for, among other things, social rights as well as the civil plurality she espouses. This is another recognition of Marshall's social citizenship, connecting with the plight of asylum-seekers in detention in Australia. While I do not advocate full political rights for asylum-seekers, I propose that social citizenship, in the form of free movement within the community and access to, at least, welfare and social institutions, should replace inhumane incarceration. By using detention as a policy of deterrence,[94] Australia has misused citizenship structures; it has focused on the legal and political aspects of citizenship but avoided responsibilities for the social aspects that Marshall, Turner and Kalantzis see as necessary for humanity and equity. This has brought criticism of Australia's human rights record[95] and exemplifies the tension between citizenship expressed in national terms and human rights expressed in international terms.

Citizenship has failed asylum-seekers in the Australian detention regime and has been used to relegate some to the category of 'other', exemplifying the tyranny of citizenship.[96] The incarceration of the boat people has denied social citizenship and violated human rights, signifying this group, who are predominantly Asian, as the 'other'. The recognition and strengthening of social rights, which the European Union has awarded to denizens and foreigners, would be the suitable outcome for detainees. This humane approach would uphold citizenship and human rights and, in Australia's case, include the 'other'.

# 8
# Detention, Exclusion and the 'Other'

Australia continues to implement a mandatory detention policy regardless of criticism from organisations such as the United Nations, the Human Rights and Equal Opportunity Commission and Amnesty International. In the face of rising numbers of asylum-seekers throughout the world, the Howard Government has increased its resolve to maintain a mandatory detention policy, announcing two new detention facilities to be built at the cost of $116 million.

Until the root causes of displacement are addressed, people will continue to flee life-threatening situations. These people are desperate: they seek asylum for their very existence and will continue to do so until conditions are safe within their homelands. As we have seen, most asylum-seekers want to return home, but will not do so until it is safe; and they will continue to undertake such hazardous journeys as the boat people to secure a humane existence. It is predicted that Australia will spend $200 million on locating, removing and detaining asylum-seekers over the next year, while it will only contribute $20 million to the UNHCR refugee effort. The money spent by Australia on maintaining detention facilities could be better spent with the UNHCR, alleviating some of the root causes that contribute to the displacement of asylum-seekers.

Incarcerating asylum-seekers in detention centres is seen as deterring would-be asylum-seekers. In Australia asylum-seekers are categorised as illegal immigrants, and refugee policy dictates that they have broken the law and are treated accordingly: like criminals. Contrary to this, those who enter Australia on a tourist or business visa, and then deliberately overstay that visa, are treated relatively leniently. The numbers in this category, most of whom arrive by air, are far greater than those who arrive by sea, yet the boat people have become the focus of hysteria and discrimination.

The contrasting treatment of the Chinese boat people and the Kosovar refugees who arrived in Australia during 1999 demonstrated this discrimination against a specific group, the 'significant other'. Although there are subtleties in this unfolding story—the boat people constitute a new wave of 'smuggled migrants', and the Kosovar refugees were returned to Kosovo—the mode of entry into Australia plays a significant part in acceptance and legality.

This book has questioned a number of assumptions, asking why detention has been used as a method of deterrence and security and why it is primarily Asians who have been detained. It has shown how a nation-state such as Australia can discriminate against its 'other' by incorporating policies that, unjustly and contrary to human rights, exclude targeted groups. The detention of boat people exposes both the inadequacies and the discriminatory basis of the administrative system that determines refugee status.

Australia has committed human rights violations by using mandatory detention. It continues to mismanage refugee policy, creating tensions between the administrative and judicial systems, leading to long delays in refugee determination and prolonged periods of detention for many asylum-seekers. The administrative system is flawed: by allocating almost complete power for refugee determination to the Immigration Minister, it causes policy to fluctuate as Ministers change. This highlights how public policy can be used as a method of control and exclusion.

Australia has also used citizenship in a discriminatory manner to exclude its 'other'. Citizenship is crucial to signify identity, and while the notion of the global citizen has gained credence and popular recognition, it is still the nation-state that determines who belongs. The Australian policy of mandatory detention denies asylum-seekers the basic social rights that constitute social citizenship, discriminating against a specific group of people, Asian boat people, by denying them access to these rights.

Human Rights Commissioner, Chris Sidoti, encapsulated the situation: 'Our policy to overseas asylum-seekers in circumstances where we can control the numbers and choose those who we take is second to none, but if they come here and seek refugee status, then our record is one of the hardest, most uncompromising and least humane'.[1]

Australia continues to discriminate against non-Anglo, non-European asylum-seekers. The Kosovar refugees were literally welcomed with open arms by Prime Minister Howard, while the Asian boat people were quickly excluded, either sent to the Port Hedland detention camp or deported, without compassion and with closed screening processes to determine refugee status. It is clear that times and attitudes have not changed when European refugees are still welcomed, either as assets or on humanitarian grounds, while Asian asylum-seekers are incarcerated or allowed entrance only on specific criteria. Similarly, the attitudes of the majority of Australians towards Asians have not changed when, at the beginning of the twenty-first century, rhetoric and policy concerning Asians echo the attitudes and discrimination incurred by the Chinese 'coolies' a hundred years ago.

Australia has taken a draconian approach in implementing a refugee detention policy. This policy is based on racist assumptions of the 'other' emanating from 'an ancient and uncompromising *fear* of uncontrolled migration into Australia, particularly from Asia and that is why we take such an uncompromising, to the point of cruel, view of those who come here uninvited'.[2] Treatment of the 'other' is an indicator of the state of health and security of a nation; Australia's continuing discriminatory treatment of its 'other' indicates a need to resolve this fear and exclusion to establish a healthy and secure nation.

# Notes

## 1 Australia's 'Other'

[1] In B. Humphries, *The Barry Humphries Book of Innocent Austral Verse*, Sun Books, Melbourne, 1968, pp. 68–9.

[2] 'Lucky Country for some', *Weekend Australian*, 15–16 May, p. 25.

[3] *Sun Herald* and *Sunday Telegraph*, 11 April 1999; P. Adams, *Late Night Live*, ABC Radio, 12 April 1999; *Age*, 12 April 1999; *Sydney Morning Herald*, 12 April 1999.

[4] *Daily Telegraph*, 7 April 1999; *Weekend Australian*, 8–9 May 1999.

[5] Human Rights and Equal Opportunity Commission Report, *Those who've come across the seas: Detention of unauthorised arrivals*, HREOC, Sydney, May 1998, p. 3.

[6] *Age*, 26 September 1896, reported that 'we shall be overrun by hordes of Asiatics'.

[7] Penguin, London, 1983. See also E. Vasta and S. Castles, *The Teeth are Smiling: The Persistence of Racism in Multicultural Australia*, p. 174; A. Triandafyllidou, 'National Identity and the "Other"', pp. 599–604.

[8] C. D'Mello *et al.*, 'Asian Immigration: Assessing the Issues', *Working Papers on Migrant and Intercultural Studies*, no. 11, Centre for Migrant and Intercultural Studies, Monash University, 1988. See also M. McGillivray and G. Smith, *Australia and Asia*, Oxford University Press, Melbourne, 1997, esp. pp. 3–4.

[9] Amnesty International, Annual Reports; HREOC, *Those who've come*, p. v.

10  Davidson, *From Subject to Citizen*, p. 149.

11  See Brawley, *The White Peril*, esp. Introduction, chs 8 and 9, and Conclusion.

12  Freeman and Jupp (eds), *Nations of Immigrants*, esp. preface.

13  ABS figures show that Australia's population grew from 7 579 000 in the 1947 census to 18 871 800 in the 1998 census.

## 2  The Wretched of the Earth

1  Saikal, *Refugees in the Modern World*, p. 11. Acknowledgment of Franz Fanon, *The Wretched of the Earth*, Macgibbon and Kee, London, 1965.

2  Saikal, *Refugees in the Modern World*, p. 3.

3  See Shawcross, 'Mass Migration and the Global Village'.

4  Kritz, Keely and Tomasi (eds), *Global Trends in Migration*, p. xix.

5  Loescher, *Refugee Movements*, p. 9. See also Rogers, 'The Future of Refugee Flows', p. 1114.

6  S. Shaw, 'The Dispossessed', *New Internationalist*, Summer 1991, p. 5.

7  Loescher, *Refugee Movements*, p. 9.

8  Rogers, 'The Future of Refugee Flows', p. 1114.

9  Castles and Miller, *The Age of Migration*, p. 3; Dowty, *Closed Borders*, p. 20; Kritz, Keely and Tomasi (eds), *Global Trends*, p. xviii; Ogata, 'Refugees', p. 2; and Cohen (ed.), *The Cambridge Survey of World Migration*, provide accounts of non-Western history of migration.

10  Bramwell (ed.), *Refugees in the Age of Total War*, p. 2. In the 'modern' period, beginning in the late fifteenth century, the European world economy came into existence, opening up long-distance trade and the global lines of communication, at the same time opening up world migration: Cohen (ed.), *The Cambridge Survey*, pp. 1–2.

11  Loescher, *Refugee Movements*, p. 32; Dowty, *Closed Borders*, p. 22.

12  D'Souza, *The Refugee Dilemma*.

13  Dowty, *Closed Borders*, pp. 22–3; James Lee in McNeil and Adams (eds), *Human Migration: Patterns and Policies*, Indiana University Press, Bloomington, 1978, pp. 20–47; Cohen (ed.), *The Cambridge Survey*, pp. 1–2.

14  Zolberg, 'International Migrants', p. 37.

15  *Ibid.*; Dowty, *Closed Borders*, pp. 36–43; Kritz, Keely, and Tomasi (eds), *Global Trends*, pp. xxii–xxiii; Castles and Miller, *The Age of Migration*, p. 48. Figures vary: see Cohen (ed.), *The Cambridge Survey*, p. 2; Dowty, *Closed Borders*, p. 38; *New Internationalist*, no. 223, September 1991, p. 24.

16  McNeil and Adams (eds), *Human Migration*, p. 246; Bramwell, *Refugees in the Age*, p. 16; Dowty, *Closed Borders*, pp. 32–3.

17  Dowty, *Closed Borders*, pp. 33–42; Marrus, *The Unwanted*, pp. 5–6; Kritz, Keely, and Tomasi (eds), *Global Trends*, p. 22; McNeil and Adams (eds), *Human Migration*, op. cit., p. 248.

18  Marrus, *The Unwanted*, pp. 8–9, discusses the use of the term 'refugee'. For sixteenth-century migration from the Low Countries, see A. Zolberg, 'State-Formation and its Victims: Refugee Movements in Early Modern Europe', Verhaegen Lecture, Erasmus University, Rotterdam, 1982; Dowty, *Closed Borders*, pp. 34–6; Zolberg, Suhrke and Aguayo, *Escape from Violence*, p. 5.

19  *Refugees*, September 1985, p. 17.

20  Zolberg, Suhrke and Aguayo, *Escape from Violence*: p. 6.

21  Ogata, 'Refugees', p. 2.

22  Zolberg, Suhrke and Aguayo, *Escape from Violence*, p. 8.

23  Zolberg, 'International Migrants', p. 38; Dowty, *Closed Borders*, pp. 42–7.

24  For a detailed analysis see Marrus, *The Unwanted*, ch. 1; Zolberg, Suhrke and Aguayo, *Escape from Violence*, ch. 1; P. Tabori, *The Anatomy of Exile: A Semantic and Historical Study*, Harrap, London, 1972. Tabori's definition of the exile (p. 27) is very close to the Convention definition.

25  Marrus, *The Unwanted*, pp. 9, 17–18; Tabori, *The Anatomy of Exile*, pp. 27–8.

26  Zolberg, 'International Migrants', p. 38; Cohen (ed.), *The Cambridge Survey*, pp. 3, 77; H. Johnstone, *British Emigration Policy: Shovelling out Paupers*, Clarendon, Oxford, 1972, p. 51.

27  For accounts of colonisation and indentured labour, see Castles and Miller (eds), *The Age of Migration*, ch. 3; Zolberg, Suhrke and Aguayo, *Escape from Violence*, pp. 8–10; Cohen (ed.), *The Cambridge Survey*, pp. 45–77; Zolberg, 'International Migrants', p. 38. Between 1835 and 1920 some 27.7 million Indians left the subcontinent for other British dominions in one of the largest and least publicised movements in history: Dowty, *Closed Borders*, p. 46.

28  Dowty, *Closed Borders*, pp. 43–4; Marrus, *The Unwanted*, pp. 8–9, 14–27; Zolberg, 'International Migrants', p. 38; Castles and Miller, *The Age of Migration*, p. 53.

29  Zolberg, 'International Migrants', p. 38.

30  'The History of Borders', *New Internationalist*, no. 223, September 1991, p. 24.

31  Zolberg, 'International Migrants', p. 39.

32  Marrus, *The Unwanted*, p. 10.

33  *Ibid.*, p. 13.

34  H. Arendt, *The Origins of Totalitarianism*, Allen and Unwin, London, 1958, p. 267; Said, 'The Mind of Winter', p. 50.

35  Ogata, 'Refugees', p. 3.

36  Marrus, *The Unwanted*, p. 51.

37  Arendt, *Origins of Totalitarianism*, p. 267.

38  Ogata, 'Refugees', p. 3.

39  *Ibid.*, p. 4.

40  Arendt, *Origins of Totalitarianism*, p. 277.

41  Ogata, 'Refugees', p. 4.

42 Decolonisation produced major refugee movements from 1950 onwards, such as mass migration associated with the partition of India, Pakistan and Bangladesh; and the mass expulsions in Africa: Bramwell, *Refugees in the Age*, pp. 34–5. See Zolberg, Suhrke and Aguayo, *Escape from Violence*, pp. 223–57; Miyoshi, 'A Borderless World?', p. 728.

43 Ogata, 'Refugees', p. 4; Goran Melander's chapter, 'The Concept of the Term "Refugee", in Bramwell, *Refugees in the Age*, pp. 7–12, gives an account of this period; K. Newland, *Refugees: The New International Politics of Displacement*, Worldwatch Paper 43, 1981, p. 7.

44 Arendt, *Origins of Totalitarianism*, p. 279; see Malkki, 'National Geographic', pp. 24–44, for an interpretation of Arendt's relation of strangeness and externality to displaced persons.

45 Xenos, 'Refugees', p. 424; Malkki, 'National Geographic', pp. 31–4.

46 Nomadology or 'nomad thought' is free or separated from identity: G. Deleuze and F. Guattari, *A Thousand Plateaus: Capitalism and Schizophrenia*, Athlone, London, 1987. See C. Miller, 'The Postidentitarian Predicament in the Footnotes of a Thousand Plateaus: Nomadology, Anthropology, and Authority, *Diacritics*, no. 23.3, Fall 1993, pp. 6–33; Rafael Perez-Torres, 'Nomads and Migrants: Negotiating a Multicultural Postmodernism', *Cultural Critique*, no. 26, Winter 1993–94, pp. 161–89.

47 Xenos, 'Refugees', p. 427.

48 Shacknove, 'Who Is a Refugee?', p. 274.

49 See Grahl-Madsen, *The Status of Refugees in International Law*, vol. 1, ch. 1, for the meaning of 'refugee' in various Western European and North American statutes.

50 For shortcomings of the UN and UNHCR, see Newland, *Refugees*, op. cit., pp. 8–9, 27–31; F. Deng, *Protecting the Dispossessed: A Challenge for the International Community*, Brookings Institution, Washington, 1993; A. Bammer, *Displacements: Cultural Identities in Question*, Indiana University Press, Bloomington, 1994.

51 In January 1998 there were 8.1 million persons of concern to the UNHCR in Africa and 7.9 million in Asia; UNHCR, *Speeches of the High Commissioner*, p. 1.

52 For refugee numbers, see J. Cuenod, 'Refugees: Development or Relief?', in Loescher and Monahan (eds), *Refugees in International Relations*, p. 219; UNHCR, *Speeches of the High Commissioner*, p. 2.

53 Article 1A (2) of the Refugee Convention.

54 Taylor, 'The Meaning of "Social Group"', fn. 23, p. 310.

55 Non-refoulment has been recognised as customary law for all refugees, even those fleeing generalised violence who do not fit one of the traditional categories of the convention; see Goodwin-Gill, 'Non-refoulement', pp. 897–920;

Article 33 of the 1951 Convention Relating to the Status of Refugees; National Population Council, *Refugee Review*, p. 139.

56   Shacknove, 'Who Is a Refugee?', p. 275.

57   Hathaway, *The Law of Refugee Status*, pp. v–vii.

58   Shacknove, 'Who Is a Refugee?', p. 275.

59   Saikal, *Refugees*, p. 5; see National Population Council, *Refugee Review*, p. 220, for another definition.

60   Bramwell, *Refugees in the Age*, p. 10.

61   *Humanitarian Assistance to Victims of Natural Disasters and Similar Emergency Situations*, G.A res. 43/131 (United Nations, 1989); and *Coordination of Humanitarian Assistance*, G.A. res. 46/182 (United Nations, December 1991), cited in Deng, *Protecting the Dispossessed*, p. 11.

62   A. Grizold, 'Solving the Refugee Problem in Slovenia', *Journal of International Relations*, 1994, vol. 1, no. 1, pp. 35–44; Cohen, 'Human Rights', pp. 4–7; D. Levinson, 'Ethnic Conflicts and Refugees', *Refugees*, August 1993, pp. 4–9.

63   Saikal, *Refugees*, p. 6.

64   Bramwell, *Refugees in the Age*, pp. 10–11; Ogata, 'Refugees', p. 5.

65   Ogata, 'Refugees', p. 5.

66   D'Souza, *The Refugee Dilemma*, p. 8.

67   Nancy Viviani in Saikal, *Refugees*, p. ii.

68   James, 'Reconstituting the Nation-State'.

69   These arguments are not the focus of this book. See Newland, *Refugees*, pp. 7–9, 27–9; Saikal, *Refugees*, pp. 6–7; M. D. Stafford, 'New Strategies for Refugees in the 1990s', *Refugees*, December 1992, pp. 10–13; A. Johnsson, 'UNHCR's Protection Role Continually Evolving', *Refugees*, April 1993, pp. 15–16; W. Wood and L. Potts, 'The UN and Migration: Falling Behind', *Political Geography*, vol. 15, no. 3/4, 1996, pp. 251–60, for accounts on the failures of the UN and its organisations. See also S. Cox, *Generations of Resistance: East Timor*, Cassell, London, 1995; D. Greenlees, 'East Timor's reluctant hero'; R. Garran, 'Hesitant Howard a Regret', *Weekend Australian*, 13–14 February 1999, p. 12.

70   Jean-Pierre Hocke, 'Refugees: As peace breaks out, funding dries up', *International Herald Tribune*, 22 August 1989. See Wood and Potts, 'The UN and Migration', p. 255, for details of UNHCR budgets.

71   Saikal, *Refugees*, p. 7.

72   *Ibid.*, p. 8; Shacknove, 'Who Is a Refugee?', p. 276.

73   The Organisation of African Unity Convention, Governing the Specific Aspects of Refugee Problems in Africa, 10 September 1969, OAU Doc.CM/ 267/Rw 1, cited in Loescher, *Refugee Movements*, p. 6; Bramwell, *Refugees in the Age*, p. 11; Gallagher, 'The Evolution', pp. 583–4.

74   The Cartagena Declaration of 1984, Geneva, UNHCR, 1985, cited in Loescher, *Refugee Movements*, p. 6; National Population Council, *Refugee Review*, p. 144; Gallagher, 'The Evolution', p. 591.

75  Shacknove, 'Who Is a Refugee?', p. 277; Deng, *Protecting the Dispossessed*, pp. 3–4.

76  D'Souza, *The Refugee Dilemma*, p. 8.

77  *Ibid.*; UNHCR, 'Global Statistics; Populations of Concern to UNHCR, 1995', pp. 1–17; see UNHCR, 'Convention Relating to the Status of Stateless Persons of 28 September 1954, *Collection of International Instruments Concerning Refugees*, pp. 59–82; Bramwell, *Refugees in the Age*, p. 32.

78  D'Souza, *The Refugee Dilemma*, p. 8; see also UNHCR, 'International Covenant on Economic, Social and Cultural Rights of 16 December and Protocol thereto', pp. 128–39.

79  D'Souza, *The Refugee Dilemma*, p. 8.

80  Bramwell, *Refugees in the Age*, p. 12.

81  D'Souza, *The Refugee Dilemma*, p. 8.

82  UNHCR, *Speeches of the High Commissioner*, p. 4.

83  M. Leopold, 'Adapting to a New World: Refugees and Forced Migration', *Development*, no. 4, 1994, pp. 9–13, p. 10.

84  UNHCR, 'Global Statistics: Populations of Concern to UNHCR, 1995', p. 2. The UNHCR includes the OAU and Cartagena definitions but only for persons *outside* their country; this still does not include internally displaced.

85  Said, 'The Mind of Winter', p. 50.

86  Castles and Miller, *The Age of Migration*, p. 4; M. Weiner, 'Peoples and States in a New Ethnic Order?', *Third World Quarterly*, vol. 13, no. 2, 1992, pp. 317–33; N. van der Gaag, 'Bullets and Borders', *New Internationalist*, March 1996, pp. 7–10.

87  For accounts of 'camp life' see Cixous, 'We Who Are Free, Are We Free?'; Lyons (ed.), *Voices, Stories, Hopes*. The author of this book acknowledges the hardships and alienation faced by detainees, experienced in a visit to Villawood Detention Centre, Sydney in 1995.

88  Said, 'The Mind of Winter', p. 51.

89  Miyoshi, 'A Borderless World', p. 728; L. Basch *et al.*, *Nations Unbound: Transnational Projects, Postcolonial Predicaments, and Deterritorialised Nation-States*, Gordon and Breach, Pennsylvania, 1994, chs 1, 7, 8.

90  UNHCR, *Speeches of the High Commissioner*, p. 2.

91  Castles and Miller, *The Age of Migration*, pp. 5–8.

92  This is analysed in greater detail in ch. 4; see also J. Widgren, 'Asylum-seekers in Europe in the Context of South-North Movements', *International Migration Review*, vol. 23, Fall 1989, pp. 599–605.

93  R. Redmond, 'Slamming Doors', *Refugees*, no. 88, January 1992, p. 23; Castles and Miller, *The Age of Migration*, p. 9; Shaw, 'The Dispossessed', pp. 4–7.

94  Castles and Miller, *The Age of Migration*, p. 10; Cornelius *et al.*, *Controlling Immigration*, p. 32; Widgren, 'Asylum-seekers in Europe', p. 604.

[95] P. L. Martin, 'Trade, Aid and Migration', *International Migration Review*, vol. 26, no. 1, 1992, p. 171.

[96] Castles and Miller, *The Age of Migration*, p. 11, Conclusion.

[97] *Ibid.*, p. 266; Widgren, 'Asylum-seekers in Europe', pp. 599–605.

[98] Castles and Miller, *The Age of Migration*, p. 266. They fail to mention criminals and drug issues in these categories.

[99] See Kitty Calavita in Cornelius *et al.*, *Controlling Immigration*, pp. 65–74.

[1] Widgren, 'Asylum-seekers in Europe', pp. 599–605.

[2] Redmond, 'Slamming Doors', p. 22; R. Swift, 'The Jealous State', *New Internationalist*, September 1991, p. 13; Castles and Miller, *The Age of Migration*, p. 267. See also M. Shaw, *Global Society and International Relations: Sociological Concepts and Political Perspectives*, Polity Press, Cambridge, 1994, ch. 1.

[3] Malkki, 'National Geographic', p. 33.

# 3 Australian Immigration and Its 'Other'

[1] Words by P. D. McCormick; cited in HREOC, *Those who've come*.

[2] See Davidson, *From Subject to Citizen*, for a similar discussion.

[3] Freeman and Jupp (eds), *Nations of Immigrants*, p. 3; Dare, *Australia*, p. 43.

[4] Australian Population and Immigration Council, *Immigration Policies*, p. 24; Armit *et al.*, *Australia and Immigration*, p. 10.

[5] Choi, *Chinese Migration*, pp. 18–19; Markus, *Australian Race Relations*, pp. 56–84. For details of these riots see Yarwood and Knowling, *Race Relations in Australia*, pp. 165–87; Yuan, *Awakening Conscience*, p. 46; Markus, *Fear and Hatred*, pp. 14–34; Buggy and Cates, *Race Relations*, chs 4, 5.

[6] Willard, *History*, pp. 20–1; Sherington, *Australia's Immigrants*, p. 30; Hawkins, *Critical Years*, p. 11.

[7] Willard, *History*, p. 99. See Yarwood and Knowling, *Race Relations*, pp. 225–55, and Evans, Saunders and Cronin, *Race Relations*, for accounts of Chinese and other coloured migrants, including the indentured Kanakas, during this time.

[8] Hawkins, *Critical Years*, p. 14.

[9] Willard, *History*, p. 120.

[10] *Bulletin*, 22 June 1901.

[11] Markus, *Australian Race Relations*, pp. 118–19.

[12] W. K. Hancock, *Australia*, Jacaranda, Melbourne, 1930, p. 59.

[13] Hawkins, *Critical Years*, p. 15; Markus, *Australian Race Relations*, p. 115. See Yarwood, *Asian Migration*, pp. 104–5, for a detailed account of the White Australia policy, Asian immigration and exclusion.

[14] Rivett (ed.), *Immigration*, p. 43.

[15] *Ibid.*, p. 24; Sherington, *Australia's Immigrants*, pp. 123–35; Rivett (ed.), *Australia*, pp. 240–1. A 1948 survey distinguished Jews from Chinese, Negroes

[sic], and various European nationalities, 58 per cent of respondents preferred to keep them out. By 1947 non-British migrants constituted only 1.9 per cent of the population, with 0.3 per cent of these from Asia: Australian Bureau of Statistics, *Census of Population*, 1947.

16  See W. Duncan and C. Janes (eds), *The Future of Immigration into Australia and New Zealand*, Angus & Robertson, Sydney, 1937; Kovaks and Cropley, *Immigrants and Society*, p. 70.

17  Freeman and Jupp (eds), *Nations of Immigrants*, p. 131; Kovaks and Cropley, *Immigrants and Society*, p. 72.

18  See Calwell, *How Many Australians Tomorrow?* and Calwell, *Immigration*, for a detailed account of government policy regarding population increase. 'Populate or perish' was not the official slogan but was used as an explanation for increased immigration; it was well known as the title of a book by J. H. Gaffney in the 1940s.

19  Cited in Sherington, *Australia's Immigrants*, p. 128.

20  Markus, *Australian Race Relations*, p. 167. Calwell defended the White Australia policy into the 1960s, claiming that it would have no consequences for foreign policy and that Australia could remain on friendly terms with Asian countries and maintain the policy: Brawley, *The White Peril*, p. 299. Pauline Hanson in her maiden speech referred in glowing terms to Calwell's exclusivist views: 'Australia to seek migrants from Europe', *Canberra Times*, 3 August 1945, p. 2.

21  Australian Population and Immigration Council, *Immigration Policies*, p. 25; Sherington, *Australia's Immigrants*, pp. 133–6.

22  Hawkins, *Critical Years*, pp. 32–1; Australian Population and Immigration Council, *Immigration Policies*, p. 26.

23  Markus, *Australian Race Relations*, p. 169.

24  Cited in Brawley, *The White Peril*, p. 257.

25  Markus, *Australian Race Relations*, pp. 169–73.

26  D. Pope, 1982, cited in Wooden, M. *et al.*, *Australian Immigration*, p. 281.

27  *Ibid.*

28  Sherington, *Australia's Immigrants*, pp. 138–9.

29  Jupp, *Exile or Refuge?*, p. 34; Lack and Templeton, *Bold Experiment*, p. 10. For a poignant account of life in Bonegilla camp, see Sluga, *Bonegilla*; Bonegilla was an immigration centre and staging camp for non-British migrants, refugees and displaced persons to be placed in jobs Australians did not want as well as a place to 'Australianise' non-British migrants, that is, an assimilation camp.

30  Calwell, *Immigration*; Lack and Templeton, *Bold Experiment*, p. 11; Sluga, *Bonegilla*, pp. 101–21.

31  Kovacs and Cropley, *Immigrants and Society*, p. 75.

32  Lack and Templeton, *Bold Experiment*, p. 13.

[33] See Jupp, *Exile or Refuge?*, pp. 34–5, for the strengths and weaknesses of post-war policy in greater detail.

[34] Freeman and Jupp, *Nations of Immigrants*, p. 18.

[35] Yarwood and Knowling, *Race Relations*, pp. 235–7. Rivett (ed.), *Australia and the Non-White Migrant*, Preface, and Rivett (ed.), *Immigration*, give a background to the White Australia policy and a proposal for change. Associations for Immigration Reform were organised in mainland states during the 1960s; see Hawkins, *Critical Years*, p. 310, n. 24; Jupp *et al.*, (eds), *The Politics*, p. 198.

[36] Appleyard *et al.*, *How Many Australians?*, p. 223, quote from Commonwealth Department of Immigration, *Australia's Immigration Policy*, p. 7.

[37] Department of Immigration and Ethnic Affairs, *1788–1978: Australia and Immigration*, p. 25.

[38] Markus, *Australian Race Relations*, p. 181.

[39] Jupp *et al.* (eds), *The Politics*, p. 226; Hawkins, *Critical Years*, p. 170.

[40] Milne and Shergold (eds), *The Great Immigration Debate*, p. 15.

[41] Lack and Templeton, *Bold Experiment*, p. 219. 'Cultural pluralism' was claimed to be first used by Jerry Zubrzyki at the National Citizenship Convention of 1968. For detailed information, see Stephen Castles, 'A New Agenda in Multiculturalism?', *Multicultural Australia Papers*, no. 61, 1987; Kukathas (ed.), *Multicultural Citizens*; Foster and Stockley, *Multiculturalism*, ch. 3; and ch. 6 of this book.

[42] Castles, 'A New Agenda?', p. 3. The Howard government is not supportive of multiculturalism. The removal of the Office of Multicultural Affairs from the Prime Minister's Department soon after taking government in March 1996 was the first indication of this. John Howard has never mentioned the word 'multiculturalism' in parliamentary debates, an indication he is personally opposed to the idea: Mr Albanese, Member for Grayndler, *Commonwealth Parliamentary Debates*, House of Representatives, 6 April 1998, p. 65.

[43] Brawley, *The White Peril*, p. 315; Markus, *Australian Race Relations*, p. 184; Murphy, *The Other Australia*, pp. 197–8.

[44] The White Australia policy was finally 'buried' in late 1973 by the Whitlam Labor Government: Brawley, *The White Peril*, pp. 297–320.

[45] Milne and Shergold, *The Great Immigration Debate*, pp. 15–16.

[46] Senate Standing Committee on Foreign Affairs and Defence, *Australia and the Refugee Problem*, pp. 89–90.

[47] Hawkins, *Critical Years*, pp. 126–7. The changing nature of immigration and the new dilemmas concerning the boat people resulted in significant government reports: the Green Paper of 1977; the Galbally Report of 1978; the Fry Report of 1982; the Fitzgerald Report of 1988; and in 1991 *Population Issues and Australia's Future: Environment, Economy and Society*, produced by the Population Issues Committee of the National Population Council.

48 Ministerial Statement to House of Representatives on Refugee Policy and Mechanisms, 24 May, 1977, point 1 of basic principles, cited in Birrell *et al.* (eds), *Refugees, Resources, Reunion*, pp. 155–6.

49 MacKellar, 'Immigrants or Refugees?', p. 5.

50 *Ibid.*, p. 6.

51 *Ibid.*, p. 4; see ch. 4 of this book for a detailed account and also M. J. R. MacKellar, Minister for Immigration and Ethnic Affairs, 'Refugee Policy and Mechanisms,' Ministerial statement, *Commonwealth Parliamentary Debates*, 24 May 1977.

52 Viviani, *The Long Journey*, p. 78.

53 *Ibid.*, p. 79; Milne and Shergold, *The Great Immigration Debate*, p. 20.

54 This bipartisan support was acknowledged in 1978 by MacKellar, Minister for Immigration and Ethnic Affairs, in his 7 June policy statement: *Australia's Immigration Policy*, p. 1.

55 Viviani, *The Long Journey*, p. 80.

56 Freeman and Jupp (eds), *Nations of Immigrants*, p. 74.

57 J. Zubrzycki, 'Immigration and the Family in a Multicultural Australia', *Australia's Multicultural Society*, La Trobe University, Melbourne, p. 2.

58 K. Bett in Freeman and Jupp (eds), *Nations of Immigrants*, p. 73. For a more detailed argument around this notion refer to Lack and Templeton, *Bold Experiment*, pp. 218–22.

59 Freeman and Jupp (eds), *Nations of Immigrants*, p. 73.

60 *Ibid.*, p. 74. For an informative discourse on economic rationalism refer to M. Pusey, *Economic Rationalism in Canberra: A Nation-Building State Changes its Mind*, Cambridge University Press, 1991.

61 Viviani, *The Long Journey*, p. 110.

62 See *Immigration Policies in Action: A Selection of Speeches by the Hon. Ian Macphee, M.P., Minister for Immigration and Ethnic Affairs*, p. 41; Viviani, *The Long Journey*, p. 112.

63 National Population Council, *Refugee Review*, p. 132.

64 *Ibid.*

65 Viviani, *The Long Journey*, p. 114.

66 *Ibid.*

67 National Population Council, *Refugee Review*, pp. 124–5.

68 Hawkins, *Critical Years*, p. 255.

69 Jupp *et al.* (eds), *The Politics*, pp. 118–19.

70 Chris Hurford, Minister for Immigration and Ethnic Affairs, *Statement to Parliament on the 1986/87 Migration Programme*, cited in Hawkins, *Critical Years*, p. 273. There were six ministers for Immigration under Hawke and one under Keating: Stewart West, 1983–84; Chris Hurford, 1984–87; Mick Young, 1987–88; Clyde Holding, 1988–89; Robert Ray, 1989–90; Gerry Hand, 1990–93; Nick Bolkus, 1993–96.

[71] Committee to Advise on Australia's Immigration Policies, *Immigration: A Commitment to Australia* (Fitzgerald Report), p. xii.

[72] Lack and Templeton, *Bold Experiment*, pp. 223–4. For critics of the report see Collins, *Migrant Hands*, p. 295. Pauline Hanson voiced similar sentiments eight years later; see ch. 5.

[73] Jupp *et al.* (eds), *The Politics*, pp. 133–4.

[74] Adelman *et al.*, *Immigration and Refugee Policy*, vol. 1, p. 289.

[75] Jupp *et al.* (eds), *The Politics*, p. 134.

[76] M. Easson, (ed.), *Australia and Immigration: Able to Grow*, Pluto Press, Sydney, 1990, p. 78.

[77] Prime Minister Hawke, quoted by Michelle Grattan, *Age*, 11 June 1990.

[78] Jupp *et al.* (eds), *The Politics*, p. 136. Gerry Hand, now retired from politics, still maintains this stance: interview on *Lateline*, ABC TV, 10 March 1999.

[79] Jupp, *Exile or Refuge?*, p. 10; National Population Council, *Refugee Review*, p. 140; and ch. 2 of this book.

[80] Ministerial Media release MPS 8/ 31 January 1992, cited in Jupp, *Exile or Refuge*, p. 13.

[81] Adelman *et al.*, *Immigration and Refugee Policy*, vol. 1, p. 276.

[82] National Population Council, *Refugee Review*, pp. 13–14; Adelman *et al.*, *Immigration and Refugee Policy*, vol. 1, pp. 255–82.

[83] Migration Reform Bill 1992, sections 54W, 54ZD, cited by K. Cronin in Jupp *et al.* (eds), *The Politics*, p. 101; *Migration Act*, section 14, notes that 'a non-citizen in the migration zone who is not a lawful non-citizen is an unlawful citizen'. The migration zone is the area consisting of the states, the territories, and Australian resource and sea installations: Crock (ed.), *Protection*, pp. 32–3. Shadow Minister of the day, Philip Ruddock, saw the role of the courts had brought about significant problems for the government. He claimed that in refugee matters it was the administrative process that should determine claims and not the judicial; see *Commonwealth Parliamentary Debates*, House of Representatives, 16 December 1992, p. 3935; *Migration Amendment Act 1992*, section 54R, cited by Cronin in Jupp *et al.* (eds), *The Politics*, p. 101.

[84] Crock (ed.), *Protection*, pp. 32–3.

[85] Cronin in Jupp *et al.* (eds), *The Politics*, p. 101; N. Poynder in Crock (ed.), *Protection*. The HREOC report, *Those who've come*, stated in its major findings that the 'mandatory detention for extended periods of almost all unlawful non-citizens who arrive by boat breaches Australia's human rights obligations under the International Covenant on Civil and Political Rights and the Convention on the Rights of the Child', pp. 14–15.

[86] Margaret Piper, 'Decision Making in the Department of Immigration: With Particular Reference to Refugee Status Determination', given at the conference *Administrative Law and Review in Public Decision-Making*, 12–13 December 1994, p. 2.

87   The framework for the tribunal was formulated in December 1992 and began operating on 1 July 1993. It was part of the *Migration Reform Act 1992* (Cth), section 31, which introduced Part 4A of the Act; M. Crock, 'Reviewing the Merits of Refugee Decisions: An Evaluation of the Refugee Review Tribunal', paper presented at the *Retreating from the Convention Conference*, Northern Territory University, 7–10 February 1997, pp. 1–4.

88   Hosking and Murphy, 'Forced Migration', p. 10.

89   D. Cox and P. Glenn, 'Illegal Immigration and Refugee Claims', in Adelman *et al.*, *Immigration and Refugee Policy*, vol. 1, pp. 306–8.

90   Joint Standing Committee on Migration, *Australia's Refugee and Humanitarian System*, paragraph 4.152, p. 148.

91   Cox and Glenn in Adelman *et al.*, *Immigration and Refugee Policy*, p. 303. Other models such as the judicial model of Canada are compared in ch. 4 of this book.

92   Amnesty International, Annual Reports; 1995–98; Poynder in Crock (ed.), *Protection*. The UN Human Rights Committee found in April 1997 that Australia had violated the rights of a boat person under the International Covenant for Civil and Political Rights by detaining him arbitrarily for more than four years: cited in Audit Report no. 32, *The Management*, p. 3.

93   *Australian*, 4 July 1996, p. 1, and 31 May 1996, p. 4; *Weekend Australian*, 6–7 July 1996, p. 21.

94   *Australian*, 4 July 1996, p. 1; DIMA, *Fact Sheet 3*, *'Recent developments'*, p. 1.

95   *Australian*, 4 July 1996, p. 2.

96   *Ibid.*, 10 July 1996, p. 4.

97   *Ibid.*, 31 May 1996, p. 4; *Advertiser*, 8 July 1996, p. 1. See also *Australian*, 8 July 1996, p. 2, and 11 July 1996, p. 10.

98   *Weekend Australian*, 6–7 July 1996, p. 21. A high proportion of the information recorded here has been obtained from research commissioned and written by BIMPR researchers who, on the whole, give a balanced and certainly professional account of issues pertaining to immigration.

99   DIMA, Fact Sheet 1, 'Immigration-the background', pp. 1–3.

1    DIMA, Fact Sheet 20, '1998–99 Migration Program planning levels', p. 2; DIMA, Fact Sheet 82, 'Immigration detention', p. 2. See Joint Standing Committee on Migration, *Asylum, Border Control and Detention*; and ch 4 of this book for more details.

2    Ch. 6 discusses the 'politics of blame'; Judith Brett in Gray and Winter, *The Resurgence of Racism*, ch. 1, discusses the 'politics of grievance'.

3    See Cronin in Jupp *et al.* (eds), *The Politics*, p. 88.

## 4   The Politics of Detention

1    UNHCR, *Guideline on Detention of Asylum-Seekers*, p. 3.

2    From a letter to Prince Charles, 7 December 1993, from David Chang; *Australian*, 28 January 1994, p. 1.

3   HREOC, *Those who've come*, p. 3.

4   See sections 88, 89 and Div. 4B of the *Migration Act*; Joint Standing Committee on Migration, *Asylum, Border Control and Detention*, foreword; DIMA, Fact Sheet 82, 'Immigration Detention', p. 1.

5   D. Richardson, 'The Detention Provisions in the Migration Act', *Migration Monitor*, nos. 29–30, June 1993, p. 13; Joint Standing Committee, *Asylum, Border Control*, p. 11.

6   Federal Race Discrimination Commissioner, *Face the Facts*, p. 17. See HREOC, *Those who've come*, p. v. International human rights standards permit detention only where necessary and requires that the individual be able to challenge the lawfulness of his or her detention in the courts. Children and other vulnerable people should be detained only in exceptional circumstances.

7   Joint Standing Committee, *Asylum, Border Control*, p. 49.

8   DIMA, Fact Sheet 1, 'Immigration', p. 9, 1; M. Crock, 'A Legal Perspective on the Evolution of Mandatory Detention', *Migration Monitor*, October 1993, p. 9; Crock (ed.), *Protection*, p. 27.

9   HREOC, *Those who've come*, pp. 18–19.

10  Crock, 'A Legal Perspective', p. 9.

11  UNHCR, Executive Committee of the High Commissioner's Programme, *Conclusion No. 44*, p. 1.

12  UNHCR *Guideline on Detention*, Guideline 3: Exceptional Grounds for Detention, UNHCR, 1996, p. 4. This is also under Article 9(1), International Convention on Civil and Political Rights; Article 37(b), CRC; Article 5(1)(f), ECHR; Article 7(3), American Convention; Article 6, African Charter; EXCOM Conclusion no. 44 (XXXVII).

13  Sub-Committee of the Whole on International Protection Note EC/ECP/44 Paragraph 51 (c).

14  See Viviani, *The Long Journey*, pp. 68–81. The initial boat landings attracted minimal media coverage but by the third, in December 1976, the press was expressing concern; the Melbourne *Sun-News Pictorial* claimed that 'today's trickle of unannounced visitors to our lonely northern coastline could well become a tide of human flotsam' and warned of the 'coming invasion of its north by hundreds, thousands and even tens of thousands of Asian refugees', cited in Viviani, p. 70.

15  Viviani, *The Long Journey*, pp. 77–81; Coughlan and McNamara (eds), *Asians in Australia*, pp. 24–8.

16  Hawkins, *Critical Years*, p. 180.

17  M. J. R. MacKellar, Minister for Immigration and Ethnic Affairs, 'Refugee Policy and Mechanisms', Ministerial statement, *Parliamentary Debates*, 24 May 1977.

18  MacKellar, 'Immigrants or Refugees?', pp. 4–6.

19  Hawkins, *Critical Years*, p. 173.

20  M. Crock in Selby (ed.), *Tomorrow's Law*, p. 32.

21  Viviani, *The Long Journey*, p. 80.

22  Hawkins, *Critical Years*, p. 174; Milne and Shergold (eds), *The Great Immigration Debate*, p. 20. Coughlan and McNamara (eds), *Asians in Australia*, p. 28, note that only about 2000 boat people out of more than half a million who fled Vietnam by boat reached Australia and yet this small number of boat people captured the popular imagination, epitomising the 'perceived uncontrolled flood from Asia'.

23  McKieran, in Crock (ed.), *Protection*, pp. 3–7. Senator Jim McKieran chaired the Joint Standing Committee on Migration whose 1994 report, *Asylum, Border Control and Detention*, affirmed Australia's mandatory detention policy. Defend, Deter, Detain refers to the defending of Australia, deterring of boat people, and detaining of those who land on Australian shores; see also Viviani, *The Indochinese*, p. 7; Freeman and Jupp (eds), *Nations of Immigrants*, p. 74.

24  *Immigration Policies in Action: A Selection of Speeches*, p. 41.

25  Viviani, *The Long Journey*, p. 112.

26  *Ibid.*, p. 81.

27  Hawkins, *Critical Years*, p. 182. This resettlement program from Southeast Asian refugee camps reduced the incentive, that is, deterred prospective boat people departing from the camps.

28  Viviani, *The Indochinese*, pp. 10–11.

29  'Boat People appear to be Cambodians', *Advertiser*, 1 December 1989, p. 16. Referred to as Cambodians by the media and government, the first group from the *Pender Bay* who arrived at Broome consisted of 10 Vietnamese, 9 Cambodians and 8 Chinese and were aged from 3 to 84 years. The second boat, codenamed the *Beagle*, also landed at Broome and consisted of 92 Cambodians, 34 Chinese and 9 Vietnamese, comprising 92 adults, 27 children and 16 babies. DIMA, Fact Sheet 81, 'Boat Arrivals since 1989', p. 1, August 1998. They will be referred to as Cambodians, as most were Cambodian nationals, in this book.

30  HREOC, *Those who've come*, p. v; DIMA, Fact Sheet 81, 'Boat Arrivals since 1989', pp. 1–7.

31  For a similar argument refer to M. Crock, 'Reviewing the Merits of Refugee Decisions: An Evaluation of the Refugee Review Tribunal', in Northern Territory University, *Retreating from the Refugee Convention: Conference Proceedings*, p. 4.

32  Nancy Viviani captures this dilemma in her aptly titled book, *The Indochinese in Australia, 1975–1995: From Burnt Boats to Barbecues*. See also Brennan, *Immigration Policy*, p. 62.

33  'Concern over boat people', *Advertiser*, 21 December 1989, p. 16.

34  'Refugee status unlikely: Evans', *Advertiser*, 16 June 1990.

35 Channel Nine's *A Current Affair*, 6 June 1990. This interview highlighted Hawke's attitude towards the Cambodians as 'queue jumpers', a label that stuck to boat people during this period.

36 Justice Keely, Federal Court Report, 15 November 1993, *Mok Gek Bouy v The Minister for Immigration, Local Government and Ethnic Affairs and Malcolm Paterson*, no. VG453 of 1992 FED no. 828; also 'Boat people: Judge slams Hawke and Evans', *Weekend Australian*, 13–14 November 1993, p. 1; Viviani, *The Indochinese*, p. 20.

37 See Working Papers prepared for the Informal Meeting on Cambodia, Jakarta, *Cambodia: An Australian Peace Proposal*; G. Evans, *Cooperating For Peace: The Global Agenda for the 1990s and Beyond*, Allen & Unwin, Sydney, 1993; G. Evans and B. Grant, *Australia's Foreign Relations in the World of the 1990s*, Melbourne University Press, 1995, ch. 13.

38 Crock in Selby (ed.), *Tomorrow's Law*, p. 35.

39 Refugee Council of Australia, 'Briefing Paper on the Boat People', May 1992, p. 11; R. Richardson, 'The Detention Provisions in the Migration Act', *Migration Monitor*, June, p. 13.

40 Reilly, Detention of Asylum-seekers, p. 2.

41 Department of Immigration, Local Government and Ethnic Affairs, *In a Changing World*, pp. 35–6; also Reilly, Detention of Asylum-seekers, pp. 2–3.

42 Crock, 'A Legal Perspective', p. 9. Detention facilities exist at Villawood Immigration Detention Centre, Sydney, with the capacity for 270 people; Maribyrnong IDC, with a capacity for 70 people; Perth IDC, with a capacity for 40 people; and the Immigration Reception and Processing Centre at Port Hedland, with a capacity for 700 people; DIMA, Fact Sheet 82, 'Immigration detention', p. 2; also Chittleborough, The Use of Detention, p. 2.

43 P. McIntosh, World Federation of Mental Health Conference, Sydney, April 1992, and the Welcome Stranger National Forum on Refugees, Sydney, June 1992.

44 Crock, 'Reviewing the Merits', p. 4.

45 Department of Immigration, *In a Changing World*, p. 36; Viviani, *The Indochinese*, p. 22.

46 Crock in Selby (ed.), *Tomorrow's Law*, p. 33.

47 The Migration Regulations Committee Report, *Australia's Refugee and Humanitarian System: Achieving a Balance Between Refuge and Control*, concluded that the Chinese students should be dealt with on a case by case basis after their four-year visas expired in 1994, a call also made by the Opposition. The report also criticised the emotive actions of former Prime Minister Hawke. See Viviani, *The Indochinese*, pp. 20–2, and G. Campbell, *Australia Betrayed*, pp. 31–4, for accounts of Hawke's actions.

48 Viviani, *The Indochinese*, pp. 20–1. As well as these Chinese students, Chinese who came to study after Tiananmen were similarly advantaged, able to claim

refugee status or to apply for a new special category of entry based on educational qualifications. Between June 1989 and November 1993 about 13 000 Chinese arrived for study and claimed they could not go back for fear of persecution. L. Hardy, 'The Refugee and Humanitarian Category', paper given at the conference *First National Immigration Outlook*, November 1990.

49   K. Rivett, *A Refugee Policy*, p. 6. Tran Van Nhu, one of the first Vietnamese boat people to arrive in 1976, was a principal of a primary school in Vietnam: Paul Lloyd, 'Faith, Hope and Charity', *Advertiser*, 27 April 1996, Insight p. 1.

50   Viviani, *The Indochinese*, p. 21; Jupp, *Exile or Refuge?*, p. 11; For a similar discussion see C. McDonald, QC, 'Australia's Declining Commitment to Refugees: Sending a Message to Asia', in Northern Territory University, *Retreating*. See S. Cooney, *The Transformation of Migration Law*, for a comprehensive analysis of the changes to immigration law after 1989.

51   Crock in Selby (ed.), *Tomorrow's Law*, pp. 33–9; Cooney, *The Transformation*, p. 33.

52   N. Poynder, 'Marooned in Port Hedland', *Alternative Law Journal*, vol. 18, no. 6, December 1993, p. 274; M. Einfeld in Crock (ed.), *Protection*, pp. 42–4.

53   'Briefing Paper on the Boat People', May 1992; 'Briefing Paper on the Boat People and Asylum Issues: For the RCA Executive Committee', May 1992, Refugee Council of Australia. See also Reilly, 'Detention of Asylum-seekers'; Chittleborough, The Use of Detention; Poynder, 'Marooned in Port Hedland'.

54   Cooney, *The Transformation*, and 'Transformation of Migration Law', paper given at the conference *Third National Immigration and Population Outlook*, Adelaide, February 1995, p. 7.

55   Crock, 'Reviewing the Merits'. The framework for the RRT was formulated in December 1992 and it began operating on 1 July 1993. It was part of *Migration Reform Act 1992* (Cth), section 31, which introduced Part 4A of the Act, pp. 1–4.

56   M. Piper, cited in Peter Fray, 'Missed the Boat', *Bulletin*, 6 September 1994, p. 30. Also in conversations between Margaret Piper and the author.

57   Margaret Piper, 'Decision Making in the Department of Immigration: With Particular Reference to Refugee Status Determination', given at the conference *Administrative Law and Review in Public Decision-Making*, 12–13 December 1994, p. 2; Crock, 'Reviewing the Merits'.

58   *Lateline*, ABC TV, 10 March 1999.

59   S. Chetty, 'The Refugee Review Tribunal: Facilitating Australia's Compliance with its Obligations Under the Refugees Convention', in Northern Territory University, *Retreating*, p. 15. See also Refugee Review Tribunal, *Homepage*, p. 1.

60   A. Reilly, 'A Brighter Horizon for Refugees', *Alternative Law Journal*, vol. 19, no. 1, 1994, p. 43; Crock, 'Climbing Jacob's Ladder', p. 340; McDonald, 'Australia's Declining Commitment'.

61 Crock (ed.), *Protection*, p. 32.
62 Crock, 'A Legal Perspective', p. 11. Between 1989 and 1993 the *Migration Act* was amended eleven times and became so complicated that few people could understand it: W. Poussard in J. Wilson *et al.*, *Australian Welfare State: Key Documents and Themes*, Macmillan, Melbourne, 1996, p. 211. See also C. Armitage, 'Laws for refugees confuse officials', *Australian*, 24 February 1995, p. 4; Cooney, *The Transformation*, p. 112; J. Lewis, 'Government Passes the Buck on Asylum-seekers', *Migration News*, no. 41, June 1996, p. 6.
63 Eve Lester, cited in F. Lewis, 'Borderline Insanity', pp. 8–9. This amending Act was enacted on Christmas Eve, 1992, as a cynical attempt by the Government to forestall any contestation: Cronin in Jupp *et al.* (eds), *The Politics*, p. 101. Also see N. Poynder in Crock (ed.), *Protection*, pp. 33–4.
64 Crock, 'Climbing Jacob's Ladder', p. 346.
65 K. Murphy, 'Who's Afraid of the Big Bad Courts?', pp. 60–1. While there has been bipartisan support for many of the restrictive changes to the *Migration Act* since 1992, the Australian Democrats, the Greens and independent senators have maintained the focus on human rights for the detainees and asylum-seekers; see Senator Brian Harradine, Media Release, *Day of Shame: Harradine*, 17 December 1992.
66 Crock, 'Climbing Jacob's Ladder', pp. 346–7; Murphy, 'Who's Afraid', p. 61.
67 McDonald, 'Australia's Declining Commitment'.
68 Australian National Audit Office, Audit Report no. 32, *The Management of Boat People*, p. 3; also HREOC, *Those who've come*, p. v.
69 Article 33: Prohibition of expulsion or return ('refoulement') from 'International Instruments and their Significance', in UNHCR, *The State of the World's Refugees*, Penguin, New York, 1993, p. 163; Crock, 'Climbing Jacob's Ladder', p. 348.
70 'Last-minute reprieve for boat people', *Advertiser*, 22 December 1992. This occurred again in late 1994 when immigration officials curtailed legal access for detainees at Port Hedland, resulting in fewer applications for review of negative primary decisions. This begs the question how many *bona fide* refugees were, and still are, returned to unsafe conditions; HREOC, *Those who've come*, pp. 224–5.
71 Joint Standing Committee, *Asylum, Border Control*, p. 1.
72 *Ibid.*, pp. xiii–xvii.
73 *Ibid.*, pp. 195, 201–14.
74 *Ibid.*, p. 199.
75 *Ibid.*, p. xiv.
76 Submissions to the Joint Standing Committee, *Inquiry into Detention Practices*. Opponents of Australia's mandatory detention policy included HREOC, the Law Council, Amnesty International, UNHCR, RCA, several legal aid com-

missions and the Australian Council of Churches: Murphy, 'Who's afraid', p. 60. The majority of submissions criticised detention, but especially note submissions 25, 26, 27, 31, 36, 38, 40, 43, 45, 57, 87, 88, 90.

77  *Ibid.*, Submissions S74 and S112, S89, S16, S96.

78  M. Lawton and K. Murphy, 'The Detention of Asylum Seekers in Australia', pp. 1–9, esp. p. 5.

79  Cronin in Jupp *et al.* (eds), *The Politics*; Murphy, 'Who's Afraid'.

80  P. Hosking and K. Murphy, 'Forced Migration', pp. 1–11, esp. p. 10; also conversations with Margaret Piper, Executive Director of the RCA.

81  Murphy, 'Who's Afraid', p. 61.

82  See G. Campbell and M. Uhlmann, *Australia Betrayed*, pp. 68–74, 36; Poynder, 'Marooned in Port Hedland', pp. 272–4; Crock (ed.), *Protection*; Fray, 'Missed the Boat', pp. 26–30.

83  *West Australian*, 21 April 1992, p. 1.

84  Hosking, 'Refugees, "Human Trafficking" and Asylum Seekers', p. 10.

85  These arguments are collected and presented in Crock (ed.), *Protection*, and also the submissions to the Joint Standing Committee, *Inquiry into Detention Practices: Submissions*, vols 1–5.

86  Justice M. Einfeld, 'Inquiry into Detention Practices', Joint Standing Committee, *Inquiry Submissions*, vol. 2, p. S818.

87  Joint Standing Committee, *Asylum, Border Control*, p. 5.

88  *Ibid.*, p. 6.

89  Only 64 Cambodian detainees took up this offer, and over 100 others remained to battle out their cases: *Weekend Australian*, 29–30 January 1994; Crock in Selby (ed.), *Tomorrow's Law*, p. 41; and RCA, 'Briefing Paper: Asylum', p. 3.

90  See Vox Populi, SBS Television, 2 February 1994; also an interview by author with John Atkinson from St Vincent de Paul who sponsored the Cambodian 'returnees', Sydney, 22 November 1994. F. Lewis, in 'Borderline Insanity', p. 9, describes the mishandling of newly released detainees in detail.

91  Viviani, *The Indochinese*, p. 25.

92  Trudy Harris, 'Cambodians: 5 year detention nightmare ends', *Weekend Australian*, 28–29 October 1995, p. 4.

93  C. Sidoti, Keynote Address, in Northern Territory University, *Retreating*, p. 9.

94  Crock in Selby (ed.), *Tomorrow's Law*, p. 42.

95  *Age*, 6 January 1995, p. 1; *Weekend Australian*, 24–25 December 1994, p. 1; *Advertiser*, 29 December 1994; *Sydney Morning Herald*, 23 November 1994, p. 5.

96  *Age*, 29 December 1994, p. 2.

97  *Australian*, 29 December 1994, p. 2.

98  For more detail see Fontaine, 'The Comprehensive Plan of Action'; M. Knowles, 'The International Conference on Indochinese Refugees and its Aftermath',

*Refugee Policy Group: Center for Policy Analysis and Research on Refugee Issues*, Issue Brief, August 1989; 'New Approaches to an Old Problem', *Refugees*, no. 74, April 1990, p. 5.

99   K. Murphy, 'Refugee Law: The Experience in the Asian Region', *Uniya Occasional Paper no. 80*, November 1994, pp. 5–7; Crock in Selby (ed.), *Tomorrow's Law*, p. 43; Lewis, 'Government Passes the Buck', p. 4.

1   *Migration Act*, sections 91A–G.

2   Lewis, 'Government Passes the Buck', p. 4; Murphy, 'Refugee Law', p. 9.

3   J. Walker, 'Bolkus defends deportations', *Weekend Australian*, 19–20 November 1994, p. 8.

4   J. Bedlington, 'What Governments Do: Facing the Practical Realities', in Northern Territory University, *Retreating*; Crock in Selby (ed.), *Tomorrow's Law*, p. 43. Criticism of the CPA focused on corrupt practices in Indonesia rendering the UNHCR's screening processes imperfect, with allegations of favourable determinations of refugee status in exchange for bribes such as sex and money: P. McGuiness, 'Boat People and the Law', *Sydney Morning Herald*, 22 November 1994, p. 16; Crock in Selby (ed.), *Tomorrow's Law*, p. 43.

5   *Advertiser*, 27 December 1994, p. 8.

6   A. Meade and K. Towers, 'Chinese gangs behind refugee racket: Bolkus', *Australian*, 29 December 1994, p. 1; K. Middleton, 'China "no" to boat people: Bolkus demands end to "racket"', *Age*, 29 December 1994, p. 1.

7   This resumed in 1999 with the arrivals of boats from southern China in a 'people-smuggling' racket with boats arriving in March, April and May; 'Welcome to an inhospitable hell', *Weekend Australian*, 29–30 May 1999, p. 7.

8   Meade and Towers, 'Chinese Gangs', p. 1.

9   See *Australian*, 'Jogger stumbles on boat people', 'Boat people foil Coastwatch', 13 December 1994, pp. 1, 2; also *Sydney Morning Herald*, 'Coastwatch surveillance queried', 'The surveillance folly, too serious to laugh about', 24 November 1994, pp. 7, 15. This also created tensions between immigration officials, the Immigration Minister and refugee advocates whom the Minister accused of 'coaching' the boat people into claiming refugee status. Refugee advocates, however, were concerned, as were immigration authorities, that if these new arrivals weren't refugees they would discredit 'real' refugees: Middleton, 'China "no" to boat people', p. 1.

10   Most one-child claims were not from boat people; interview with Margaret Piper, Executive Director, RCA, 10 June 1998.

11   December 1994, *MIEA v Respondent A and others* (1994) 127 ALR 383.

12   Senator Bolkus, cited in 'China accepts boat people's return', *Age*, 2 February 1995, p. 4.

13   For an insightful account of the one-child policy and Australia's response, see M. T. Reist, 'Debunking the Myths: Why Do they Come?', in Northern Territory University, *Retreating*; *Age*, 31 December 1994, p. 1; Eve Lester, quoted

in 'Bolkus reaction to boat people is shameful', *Age*, 6 January 1995, p. 10; 'Refugee laws come under fire', *Weekend Australian*, 1–2 April 1995, p. 5; 'Bishops fear Migration Bill will erode rights', *Australian*, 24 March 1995, p. 5; 'Opposition will seek to amend refugee bill', *Australian*, 8 March 1995, p. 2; 'Harradine may quit if refugee Bill passes', *Weekend Australian*, 25–26 March 1995, p. 2.

14  Senator Bolkus, 'Refugee Bills reinforce human rights commitment', *Australian*, 2 March 1995, p. 11.

15  Reist, 'Debunking the Myths'; Senator Bolkus, quoted in 'China accepts boat people's return', *Age*, 2 February 1995, p. 4; 'Tougher laws on refugees', *Age*, 31 December 1994, p. 1; 'Boat people will face scrutiny by Immigration', *Canberra Times*, 20 January 1995, p. 2; 'Laws to prevent influx of refugees', *Weekend Australian*, 31 December–1 January 1995, pp. 1–2.

16  Cited in 'Tougher laws on refugees', *Age*, 31 December 1994, p. 1.

17  'Boat people slip through security', *Advertiser*, 11 March 1995, p. 10; '52 boat people face swift deportation', *Weekend Australian*, 11–12 March 1995, p. 13.

18  Justice Nicholson, cited in 'Judge damns refugee camps', *Australian*, 20 July 1995, p. 1; 'Call for justice echoes in community', *Australian*, 21 July 1995, p. 2: a poignant reminder of David Chang's words to Prince Charles.

19  Natalie O'Brien, 'Boat people protesters denied food', *Australian*, 3 July 1995, p. 3; 'Boat people protesters get treatment for exhaustion', *Australian*, 4 July 1995, p. 5; Colleen Egan, 'Security "provoked" refugee violence', *Australian*, 10 July 1995, p. 2; Maria Ceresa, 'Bolkus accused of fudging boat people costs', *Australian*, 11 April 1996, p. 7; Maria Ceresa, 'Reassured boat people deported', *Australian*, 9 June 1996 p. 7; Penelope Green, 'Court rules in favour of deporting boat people', *Australian*, 29 February 1996, p. 2.

20  HREOC, *Those who've come*, pp. 265–8; Australian National Audit Office, Audit Report no. 32, *The Management*, p. 9.

21  HREOC, *Those who've come*, pp. 224–5; *RMS News*, August 1996, p. 3.

22  HREOC, *Those who've come*, pp. 267–9. Of the 822 Chinese boat people who arrived, only 15 remained (detained) and the others were returned; see E. Lester, 'Singing Our Song', *Uniya Focus*, no. 19, June 1998.

23  Gabrielle Chan, 'Ruddock targets refugee log jam', *Australian*, 31 May 1996, p. 4; 'Ruddock moves on refugee appeals', *Australian*, 18 April, 1996, p. 12; Maris Ceresa, 'Overhaul for refugee tribunal', *Australian*, 17 April 1996, p. 1. By June 1998 the amalgamation of review tribunals was the main initiative of the government; to date the review tribunals, including the RRT, have remained relatively untouched but under threat: information from Margaret Piper, June 1998.

24  For a more comprehensive outline of the model, see HREOC, *Those who've come*, pp. 247–56.

## 5  International Comparisons

[1]  Cornelius *et al.* (eds), *Controlling Immigration*, p. 7.

[2]  Daniel Defoe, 'The True-Born Englishman', in H. Morley (ed.), *The Earlier Life and Chief Earlier Works of Daniel Defoe*, Routledge, London, 1899, pp. 175–218.

[3]  Z. Layton-Henry in Cornelius *et al.* (eds), *Controlling Immigration*, p. 281.

[4]  See Z. Layton-Henry, *The Politics of Immigration: Immigration, 'Race' and 'Race' Relations in Post-War Britain*, Blackwell, Oxford, 1992, esp. ch. 2.

[5]  Layton-Henry in Cornelius *et al.* (eds), *Controlling Immigration*, pp. 292–3.

[6]  National Population Council, *Refugee Review*, p. 111.

[7]  M. Piper in Crock (ed.), *Protection*, p. 121.

[8]  United Kingdom, Asylum Directorate: Immigration and Nationality Directorate, Home Office, *Briefing Paper*, pp. 3–4.

[9]  *Ibid.*, p. 5.

[10]  M. Piper, 'Outline of Specific Determination Procedures for Selected Countries', *Uniya Paper.*

[11]  National Population Council, *Refugee Review*, p. 112.

[12]  Amnesty International, *Home Page, United Kingdom: Arbitrary detention of asylum-seekers*, 30 January 1997.

[13]  French Minister of the Interior, Pasqua, cited by Hollifield in Cornelius *et al.* (eds), *Controlling Immigration*, p. 171.

[14]  Silverman, *Deconstructing*, p. 10; see also A. Hargreaves, *Immigration, 'Race' and Ethnicity in Contemporary France.*

[15]  Hollifield in Cornelius *et al.* (eds), *Controlling Immigration*, p. 172.

[16]  See Nonna Meyer in Hargreaves and Leaman, *Racism, Ethnicity*. The New Right has racialised immigration through the discourse of cultural differentiation and new nationalism which Le Pen himself has labelled as nationalist: Silverman, *Deconstructing*, p. 167.

[17]  See Hollifield in Cornelius *et al.* (eds), *Controlling Immigration*, p. 155.

[18]  *Ibid.*, p. 167.

[19]  Silverman, *Deconstructing*, pp. 38–9.

[20]  *Ibid.*; Hollifield in Cornelius *et al.* (eds), *Controlling Immigration*, p. 150; National Population Council, *Refugee Review*, p. 109.

[21]  Piper, 'Outline'.

[22]  Also called 'international zones'; A. Cruz in Tomasi (ed.), *In Defense*, vol. 17, pp. 174–5.

[23]  Piper in Crock (ed.), *Protection*, p. 119.

[24]  The European Union is still evolving. Defined in simplistic terms as a set of inter-governmental institutions, it is also a unique arrangement between states, which benefits the majority of individuals within those states, without

threatening national sovereignty. See Taylor, *The European Union*, pp. 1–2; European Commission, *Background Report, The Growth of the EU*, p. 1; European Commission, *Background Report, Brussels: Myths and Realities*, p. 2; Hargreaves and Leaman, *Racism, Ethnicity*, p. xiii.

25  European Commission, *Maastricht Treaty: Final Act*, pp. 1–12. The Schengen Agreement created a frontier-free space for the movement of goods, services and persons, and harmonised a wide range of policies, including controls on immigration from third countries. See Collinson, *Europe*, p. 111; Layton-Henry, *The Politics of Immigration*, pp. 231–4; Ursula Levelt in M. Martiniello, *Migration Citizenship and Ethno-National Identities in the European Union*, pp. 199–212.

26  Council of the European Communities, *Single European Act and Final Act*, Office for Official Publications of the EC, Article 8a; the emphasis is mine. See also Collinson, *Beyond Borders*, p. 37.

27  Cornelius *et al.* (eds), *Controlling Immigration*, p. 33.

28  Collinson, *Europe*, pp. 112–13; D. Joly in Cohen (ed.), *The Cambridge Survey*, p. 497; Taylor, *The European Union*, p. 62; Cornelius *et al.* (eds), *Controlling Immigration*, p. 32.

29  'Europe in harmony against asylum-seekers', *Australian*, 16 January 1996, p. 7; Joly in Cohen (ed.), *The Cambridge Survey*, p. 498; Collinson, *Europe*, p. 138.

30  See Antonio Cruz in Tomasi (ed.), *In Defense*, vol. 17, p. 171–98 for a detailed account; also Joly in Cohen (ed.), *The Cambridge Survey*, p. 497; *Guardian*, 13 November 1996, p. 6; UNHCR Press Release, REF/1100, 10 March 1995.

31  ECRE Report, *Arrivals/Statistics*, 1996, part III, Legal Developments, no. 3, Detention.

32  UNHCR, Press Release, REF/1128, 24 November 1995; International Council of Voluntary Agencies, 'The Pursuit and Implementation of Durable Solutions', part of the NGO Statement to the 47th Session of the Executive Committee of the UNHCR, Geneva, October 1996, p. 17.

33  See *Refugees*, no. 73, March 1990, and no. 83, March 1991, for xenophobic concerns; also Helsinki Rights Watch, *Foreigners Out*; Sigrid Baringhorst in Hargreaves and Leaman, *Racism, Ethnicity*.

34  Inscription at the base of the Statue of Liberty in New York Harbour by Emma Lazarus from a sonnet, 'The New Colossus', in Ungar, *Fresh Blood*, pp. 105–6.

35  Freeman and Jupp (eds), *Nations of Immigrants*, p. 88.

36  Cornelius *et al.* (eds), *Controlling Immigration*, p. 87. A *Newsweek* poll in 1993 found that 60 per cent of Americans thought that levels of immigration were too high, 59 per cent said that many immigrants end up on welfare, and only 20 per cent thought the country a 'melting pot': *Newsweek*, 9 August 1993, p. 18.

37  Cornelius *et al.* (eds), *Controlling Immigration*, p. 92. There is also a side-door entry, including the guest-worker category, prevalent in the United States, Germany and France.

38  Loescher, *Beyond Charity*, p. 99.

39  Tucker *et al.*, *Immigration*, pp. 73, 114; Loescher, *Beyond Charity*, p. 101.

40  Bureau of Population, Refugees, and Migration, Department of State, *Fact Sheet: Who is a Refugee?*; also Tucker *et al.*, *Immigration*, p. 75.; Le May, *Anatomy*, p. 17.

41  Zucker and Zucker in Adelman (ed.), *Refugee Policy*, p. 224.

42  Le May, *Anatomy*, p. 154; US INS, *Fact Sheet: Illegal Immigration Reform*, p. 2.

43  Lobby groups such as the anti-abortionists influenced the 1996 Act; see Von Sternberg in Tomasi (ed.), *In Defense*, vol. 18, pp. 177–80, 116; Le May, *Anatomy*, p. 154; Zucker and Zucker in Adelman (ed.), *Refugee Policy*, pp. 224–5; Zolberg in Tucker *et al.*, *Immigration*, p. 116; Loescher, *Beyond Charity*, pp. 100–2.

44  Arthur Helton in Adelman (ed.), *Refugee Policy*, pp. 227–9.

45  *Ibid.*, p. 255.

46  Loescher, *Beyond Charity*, pp. 101–2.

47  Keely in D. Kubat (ed.), *The Politics of Migration Policies*, Centre for Migration Studies, New York, 1993, p. 73.

48  J. De Wind and D. H. Kinley, *Aiding Migration*, Westview Press, Boulder, 1988, p. 6.

49  Loescher, *Beyond Charity*, pp. 102–5; UNHCR, *The State of the World's Refugees*, p. 42.

50  McKinley in Tomasi (ed.), *In Defense*, vol. 18, p. 204. This became known as the 'Caribbean Crisis'.

51  Legomsky, 'The New Techniques for Managing High-Volume Asylum Systems', p. 678.

52  *Ibid.*; McKinley in Tomasi (ed.), *In Defense*, vol. 18, p. 209. The CPA was discussed in ch. 4; for further information, see US, Bureau of Population, Refugees and Migration, *1996 Overview on Population*, p. 2.

53  *New York Times*, 13 November 1954, p. 20; Helton in Adelman (ed.), *Refugee Policy*, p. 254.

54  Helton in Adelman (ed.), *Refugee Policy*, p. 254. A smaller detention and immigration centre existed on Angel Island in San Francisco Harbor. Ellis Island became the major centre.

55  *Leng May Ma v. Barber*, 357 US 190 (1958), cited by Helton in Adelman (ed.), *Refugee Policy*, p. 254; the emphasis is mine.

56  *Ibid.*, p. 255; Helton, 'Making Refugee Detention Policy', p. 14; Loescher, *Beyond Charity*, pp. 102–3.

57 Zucker and Zucker in Cohen (ed.), *The Cambridge Survey*, p. 447; Loescher, *Beyond Charity*, pp. 103–4; Le May, *Anatomy*, pp. 20–1; Calavita in Cornelius *et al.* (eds), *Controlling Immigration*, p. 64.

58 Le May, *Anatomy*, p. 23; Calavita in Cornelius *et al.* (eds), *Controlling Immigration*, pp. 59–61, 68. See D. Mattingly, 'Maid in the USA', *New Internationalist*, no. 305, September 1998, pp. 14–15, for a discussion on contemporary cheap domestic labour for middle-class American families.

59 Calavita in Cornelius *et al.* (eds), *Controlling Immigration*, pp. 65–74.

60 *Ibid.*, p. 63. Newly arrived immigrants were blamed for social ills in many Western countries.

61 Helton in Adelman (ed.), *Refugee Policy*, p. 256; Helton, 'Making Refugee Detention Policy', p. 14.

62 Peter Schuck in Freeman and Jupp (eds), *Nations of Immigrants*, p. 54. Legal immigration rose from an annual level of 534 000 before the 1990 Act to 915 900 in 1996: Cornelius *et al.* (eds), *Controlling Immigration*, pp. 74–5; also US INS, *Highlights*, p. 1; US, *International Policy: 1996 Overview on Population*, pp. 2–3.

63 Le May, *Anatomy*, pp. 143, 154; Phyllis Coven in Tomasi (ed.), *In Defense*, vol. 18, pp. 157–63.

64 Piper, 'Outline'.

65 Paul Schmidt and Molly Clark in Tomasi (ed.), *In Defense*, vol. 18, pp. 164–8.

66 Piper, 'Outline'.

67 Helton, 'Making Refugee Detention Policy', p. 15.

68 *Ibid.*

69 *Ibid.*, p. 17; the emphasis is mine.

70 In 1996 the INS estimated five million undocumented immigrants residing in the United States, which is about 1.9 per cent of the total US population. It is estimated that 41 per cent of the undocumented population, in 1996, were non-immigrant overstayers: US INS, *Illegal Alien Resident Population*, p. 1.

71 See 'Immigrant Rights and Hidden Agendas', in *Guardian*, 13 November 1996, pp. 6–7; Cameron Stewart, 'Migrant Trap', *Australian*, 1 November 1996, p. 15; US INS, *The Illegal Immigration Reform and Immigrant Responsibility Act of 1996*.

72 Inscription in the Memorial Chamber of the Peace; V. Knowles, *Strangers at Our Gates*, p. ix.

73 Garcia y Griego in Cornelius *et al.* (eds), *Controlling Immigration*, pp. 127, 136; Cox and Glenn in Adelman *et al.*, *Immigration and Refugee Policy*, vol. 1, pp. 283–4; National Population Council, *Refugee Review*, pp. 106–7.

74 Cox and Glenn in Adelman *et al.*, *Immigration and Refugee Policy*, vol. 1, p. 298.

[75] Immigration and Refugee Board of Canada, *Immigration and Refugee Board: General Background*, p. 1; Hawkins, *Critical Years*, pp. 190–1; Cox and Glenn in Adelman *et al.*, *Immigration*, vol. 1, pp. 292–305.

[76] Cox and Glenn in Adelman *et al.*, *Immigration*, vol. 1, p. 298.

[77] Immigration Objectives in the Act highlight ten points: Department of Justice of Canada, *Immigration Act*, chs./I/1–2, p. 7.

[78] Knowles, *Strangers at Our Gates*, p. 160.

[79] *Immigration Act*, Part I, Canadian Immigration Policy, Objectives, chs I/1–2, pp. 7–8; Part IV, Claims and Appeals, chs 1–2, pp. 57–82.

[80] Immigration and Refugee Board of Canada, *General Background*, p. 1; Garcia y Griego states that Canada's immigration policy-making apparatus has demonstrated 'unusual flexibility and agility', in Cornelius *et al.* (eds), *Controlling Immigration*, p. 121.

[81] Immigration and Refugee Board of Canada, *Convention Refugee Determination*, p. 1; the emphasis is mine.

[82] *Ibid.*, p. 2.

[83] Immigration and Refugee Board of Canada, *General Background*, p. 1.

[84] The CRDD hears an average of 25 000 claims per year across Canada. Since its inception, in 1989, the IRB has granted, on average, refugee status to approximately 12 500 persons annually: *ibid*.

[85] National Population Council, *Refugee Review*, pp. 106–7; Garcia y Griego in Cornelius *et al.* (eds), *Controlling Immigration*, pp. 137–8.

[86] Knowles, *Strangers at Our Gates*, p. 171; Cox and Glenn in Adelman *et al.*, *Immigration*, vol. 1, p. 305.

[87] Garcia y Griego in Cornelius *et al.* (eds), *Controlling Immigration*, p. 128; Holton and Lanphier in Adelman *et al.*, *Immigration*, vol. 1, p. 129.

[88] Canada, House of Commons, *Debates*, 10 December 1986, p. 1976.

[89] 'Leapfrogging' parallels Bob Hawke's phrase 'jumping the queue', used in Australia around the same time. Headlines such as 'Refugees flooding Canada's borders could hit 30 000', *Toronto Star*, 18 June 1987, resembled Australian newspaper headlines. For a detailed account see Knowles, *Strangers at Our Gates*, pp. 173–4; Garcia y Griego in Cornelius *et al.* (eds), *Controlling Immigration*, pp. 136–7.

[90] This has since reverted to the previous system where, after the Refugee Determination Hearing, the claim is heard by the two-member panel in the Normal Process where only one is needed to agree. If the claim is unsuccessful at this stage the claimant moves to the next stage, Special Circumstances, where the two-member panel need to agree for the claim to continue: Immigration and Refugee Board of Canada, *Convention Refugee Determination*, p. 1.

[91] Garcia y Griego in Cornelius *et al.* (eds), *Controlling Immigration*, pp. 138–9.

[92] Canada hosted the Inter-Governmental Consultations on Asylum, Refugee and Migration Policies in Europe, North America and Australia in June 1992. This

consisted of sixteen Western states, comprising 13 European governments, Canada, Australia and the United States: Keely and Stanton-Russell in Tomasi (ed.), *In Defense*, vol. 18, p. 128.

93  UNHCR, *Resettlement Handbook*, p. 2; Garcia y Griego in Cornelius *et al.* (eds), *Controlling Immigration*, p. 130; Piper, 'Outline'. See section 103.1–1 of the *Immigration Act*, ch./1/2–2, p. 108; sections 503(1) and 515(10) of the *Criminal Code*, R.S.C. 1985, c.C-46; Immigration and Refugee Board of Canada, *Guidelines on Detention*, p. 1; Helton in Adelman (ed.), *Refugee Policy*, p. 260; Piper in Crock (ed.), *Protection*, pp. 117–18.

94  Immigration and Refugee Board of Canada, *Guidelines on Detention*, p. 5, p. 1, esp. rules 18, 28, 29, and 30.

95  *Ibid.*, p. 5. Adjudicators, as far as practicable, must follow the claim to the final decision, becoming familiar with the case.

96  See section 103.1–14 of the *Immigration Act*, p. 110; Piper, 'Outline'; 1995 World Refugee Survey, *USCR*, 1995, pp. 186–7.

97  De Voretz, *Diminishing Returns*, p. 23.

98  Frideres, 'Canada's Changing Immigration Policy', pp. 464–5. A paper by M. Burstein, 'The Canadian Immigration Experience Today', Third National Immigration and Population Outlook Conference, discusses the changing nature of Canadian immigration policy, highlighting the shift from family to economic immigration. See also Knowles, *Strangers at Our Gates*, pp. 176–7.

# 6 The Politics of Race

1  Maiden speech by Pauline Hanson, MP, 10 September 1996; also Merritt, *Pauline Hanson*, p. 7; *Pauline Hanson's Maiden Speech*, www.gwb/news/photo/ phtalk, p. 3.

2  For information on settler societies, see D. Stasiulis and N. Yuval-Davis, *Unsettling Settler Societies: Articulations of Gender, Race, Ethnicity and Class,* Sage, London, 1995, pp. 3–4. Stephen Fitzgerald notes that the 'immigration debate' sparked by Hanson was not a serious debate about immigration or multiculturalism but a sparring match 'about racism': *Is Australia an Asian Country?*, p. viii; also Jupp in Nile (ed.), *Australian Civilisation*, p. 79. Zelinka, *Understanding Racism*, describes the 'irrational fear of Asian immigration or "invasion from the north"'.

3  Yarwood and Knowling, *Race Relations*, p. 9; G. Leech, 'The First Boat People', *Australian Magazine*, 18–19 July 1998, pp. 17–21. Dare, *Australia*, pp. 7–8, describes early human habitation at Lake Mungo in New South Wales.

4  Paul Lloyd, 'Faith, Hope, Charity', *Advertiser*, 27 April 1996, Insight, p. 1. The Director of the Australian Refugee Association, Kevin Liston, highlights the courage of boat people who leave their homeland to brave treacherous sea voyages in an act of desperation and courage, risking their lives in hope of

freedom and a just life. Liston believes the Vietnamese boat people will eventually be seen as important symbols of Australia's nationhood, recognised as real Australian heroes.

5   See Yarwood and Knowling, *Race Relations*, esp. ch. 1, and Buggy and Cates, *Race Relations*, esp. chs 1–3, for early colonisation and the effects on Indigenous peoples.

6   Thompson, *Fair Enough*, pp. 28–9; A. Jakubowicz (ed.), *Racism, Ethnicity and the Media*, p. 3.

7   *Inverell Times*, 30 December 1903, cited in Benmayor and Skotnes (eds), *Migration and Identity*, p. 85.

8   Zelinka, *Understanding Racism*, p. 8. See Evans, Saunders, and Cronin, *Race Relations*, Pt 2, for discrimination against Melanesians and Kanakas.

9   Victoria Act no. 41, 1857; Choi, *Chinese Migration*, pp. 18–21; Markus, *Australian Race Relations*, pp. 56–84; J. Webb and A. Enstice, *Aliens and Savages*, pp. 130–67; Australian Population and Immigration Council, *Immigration Policies and Australia's Population: A Green Paper*, p. 23. In the United States a similar backlash occurred against Chinese working the goldfields of California; see Choi, *Chinese Migration*, p. xii, and Markus, *Fear and Hatred*.

10  *The Empire*, Sydney, February 1861, cited in Willard, *History*, p. 19.

11  Markus, *Australian Race Relations*, p. 59; Bereson and Matheson, *Racism*, pp. 14–15.

12  See Yarwood and Knowling, *Race Relations*, pp. 165–87; Yuan, *Awakening Conscience*, p. 46; Markus, *Fear and Hatred*, pp. 14–34; Buggy and Cates, *Race Relations*, chs 4, 5; Evans, Saunders and Cronin, *Race Relations*, p. 241 and ch. 3.

13  Willard, *History*, pp. 20–1. This resonates with the rhetoric used by Pauline Hanson in her maiden speech to parliament, 10 September 1996. See also Murphy, 'Are We Being Swamped?'; Markus, *Australian Race Relations*, p. 59; Sherington, *Australia's Immigrants*, p. 30; Hawkins, *Critical Years*, p. 11.

14  Parkes cited in Rivett (ed.), *Immigration*, p. 9; also Markus, *Australian Race Relations*, pp. 83–4, for another account of this incident.

15  Bereson and Matheson, *Racism*, pp. 15–16; Murphy, *The Other Australia*, pp. 28–30.

16  Cited in London, *Non-White Immigration*, p. 12. Unions supported this view. The Trade Union Congresses held between 1879 and 1891 passed resolutions regarding the exclusion of non-Australian workers; see Zelinka, *Understanding Racism*, p. 15.

17  Murphy, *The Other Australia*, p. 34; Stasiulis and Yuval-Davis, *Unsettling Settler Societies*, p. 73. See Webb and Enstice, *Aliens and Savages*, pp. 64–8, 159–66, for an account of social Darwinian thought and practice in early colonial Australia.

18  Cited in Yarwood and Knowling, *Race Relations*, p. 178.

19  Cited in Yarwood and Knowling, *Race Relations*, p. 185. The *Bulletin* signified Australia's 'whiteness' by defiantly proclaiming on its masthead 'Australia for the white man', which remained until 1961; see Phillip Adams, 'Our Bigotry Has Never Been Silenced', *Weekend Australian*, 12–13 October 1996, Review, p. 2. J. Woods, member for Stawell, Victoria, in 1881, expressed a low opinion of the Chinese: Buggy and Cates, *Race Relations*, p. 112.

20  Cited in Yarwood and Knowling, *Race Relations*, p. 187.

21  Nile (ed.), *Australian Civilisation*, pp. 11–12.

22  *Ibid.*, p. 12.

23  H. Irving, *To Constitute a Nation: A Cultural History of Australia's Constitution*, Cambridge University Press, 1997, p. 81.

24  *Ibid.*, p. 109.

25  See Palfreeman, *The Administration of the White Australia Policy*, pp. 5–6; K. Rivett (ed.), *Australia*, p. 20; Hawkins, *Critical Years*, p. 15; Markus, *Australian Race Relations*, p. 115.

26  B. Anderson, *Imagined Communities*, Verso, London, 1983; Irving, *To Constitute a Nation*, p. 114; Vasta and Castles (eds), *The Teeth are Smiling*, p. 176.

27  Prime Minister Barton introduced the Immigration Restriction Bill on 7 August 1901 and it was assented to by the Governor-General on 23 December 1901.

28  Markus and Ricklefs, *Surrender Australia?*, p. 12.

29  Nile (ed.), *Australian Civilisation*, p. 79.

30  See Yarwood and Knowling, *Race Relations*, pp. 227–8, for these allegations.

31  *Ibid.*, p. 228.

32  See J. Quick, *The Federal Movement in Australia*, Angus & Robertson, Sydney, 1901; Quick and Garran, *The Annotated Constitution of the Australian Commonwealth*, 1901.

33  Yuan, *Awakening Conscience*, p. 60; Webb and Enstice, *Aliens and Savages*, p. 170.

34  Thompson, *Fair Enough*, p. 172.

35  Palfreeman, *The Administration of the White Australia Policy*, p. 81. The Natal Method, adopted by the Government of Natal in 1897 to exclude immigrants from the Indian subcontinent, was easily manipulated by the authorities to achieve any desired result: Rivett (ed.), *Immigration*, p. 13; also Yarwood, 'The Dictation Test'; Hawkins, *Critical Years*, p. 15; Choi, *Chinese Migration*, p. 27; Markus, *Australian Race Relations*, p. 115.

36  Palfreeman, *The Administration of the White Australia Policy*, p. 81; Webb and Enstice, *Aliens and Savages*, p. 170. After the test was removed in 1958 there were calls to reinstate a test in one form or another: Glenn Schloss 'English Test for Citizenship Urged', *Advertiser*, 13 October 1996, p. 25. The Howard Coalition Government introduced a tighter language test when it came to

power in 1996, which was compared to the discriminatory dictation test. Concern was expressed by migrant groups about the increases in the language test: Anne O'Donaghue, *Australian*, 10 July 1996, p. 4.

37  Yuan, *Awakening Conscience*, p. 67; Irving, *To Constitute a Nation*, pp. 114–15; Webb and Enstice, *Aliens and Savages*, p. 170; Yarwood, *Asian Migration*, p. 2.

38  Brian Fitzpatrick, quoted in Thompson, *Fair Enough*, pp. 58–9.

39  *Ibid.*, p. 252.

40  Jupp in J. Wilson *et al.* (eds), *The Australian Welfare State: Key Documents and Themes*, Macmillan, Melbourne, 1996, p. 177.

41  London, *Non-White Immigration*, p. 21; Yarwood and Knowling, *Race Relations*, pp. 237–8.

42  Miles quoted in Vasta and Castles (eds), *The Teeth are Smiling*, p. 176; Zelinka, *Understanding Racism*, p. 9; Jupp in Wilson *et al.* (eds), *The Australian Welfare State*, pp. 174–89.

43  *Age*, 26 September 1896, cited in Markus, *Fear and Hatred*, p. 260; the emphasis is mine.

44  Foster and Stockley, *Multiculturalism*, p. 26; London, *Non-White Immigration*, p. 12. See also Yarwood, *Asian Migration*, p. 62.

45  Yarwood, *Asian Migration*, p. 66.

46  Markus, *Australian Race Relations*, p. 110.

47  Palfreeman, *The Administration of the White Australia Policy*, pp. 8–9; Foster and Stockley, *Multiculturalism*, p. 26.

48  Cited in Murphy, *The Other Australians*, p. 53. See London, *Non-White Immigration*, pp. 14–17, for details of events during the 1930s and 1940s.

49  Calwell, *Immigration*; Foster and Stockley, *Multiculturalism*, p. 26; Murphy, *The Other Australia*, pp. 58–60. See also Webb and Enstice, *Aliens and Savages*, p. 205.

50  Vann Woodward cited in Markus, *Australian Race Relations*, p. 155.

51  A. Calwell, *How Many Australians Tomorrow?*, and Calwell, *Immigration*, provide details of policy regarding population increase. See also Murphy, *The Other Australia*, p. 135.

52  Murphy, *The Other Australia*, p. 105; Markus, *Australian Race Relations*, p. 167; Palfreeman, *The Administration of the White Australia Policy*, pp. 27–30.

53  Rivett (ed.), *Australia*, p. 26; Hawkins, *Critical Years*, p. 33; Markus, *Australian Race Relations*, p. 156.

54  UNESCO, *Race and Science*, Columbia University Press, New York, pp. 500–1.

55  Rivett (ed.), *Australia*, pp. 198–204; Murphy, *The Other Australia*, pp. 133–61; Markus, *Australian Race Relations*, pp. 155–73.

56  See the *Australian*, 28 June 1965, for views of the unions; Palfreeman, *The Administration of the White Australia Policy*, pp. 119–20.

57 Markus, *Australian Race Relations*, p. 160; Jupp, *Understanding Australian Multiculturalism*, p. 5; Murphy, *The Other Australia*, pp. 165–72.

58 Rivett (ed.), *Australia*, preface; also Rivett (ed.), *Immigration*, for a proposal for change. Associations for Immigration Reform were organised in mainland states during the 1960s; see Hawkins, *Critical Years*, p. 310, n. 24; London, *Non-White Immigration*, p. 18; Murphy, *The Other Australia*, p. 173.

59 The Act, no. 52 of 1975, section 9, cited in Markus, *Australian Race Relations*, p. 184.

60 Thomas in Coughlan and McNamara (eds), *Asians in Australia*, pp. 274–5.

61 *Ibid.*

62 Markus and Rasmussen (eds), *Prejudice in the Public Arena*, pp. 73–4.

63 Foster and Stockley, *Multiculturalism*, p. 51.

64 *Sydney Morning Herald*, 21 January 1971, cited in Rivett (ed.), *Australia*, pp. 31–2.

65 *Sydney Morning Herald*, 21 June 1971, cited in *ibid.*, p. 33.

66 Standing Committee on Multiculturalism, *Multiculturalism: Building the Canadian Mosaic*, Queens Printer for Canada, Ottawa, 1987, p. 87, cited by Hindess in Kukathas (ed.), *Multicultural Citizens*, p. 33. Jupp, *Understanding Australian Multiculturalism*, provides a succinct history of the birth of Australian multiculturalism. See also Berry *et al.*, *Multiculturalism and Ethnic Attitudes in Canada.*

67 McAllister in Kukathas (ed.), *Multicultural Citizens*, p. 50; Hawkins, *Critical Years*, pp. 231–2.

68 Yarwood and Knowling, *Race Relations*, p. 289; Foster and Stockley, *Multiculturalism*, esp. ch. 3; Murphy, *The Other Australians*, pp. 197–8.

69 McAllister in Kukathas (ed.), *Multicultural Citizens*, p. 52.

70 Cited in Markus, *Australian Race Relations*, p. 183. Also Murphy, *The Other Australia*, p. 201.

71 Markus, *Australian Race Relations*, p. 187; Foster and Stockley, *Multiculturalism*, pp. 67–83; Freeman and Jupp, *Nations of Immigrants*, pp. 132–4.

72 Markus, *Australian Race Relations*, p. 191.

73 See Viviani, *The Long Journey*, chs 4 and 5; Hawkins, *Critical Years*, pp. 170–4, 177–88; and Markus, *Australian Race Relations*, p. 192, for detail of this period.

74 Viviani, *The Indochinese*, p. 8.

75 *Ibid.*, pp. 143–8.

76 Betts, *Ideology and Immigration*, pp. 142–3; Vinson, Leech and Lester, 'The Number of Boat People', pp. 1–4; Manne, 'Indochinese Refugees and the Australian Political Culture', pp. 10–14.

77 See Blainey, 'The Asianisation of Australia', *Age*, 20 March 1984. Ironically, but understandably, this title became synonymous with Blainey's attack on Asian immigration and multiculturalism. See also Richard Goodwin, 'Too

Many Asians: Immigration Policy Questioned', *Warrnambool Standard*, 19 March 1984; S. Castles, 'A New Agenda in Multiculturalism?', *Multicultural Australia Papers*, no. 61, June 1987, Clearing House on Migration Issues, Richmond, Vic., p. 1.

78 Singer (ed.), *The Immigration Debate*, p. 1.

79 Castles in Freeman and Jupp, *Nations of Immigrants*, p. 188; Singer (ed.), *The Immigration Debate*, p. 1; Goodwin, 'Too Many Asians'.

80 Blainey, *All for Australia*, pp. 123–4; also Jupp, *Ghettoes, Tribes and Prophets*, p. 1. For another argument about family reunion see Betts, in D. Goodman *et al.*, *Multicultural Australia: The Challenges of Change*, Scribe, Newham, 1991.

81 Theophanous, *Understanding Multiculturalism*, p. 34.

82 See Singer, *The Immigration Debate*; Blainey, *All for Australia*, pp. 159–60.

83 Blainey, *All for Australia*, pp. 22–3, 130; Theophanous, *Understanding Multiculturalism*, pp. 35–7; Markus and Ricklefs (eds), *Surrender Australia?*, p. 23.

84 See the 1997 Housing Industry Association Report, Castles, Iredale, Withers and Foster, *Australia and Immigration*, which concludes that the myth that immigrants take jobs, create social division and live on welfare is not a reality. See also P. Ruthven, *Australian Financial Review*, 14 October 1996; R. Holton, 'Public Disorder in Australia between 1985 and 1989 with Particular Reference to Immigration and Multiculturalism', *Working Papers on Multiculturalism*, no. 17, Office of Multicultural Affairs, Department of the Prime Minister and Cabinet, 1991, p. 13; Paul Kelly, 'The immigration puzzle', *Weekend Australian*, 24–25 May 1997, p. 21.

85 R. Rasmussen and K. Tang in C. D'Mello *et al.*, 'Asian Immigration: Assessing the Issues', *Working Papers on Migrant and Intercultural Studies*, no. 11, Centre for Migrant and Intercultural Studies, Monash University, 1988, p. 9.

86 Blainey, *All for Australia*, pp. 156–61.

87 Michael Hodgman, Shadow Minister for Immigration and Ethnic Affairs, *Australian*, 5 March 1984, Letters to the Editor; 'Immigration should be banned', *Age*, 20 March 1984; see also G. Robinson, 'Racism: Beaten Senseless by the Media', *New Journalist*, no. 44, November 1984, p. 15; Theophanous, *Understanding Multiculturalism*, pp. 35–6.

88 *Age*, 12 May 1984; *Australian*, 3 April 1984; Theophanous, *Understanding Multiculturalism*, p. 35; Blainey, *All for Australia*, pp. 34–5.

89 K. Laster, 'Geoffrey Blainey and the Asianisation of Australia: A Debate Half Won', in *Migration Action*, vol. 7, no. 2, 1984, p. 4.

90 *Australian*, 3 April 1984.

91 Ricklefs in Markus and Ricklefs (eds), *Surrender Australia?*, pp. 36–48.

92 Mackie in Coughlan and McNamara (eds), *Asians in Australia*, p. 30.

93 Interview with Henry Reynolds on 3AR Melbourne, 4 October 1984, cited in Markus and Ricklefs (eds), *Surrender Australia?*, p. 40.

94 Ricklefs in Markus and Ricklefs (eds), *Surrender Australia?*, pp. 46–8. In 1995 Blainey still defended his 1984 remarks, even extending them by including Indigenous issues; see Catherine Armitage, 'Blainey denounces "racist" Aboriginal groups', *Australian*, 29 May 1995, pp. 1–2.

95 Cited in P. Kelly, *The End of Certainty*, Allen & Unwin, Sydney, 1992, p. 423; the italics are mine. See also Mackie in Coughlan and McNamara (eds), *Asians in Australia*, p. 34.

96 Lack and Templeton, *Bold Experiment*, p. 223.

97 Committee to Advise on Australia's Immigration Policies, *Immigration* (Fitzgerald Report), pp. xii, 1.

98 Lack and Templeton, *Bold Experiment*, pp. 223–4. Critics of the report condemned its selective presentation of multiculturalism; see Collins, *Migrant Hands*, esp. p. 295.

99 Lack and Templeton, *Bold Experiment*, p. 225.

1 Committee to Advise on Australia's Immigration Policies, *Immigration* (Fitzgerald Report), p. 14; also cited in Wooden *et al.*, *Australian Immigration*, p. 291.

2 Freeman and Jupp (eds), *Nations of Immigrants*, pp. 142–3.

3 Mackie in Coughlan and McNamara (eds), *Asians in Australia*, p. 36; see Crock (ed.), *Protection*, for further details.

4 'Yellow peril again', *Courier Mail*, 29 November 1977; 'Boat people flood feared', *Age*, 6 January 1995; 'Fears of 20 000 boat people', *Advertiser*, 26 November 1994; 'New fighting spawns flood of refugees', *Advertiser*, 25 June 1993.

5 Mackie in Coughlan and McNamara (eds), *Asians in Australia*, p. 39; Campbell and Uhlmann, *Australia Betrayed*; M. Steketee, 'The New Voices: A Culture of Blame', *Weekend Australian*, 12–13 October 1996, p. 22. Anti-Asian protests were held at 1995 Third National Immigration and Population Outlook Conference in Adelaide by National Action, who called for a cessation of immigration, especially Asian.

6 Maiden speech by Pauline Hanson, MP, *Commonwealth Parliamentary Debates*, 10 September 1996; *Pauline Hanson's Maiden Speech*, http://www.gwb.com.au/gwb/news/photo/phtalk, p. 3. For details of book and reviews see Merritt, *Pauline Hanson*. Although not written by Pauline Hanson, the book sets out her manifesto, including her maiden speech, other speeches, and a section by Members of the Pauline Hanson Support Group. Gerard Henderson, 'The ugly, paranoid Hanson manifesto', *Advertiser*, 3 May 1997, p. 28, reviews the book, saying that Hanson has declared her support for the contents. See also David Penberthy, in 'Look closely: Pauline's truth is not pretty', *Advertiser*, 3 May 1997, p. 23 Robert Manne, 'Extreme views the Right must reject', *Weekend Australian*, 26–27 April 1997, pp. 21–2.

7    Langton in Adams (ed.), *The Retreat from Tolerance*, p. 92; Jamie Walker, 'Hanson rhetoric revitalises angry Right', *Weekend Australian*, 12–13 October 1996.

8    For an argument on this issue, see P. Ahluwalia and G. McCarthy, Political Correctness: Pauline Hanson and the Construction of Australian Identity, unpublished paper, 1997. Politics Department, University of Adelaide.

9    Rex Jory, 'Hanson also has rights', *Advertiser*, 13 May 1997, p. 6; Hugh Mackay, 'I don't agree with her on everything, but . . .', *Weekend Australian*, 17–18 May 1997, p. 2. Kate Legge, 'The passion is back in politics', *Australian*, 30 May 1997, p. 17, argues that Hanson is part of an argument that we, as a nation, have to have to determine our identity. See also Phillip Adams, 'This is personal, Pauline', *Weekend Australian*, 24–25 May 1997.

10   Matthew Cook, 'Searching for scapegoats', in Letters, *Sydney Morning Herald*, 23 May 1997.

11   Merritt, *Pauline Hanson*, p. 125; Vinson, 'The Hanson Effect'.

12   Castles, Iredale, Withers and Foster (eds), *Australia and Immigration*, p. 2. The Bureau of Immigration and Population Research released figures in November 1994 indicating that the three largest source countries for settler arrivals in 1993–94 were the UK (12.8%), New Zealand, (11.1%) and Viet Nam, (7.8%); *Immigration Update*, p. 1. See also Murphy, 'Are We Being Swamped'; P. Smark, 'Facts spoil populist story on immigration', *Sydney Morning Herald*, 24 May 1997, p. 41.

13   Louise Dodson and Peter Hartcher, 'Hanson wrong: PM speaks out', *Australian Financial Review*, 9 May 1997, p. 3; Mike Steketee, 'Coalition's quiet Hansonism undermines Pauline's pitch', *Weekend Australian*, 17–18 May 1997, p. 6; Editorial, 'Ending the politics of racism', *Weekend Australian*, 12–13 October 1996, p. 20; Phillip Adams, 'Our bigotry has never been silenced', *Weekend Australian*, Review, 12–13 October 1996, p. 2.

14   Paul Kelly, 'The Asian Imperative', *Weekend Australian*, 10–11 May 1997, p. 25.

15   'Indonesian warning on racism', *Weekend Australian*, 17–18 May 1997, p. 2. The *Weekend Australian* presented a special edition titled 'A Divided Nation', May 31–June 1, 1997, indicating the state of the Australian nation. See also *Weekend Australian*, 10–11 May 1997, p. 20.

16   Langton in Adams (ed.), *The Retreat from Tolerance*, p. 91.

17   See J. Stapelton, 'Lighter side of racism encourages kids to fight back', *Australian*, 27 June 1997, p. 3; Beatrice Faust, 'Hatred is not the answer', *Weekend Australian*, 3–4 May 1997; Kimina Lyall, 'Words translate to ugly deeds on hate street', *Weekend Australian*, 12–13 October 1996, p. 9; 'PM blamed for rise in race abuse complaints', *Advertiser*, 12 October 1996, p. 8; Susan Jeanes in Comment, 'One Nation's victims', *Advertiser*, 14 May 1997,

p. 17; Phillip Adams, 'Oh, Magoo, you've done it again', *Weekend Australian*, 17–18 May 1997; *Advertiser*, 26 April 1997, p. 6; *Weekend Australian*, 17–18 May 1997, p. 2; *Weekend Australian*, 10–11 May 1997, p. 20; Fitzgerald, *Is Australia an Asian Country?*

18  *Weekend Australian*, 10–11 May 1997, p. 20; Hugh Mackay, 'A Kind of Adolescence', *Reinventing Australia*, pp. 199–213. While this appears a simplistic analogy it is a useful one as adolescence signifies identity crises around insecurities, fears and change; all that can be related to Australian identity and the increasing levels of anxieties within the community.

19  Multiculturalism, as a policy, disappeared once the Howard Government was elected in March 1996. See also Jones in E. Laquian *et al.*, *The Silent Debate*, p. 263; Professor Jock Collins cited in David Leser, 'Welcome to Australia', *Age*, *Good Weekend*, 12 September 1998, p. 22.

20  J. Camilleri, *An Introduction to Australian Foreign Policy*, Jacaranda Press, Brisbane, 1975, p. 12.

21  Betts, *Ideology and Immigration*, chs 5, 7.

22  Jeff Turner, 'Hanson, the future fear', *Advertiser*, 24 April 1997, p. 9, compares Hanson with the French far right demagogue Jean-Marie Le Pen.

23  Kukathas (ed.), *Multicultural Citizens*, p. 149.

24  Castles, Kalantzis, Cope and Morrisey, *Mistaken Identity*, pp. 116, 128–37.

25  See Fitzgerald, *Is Australia an Asian Country?*, for details of Australian relations with Asia.

26  See Jupp, *Understanding Australian Multiculturalism*, p. 1, and Webb and Enstice, *Aliens and Savages*, for details of prejudices and racism in Australian settler history. The rhetoric of Pauline Hanson in the late twentieth century echoes uncannily the rhetoric of William Lane, *White or Yellow? A Story of the Race War of A.D. 1908*, serialised in *Boomerang*, 18 February – 5 May 1888, Brisbane.

## 7  The Politics of Belonging

1  Luke, 'Televisual Democracy', p. 72.

2  Horne in Jorden, *Redefining Australians*, p. viii. For a comprehensive and theoretical account of national identity, see A. Smith, *National Identity*, Penguin, London, 1991; for citizenship and aliens, see Bosniak, 'The Citizenship of Aliens', pp. 29–35.

3  Bosniak, 'The Citizenship of Aliens', p. 29.

4  Capling, Considine and Crozier, *Australian Politics*, p. 129.

5  B. Sullivan and G. Whitehouse (eds), *Gender, Politics and Citizenship in the 1990s*, UNSW Press, Sydney, 1996, p. 15. McAllister in B. Galligan, I. McAllister, and J. Ravenhill (eds), *New Developments in Australian Politics*,

Macmillan, Melbourne, 1997, pp. 13–16, discusses a contemporary Australian identity.

6   Jorden, *Redefining Australians*, p. 1; Joint Standing Committee on Migration, *Australians All*, pp. 15–18. Australia's first citizen was Prime Minister Ben Chifley, awarded citizenship on 3 February 1949: *Post Migration*, June 1995, p. 5.

7   J. Wolmark, *Aliens and Others: Science Fiction, Feminism and Postmodernism*, University of Iowa Press, Iowa City, 1994, p. 27.

8   Amnesty International, Annual Reports; HREOC, *Those who've come*, p. v; Lester, 'Arbitrary Detention of Boat People'; Lester and Vinson, 'The Twilight Zone of Human Rights'; Australian National Audit Office, Audit Report no. 32, *The Management of Boat People*, p. 3.

9   Capling, Considine and Crozier, *Australian Politics*, pp. 6–10.

10  Van Steenbergen (ed.), *The Condition of Citizenship*, pp. 1–9; Wexler in Turner, *Theories of Modernity and Postmodernity*, pp. 164–76; Bosniak, 'The Citizenship of Aliens', p. 29; W. Kymlicka and W. Norman, 'Return of the Citizen: a Survey of Recent Work on Citizenship Theory', *Ethics*, 104, January 1994, p. 352.

11  Clark, *Citizenship*, pp. 4–5. See also Aristotle, *The Politics* (trans. Ernest Barker), 1960, Clarendon Press, Oxford, Book III, xiii, sec. 12; Riesenberg, *Citizenship in the Western Tradition*, esp. Introduction.

12  Davidson, *From Subject to Citizen*, pp. 16–18; Walzer in P. Brown and H. Shue (eds), *Boundaries: National Autonomy and its Limits*, Rowman and Littlefield, New Jersey, 1981, pp. 24–6.

13  Riesenberg, *Citizenship in the Western Tradition*, pp. xviii–xix; Hindess in Kukathas (ed.), *Multicultural Citizens*, p. 37; Hammar, *Democracy and the Nation State*, pp. 46–51.

14  Dahrendorf in Van Steenbergen (ed.), *The Condition of Citizenship*, pp. 12–13. Fraser and Gordon in James (ed.), *Critical Politics*, pp. 59–76, argue for retaining social citizenship as a synthesiser of the core normative notions of liberal and communitarian ideals and values. They argue that social citizenship in the form of situating the 'social' in democracy has the ability to integrate justice and solidarity.

15  Marshall, *Citizenship*, pp. 8–9.

16  Davidson in James (ed.), *Critical Politics*, p. 113.

17  Marshall, *Citizenship*, p. 11.

18  Hammar, *Democracy and the Nation State*, p. 53.

19  Capling, Considine, and Crozier, *Australian Politics*, pp. 6–10.

20  Marshall, *Citizenship*, p. 14; Linklater in P. Keal (ed.), *Ethics and Foreign Policy*, Allen & Unwin, Sydney, 1992, p. 24.

21  Van Steenbergen (ed.), *The Condition of Citizenship*, p. 3.

22  Fraser and Gordon in *ibid.*, p. 93.

23  *Ibid.*

24  Fraser and Gordon in James, *Critical Politics*, p. 66; M. Mann, 'Ruling Class Strategies and Citizenship', *Sociology*, 21, 1987, pp. 339–54.

25  Turner in C. Mouffe, *Dimensions of Radical Democracy*, Verso, London, 1992, p. 40. This is not the focus of this discussion but a valid point to take in consideration.

26  Fraser and Gordon in Van Steenbergen (ed.), *The Condition of Citizenship*, p. 93.

27  Davidson, *From Subject to Citizen*, p. 31.

28  Hindess in Kukathas (ed.), *Multicultural Citizens*, pp. 41–2.

29  Pranger, *The Eclipse of Citizenship*, p. 9.

30  Habermas, 'Citizenship and National Identity, p. 13; P. Muus (ed.), *Exclusion and Inclusion of Refugees in Contemporary Europe*, ch. 12.

31  Hindess in Kukathas (ed.), *Multicultural Citizens*, pp. 41–2.

32  Turner, *Citizenship and Capitalism*, p. 85; P. James, 'Reconstituting the Nation-State', p. 70.

33  Turner, *Citizenship and Capitalism*, p. 85; the emphasis is mine.

34  Poynder in Crock (ed.), *Protection*, ch. 8; Amnesty International, *Human Rights Reports*, 1994 to 1998; HREOC, *Those who've come*, p. v; Australian National Audit Office, Audit Report no. 32, *The Management*, p. 3.

35  C. Taylor, *Multiculturalism and 'The Politics of Recognition'*, Princeton University Press, 1992, pp. 25–6; Walzer in Brown and Shue (eds), *Boundaries: National Autonomy and its Limits*, p. 13. The ill-effects of detaining asylum-seekers are well documented: see Crock (ed.), *Protection*, part 3. Personal interviews with Detainees at Villawood Detention Centre in Sydney during 1995 confirmed the level of anguish, hopelessness and depression faced by detainees.

36  Turner, *Orientalism, Postmodernism and Globalism*, pp. 112–13; G. Sharp, 'At the Centre of Globalisation', *Arena*, no. 4, 1994–95, p. 2; Ogata, in UNHCR, *Speeches of the High Commissioner*, p. 5.

37  B. Anderson, *Imagined Communities*, Verso, London, 1993.

38  James, 'Reconstituting the Nation-State', p. 74. A similar discussion is presented by Martin Shaw in *Global Society and International Relations: Sociological Concepts and Political Perspectives*, Blackwell, Oxford, 1994, esp. p. 13.

39  Turner, *Orientalism, Postmodernism and Globalism*, p. 183; the emphasis is mine.

40  Helsinki Rights Watch, *Foreigners Out*.

41  Turner, *Orientalism, Postmodernism and Globalism*, p. 184.

42  *Ibid.*; the italics are mine. See also Giddens in D. Miliband (ed.), *Reinventing the Left*, Polity Press, Cambridge, 1994, p. 5.

43  Turner in Van Steenbergen (ed.), *The Condition of Citizenship*, pp. 9, 154–5.

44  D. Held (ed.), *Political Theory Today*, Polity Press, Oxford, 1991, p. 206; D. Archibugi and D. Held, *Cosmopolitan Democracy: An Agenda for a New World*

*Order*, Polity Press, Cambridge, 1995, p. 100. Falk, *On Human Governance*, pp. 106–7, discusses the democratisation of the global decision-making processes attached to the processes of globalisation.

[45] C. W. Kegley and E. R. Wittkopf, cited in Held, *Political Theory Today*, p. 207.

[46] Fraser and Gordon in Van Steenbergen (ed.), *The Condition of Citizenship*, ch. 8; W. Kymlicka and W. Norman, 'Return of the Citizen: a Survey of Recent Work on Citizenship Theory', *Ethics*, 104, January 1994, p. 355; King and Waldron, 'Citizenship, Social Citizenship and the Defence of the Welfare State', pp. 415–43; P. Coover, I. Crewe, I. and D. Searing, 'The Nature of Citizenship in the United States and Great Britain', *Journal of Politics*, 53, 1991, pp. 800–32, esp. p. 804.

[47] National Action, a neo-Nazi group, demonstrated at the Third National Immigration and Population Outlook Conference in Adelaide during February 1995 for a decrease in Asian immigration, attracting a high level of media coverage.

[48] Turner in Van Steenbergen (ed.), *The Condition of Citizenship*, p. 157.

[49] P. Donati, *International Sociology*, vol. 10, no. 3, 1995, p. 300.

[50] Turner in Van Steenbergen (ed.), *The Condition of Citizenship*, p. 159.

[51] Turner sees educational institutions, especially universities, as playing a crucial role in cultural citizenship, being an essential aspect of the socialisation of children and adults into this national system of values: *ibid.*

[52] *Ibid.*, pp. 158–9.

[53] Turner, *Citizenship and Capitalism*, pp. 97–8. Stuart Hall and David Held also recognise the role that social movements play in the politics of citizenship in contemporary times, reflecting that citizenship will need to 'come to terms' with the problems posed by 'difference'; S. Hall and J. Martin (eds), *New Times: The Changing Face of Politics in the 1990s*, Verso, London, 1990, p. 176. See also Giroux, 'Living Dangerously', pp. 1–28.

[54] Turner in Van Steenbergen (ed.), *The Condition of Citizenship*, p. 166. This resonates with the 'cosmopolitan democracy' of David Held, in which there is shift to democratise the global arenas of decision-making that are dominated by state and market forces; Archibugi and Held, *Cosmopolitan Democracy: An Agenda for a New World Order*, pp. 12–15, 106–17; Held (ed.), *Political Theory Today*, pp. 204–12. Falk has a similar argument in *On Human Governance*, pp. 106–7.

[55] Turner in Van Steenbergen (ed.), *The Condition of Citizenship*, p. 166.

[56] *Ibid.*; Turner, *Citizenship and Capitalism*, p. 92; Falk, *On Human Governance*, pp. 3–7.

[57] Habermas in A. Gutman, *Multiculturalism: Examining the Politics of Recognition*, Princeton University Press, 1994, pp. 116–17; Hall and Martin (eds), *New Times: The Changing Face of Politics in the 1990s*, p. 176.

58  Turner, *Citizenship and Capitalism*, pp. 11–12.

59  *Ibid.*, p. 133.

60  Van Gunsteren, 'Admission to Citizenship', p. 731.

61  Walzer, *Spheres of Justice*, p. 62.

62  See 'Hell on Earth', *Weekend Australian*, 2–3 November 1996, p. 25; B. Rosenthal, 'Great Lakes awash with the homeless', *Weekend Australian*, 26–27 October 1996, p. 15. By April 1998 the UNHCR reported over 600 000 Rwandans as refugees in Rwanda, with over 50 000 people displaced in the Democratic Republic of Congo: UNHCR *Country Updates*, p. 1. Between 1996 and 1998 some 2 million refugees returned to Rwanda: pp. 5–6.

63  Coonatilake in J. Pieterse (ed.), *The Decolonization of Imagination: Culture, Knowledge and Power*, Zed Books, London, 1995, p. 232.

64  Van Gunstereen, 'Admission to Citizenship', p. 731.

65  Turner, *Capitalism and Citizenship*, p. 103.

66  *Ibid.*, p. 105.

67  *Ibid.*, p. 92.

68  Semiotics is defined as a *meaning-making* system constructed through discourses, language and linguistics: C. Poynton, *Language and Gender: Making the Difference*, Deakin University Press, 1985, ch. 1.

69  Wexler in Turner, *Theories of Modernity and Postmodernity*, p. 171.

70  *Ibid.*, p. 165. See also Baudrillard in J. Fekete (ed.), *The Structural Allegory: Reconstructive Encounters with the New French Thought*, Minneapolis, University of Minnnesota Press, 1984, pp. 54–73.

71  Luke, 'Televisual Democracy', p. 72.

72  Wexler in Turner, *Theories of Modernity and Postmodernity*, pp. 165–7. See also George Yudice, 'Civil Society, Consumption, and Governmentality in an Age of Global Restructuring', *Social Text*, 45, vol. 14, no. 4, Winter 1995.

73  Luke, 'Televisual Democracy', p. 62.

74  The spread of telecommunications in the form of cable and satellite TV and the internet has made it possible for many people to witness major events throughout the world. While it is still the minority of people, in a global sense, who own a TV, computer or telephone, access to these communications is spreading, with village people watching world events on a community TV.

75  There are similarities with the theories of social control of Michel Foucault, *The Archaeology of Knowledge*, Pantheon, London, 1972, and *Discipline and Punish: The Birth of the Prison*, Penguin, London, 1977.

76  Falk in Van Steenbergen (ed.), *The Condition of Citizenship*, p. 139.

77  *Ibid.*, p. 138. See also L. Basch, N. Schiller, and C. Blanc, *Unbound: Transnational Projects, Postcolonial Predicaments, and Deterritorialized Nation-States*, Gordon and Breach, Pennsylvania, 1994, for a comprehensive account of the 'transnational'.

78 Davidson in James (ed.), *Critical Politics*, pp. 114, 115.

79 UNHCR, *The State of the World's Refugees, 1993: The Challenge of Protection*, Penguin, New York, 1993. Personal interviews with detainees at the Villawood Detention Centre confirmed this, with the majority of detainees preferring to return to their homeland, in this case Cambodia, China and Turkey.

80 Xenos, 'Refugees', p. 427; H. Arendt, *The Origins of Totalitarianism*, Allen & Unwin, London, 2nd edn, 1958, ch. 9.

81 Arendt, *The Origins of Totalitarianism*, p. 293.

82 Xenos, 'Refugees', p. 427.

83 T. Spybey, *Globalization and World Society*, Polity Press, Cambridge, 1996, p. 169.

84 See their essay 'Reclaiming Social Citizenship: Beyond the Ideology of Contract Versus Charity' in James (ed.), *Critical Politics*.

85 *Ibid.*, p. 59.

86 Rea in M. Martiniello, *Migration, Citizenship*, pp. 179–81, ch. X. Muus (ed.), *Exclusion and Inclusion of Refugees in Contemporary Europe*, provides a comprehensive analysis of EU refugee policies.

87 Rea in Martiniello, *Migration, Citizenship*, ch. 10.

88 M. Kalantzis, 'Civic Pluralism: Australia's Opportunity', in Bureau of Immigration, Multiculturalism and Population Research, papers from the Third National Immigration and Population Outlook Conference, pp. 1–5. Laksiri Jayasuriya presents a similar proposal with a 'democratic pluralism' as a method of inclusion in Nile (ed.), *Australian Civilisation*, pp. 93–109.

89 Kalantzis, 'Civic Pluralism', p. 2.

90 *Ibid.*, p. 4. In Kalantzis' theory there is no call to assimilate, but see ch. 6 above.

91 See James, 'Reconstituting the Nation-State'.

92 Kalantzis, 'Civic Pluralism', p. 4.

93 *Ibid.*, p. 5.

94 The Attorney-General's Department adopted this reasoning in its submission to the Joint Standing Committee on Migration, summarising the legitimate reasons for detaining a non-citizen as being: (i) to control migration flows (ii) to facilitate expulsion of deportees who have exhausted all avenues of review, and (iii) to prevent persons from absconding (p. 14). It also remarked that 'detention for the objective of deterring other possible asylum-seekers is inconsistent with the objects and purposes of the Refugee Convention': *Commonwealth Parliamentary Debates*, House of Representatives, 5 May 1992, p. 2372.

95 Poynder in Crock (ed.), *Protection*; Amnesty International, Annual Reports; 'Refugees not criminals', *Age*, 20 June 1994, p. 4; HREOC, *Those who've come*, p. v; Lester and Vinson, 'The Twilight Zone of Human Rights'; Australian National Audit Office, Audit Report no. 32, *The Management*, p. 3.

96 See Davidson in James (ed.), *Critical Politics*, p. 111. Michael Walzer refers to the tyranny of citizenship in Brown and Shue (eds), *Boundaries: National Autonomy and its Limits*, p. 25.

## 8 Detention, Exclusion and the 'Other'

1 Commissioner Chris Sidoti quoted by Roy Eccleston, 'Lucky country for some', *Weekend Australian*, 15–16 May 1999, p. 25.

2 *Ibid.*; the emphasis is mine.

# Select Bibliography

## Unpublished Sources

Amnesty International, Arbitrary Detention of Vietnamese Asylum Seekers, Hong Kong, April 1994.

—— Australian Government Urged to Change its Policy of Automatic Detention of Asylum Seekers, Media Release, 17 June 1994.

Australian Democrats, Democrats Oppose Migration Bill, Press Release, 21 June 1994.

Bureau of Immigration and Population Research, papers from the Third National Immigration and Population Outlook Conference, 22–24 February 1995.

—— papers from the Second National Immigration and Population Outlook Conference, 11–13 November 1992.

Chittleborough, M., The Use of Detention for Holding People Seeking Refugee Status, Survivors of Trauma and Torture Assistance and Rehabilitation Service, Adelaide, 1992.

Refugee Council of Australia, Position Paper with Respect to Asylum-Seekers and the Refugee Determination Procedure, May 1992.

—— The Asylum Dilemma: Background Information, February 1993.

—— Position Paper on Screened-Out Asylum Seekers: With particular reference to those who have been detained while there claims have been processed, July 1993.

—— Briefing Paper: Asylum, February 1994.

—— Asylum, Border Control and Detention: RCOA Response to the Report, March 1994.

—— Bureau of Immigration and Population Research Forum: Asylum Seekers in Australia, 20 April 1994.

—— Senator Bolkus Shifts the Goalposts Again, Media Release, 14 June 1994.

Reilly, A., Detention of Asylum-seekers: A Questionable Policy, South Brisbane Immigration and Community Legal Service, 1993.

## Government Documents

Australian Population and Immigration Council, *Immigration Policies and Australia's Population; A Green Paper*, AGPS, Canberra, 1977.

Bureau of Immigration and Population Research, *Australian Immigration, Consolidated Statistics*, no. 17.

Committee to Advise on Australia's Immigration Policies, *Immigration: A Commitment to Australia* (Fitzgerald Report), AGPS, Canberra, 1988.

Commonwealth Department of Immigration, *Australia's Immigration Policy,* Immigration Reference Paper, 1970.

Department of Immigration and Ethnic Affairs, *1788–1978: Australia and Immigration,* AGPS, Canberra, 1978.

—— *Australia's Refugee Resettlement Programs; An Outline*, Canberra, 1988.

Department of Immigration, Local Government and Ethnic Affairs, *In a Changing World: Australia's Refugee and Humanitarian Initiatives*, Canberra, 1992.

Federal Race Discrimination Commissioner, *Face the Facts: Some Questions and Answers about Immigration, Refugees and Indigenous Affairs*, AGPS, Canberra, 1997.

Foster, W., *Macroeconomic Effects of Change in the Size and Composition of Australia's Migrant Intake: Results from the extended Access Economics Murphy Model*, Research Paper for the Bureau of Immigration Research, 1992.

Human Rights and Equal Opportunity Commission, *Those who've come across the seas: detention of unauthorised arrivals*, Commonwealth of Australia, 1998.

Joint Committee on Foreign Affairs, Defence and Trade, *A Review of Australia's Efforts to Promote and Protect Human Rights*, Parliament of the Commonwealth of Australia, Canberra, 1992.

Joint Standing Committee on Migration, *Australia's Refugee and Humanitarian System: Achieving a Balance Between Refuge and Control*, AGPS, Canberra, 1992.

—— *Inquiry into Detention Practices: Submissions*, 5 vols, 1994.

—— *Asylum, Border Control and Detention*, AGPS, Canberra, 1994.

—— *Australians All: Enhancing Australian Citizenship*, AGPS, Canberra, 1994.

Jupp, J., *Ghettoes, Tribes and Prophets*, Office of Multicultural Affairs, Department of the Prime Minister and Cabinet, 1990.

MacKellar, M. J. R. (Minister for Immigration), 'Immigrants or Refugees?', paper delivered at the Australian Institute of International Affairs Seminar on 'Immigrants and Refugees', 1978.

Macphee, I., *Immigration Policies in Action: A Selection of Speeches by the Hon. Ian Macphee, MP, Minister for Immigration and Ethnic Affairs, 1979–1982*, AGPS, Canberra, 1982.

National Population Council, *Refugee Review*, Canberra, 1991.

Senate Standing Committee on Foreign Affairs and Defence, *Australia and the Refugee Problem*, Parliamentary Paper no. 329/1976, AGPS, Canberra, 1976.

Trieu Dan, N., *Indo-Chinese Refugees in France: A Study and Some Comparisons with Australia*, Information Paper, Victorian Ministry of Immigration and Ethnic Affairs, 1982.

United Kingdom, Asylum Directorate: Immigration and Nationality Directorate, Home Office, *Briefing Paper*, October 1996.

Williams, L. S., and McKenzie, F., *Understanding Australia's Population*, Bureau of Immigration, Multicultural and Population Research, AGPS, Canberra, 1996.

Working Papers prepared for the Informal Meeting on Cambodia, *Cambodia: An Australian Peace Proposal*, Jakarta, 26–28 February 1990, AGPS, Canberra.

## Published Works

Adams, P. (ed.), *The Retreat from Tolerance: A Snapshot of Australian Society*, ABC Books, Sydney, 1997.

Adelman, H., 'Refuge or Asylum: A Philosophical Perspective', *Journal of Refugee Studies*, vol. 1, no. 1, pp. 7–19.

—— 'The Right of Repatriation-Canadian Refugee Policy: The Case of Rwanda', *International Migration Review*, vol. 30, no. 1, Spring 1996, pp. 289–309.

—— (ed.), *Refugee Policy: Canada and the United States*, York Lane Press, Ontario, 1991.

Adelman, H. *et al.*, *Immigration and Refugee Policy: Australia and Canada Compared*, 2 vols, Melbourne University Press, 1994.

Amnesty International, *Refugees: Human Rights Have No Borders*, Amnesty International Publications, London, 1997.

Appleyard, R. T., *et al.*, *How Many Australians? Immigration and Growth*, Angus and Robertson, Melbourne, 1971.

Arendt, H., *The Origins of Totalitarianism*, Allen and Unwin, London, 1958.

Armit, M., *et al.*, *Australia and Immigration, 1788 to 1988*, AGPS, Canberra, 1988.

Balibar, E., 'Propositions on Citizenship', *Ethics*, vol. 98, no. 4, July 1988, pp. 723–30.

Barbalet, J. M., *Citizenship: Rights, Struggle and Class Inequality*, Open University Press, Milton Keynes, 1988.

Benmayor, R., and Skotnes, A. (eds), *Migration and Identity*, vol. 3, International Yearbook of Oral History and Life Stories, Oxford University Press, 1994.

Bereson, I., and Matheson, A., *Racism: An Australian Perspective*, Hawker Brownlow Education, Victoria, 1992.

Berry, J., *et al.*, *Multiculturalism and Ethnic Attitudes in Canada*, Canadian Government Printers, Ottawa, 1977.

Betts, K., *Ideology and Immigration: Australia 1976 to 1987*, Melbourne University Press, 1988.

Birrell, R., *et al.* (eds), *Refugees, Resources, Reunion: Australia's Immigration Dilemmas*, VCTA Publishing, Fitzroy, Vic., 1979.

Blainey, G., *All for Australia*, Methuen Haynes, Sydney, 1984.

Bosniak, L. 'The Citizenship of Aliens', *Social Text*, 56, vol. 16, no. 3, Fall 1998.

Bramwell, A. C. (ed.), *Refugees in the Age of Total War*, Unwin Hyman, London, 1988.

Brawley, S., *The White Peril: Foreign Relations and Asian Immigration to Australasia and North America, 1919–1978*, New South Wales University Press, Sydney, 1995.

Brennan, F., *Immigration Policy: The Moral and Ethical Dimensions*, Australian Catholic University and Bureau of Immigration and Population Research, Sydney, 1993.

Buggy, T., and Cates, J., *Race Relations in Colonial Australia: An Enquiry Approach*, Nelson, Melbourne, 1982.

Calwell, A., *How Many Australians Tomorrow?* Reed and Harris, Melbourne, 1945.

—— *Immigration: Policy and Progress*, Department of Immigration, Canberra, 1949.

Camilleri, J. A., and Falk, J., *The End of Sovereignty?* Edward Elgar, Aldershot, 1992.

Campbell, G., and Uhlmann, M., *Australia Betrayed*, Foundation Press, Perth, 1995.

Capling, A., Considine, M., and Crozier, M., *Australian Politics in the Global Era*, Longman, Melbourne, 1998.

Carens, J. H., 'Aliens and Citizens: The Case for Open Borders', *Review of Politics*, vol. 49, no. 2, Spring 1987, pp. 251–73.

Castles, S., Iredale, R., Withers, G., and Foster, W., *Australia and Immigration: A Partnership*, Housing Industry Association, 1997.

Castles, S., Kalantzis, M., Cope, W., and Morrissey, M. (eds), *Mistaken Identity: Multiculturalism and the Demise of Nationalism in Australia*, Pluto Press, Sydney, 1988.

Castles, S., and Miller, M. J., *The Age of Migration: International Population Movements in the Modern World*, Macmillan, London, 1993.

Choi, C. Y., *Chinese Migration and Settlement in Australia,* Sydney University Press, 1975.

Churgin, M. J., 'Mass Exoduses: The Response of the United States', *International Migration Review*, vol. 30, no. 1, Spring 1996, pp. 310–24.

Cixous, H., 'We Who Are Free, Are We Free?', *Critical Inquiry*, no. 19, Winter 1993.

Clark, P. B., *Citizenship*, Pluto Press, London, 1994.

Cohen, R., 'Human Rights and Humanitarian Action Go Hand in Hand', *Refugees*, April 1993, pp. 4–7.

Cohen, R. (ed.), *The Cambridge Survey of World Migration*, Cambridge University Press, 1995.

Collins, J., *Migrant Hands in a Distant Land: Australia's Post-War Immigration*, Pluto Press, Sydney, 1988.

Collinson, S., *Europe and International Migration*, Pinter, London, 1993.

—— *Beyond Borders: West European Migration Policy Towards the 21st Century*, Royal Institute of International Affairs, London, 1993.

Cooney, S., *The Transformation of Migration Law*, AGPS, Canberra, 1995.

Cornelius, W. A., *et al.* (eds), *Controlling Immigration: A Global Perspective*, Stanford University Press, 1992.

Coughlan, J., and McNamara, D. (eds), *Asians in Australia: Patterns of Migration and Settlement*, Macmillan, Melbourne, 1997.

Crock, M., 'Climbing Jacob's Ladder: The High Court and the Administrative Detention of Asylum Seekers in Australia', *Sydney Law Review*, vol. 15, no. 3, September 1993, pp. 338–56.

Crock, M. (ed.), *Protection or Punishment? The Detention of Asylum Seekers in Australia*, Federation Press, Sydney, 1993.

Curthoys, A., and Markus, A. (eds), *Who Are Our Enemies? Racism and the Australian Working Class*, Hale & Iremonger, Neutral Bay, NSW, 1978.

Dare, T., *Australia: A Nation of Immigrants*, Child & Associates, Australia, 1988.

Davidson, A., *From Subject to Citizen: Australian Citizenship in the Twentieth Century*, Cambridge University Press, 1997.

Day, L. H., 'Australia's Obligation to Refugees', *Working Papers in Demography*, Research School of Social Sciences, Australian National University.

De Voretz, D. J. (ed.), *Diminishing Returns: The Economics of Canada's Recent Immigration Policy*, Policy Study 24, C. D. Howe Institute, Laurier Institution, Vancouver, 1995.

Dique, J. C., *Migration: The Quiet Invasion*, Veritas, Australia, 1985.

Dowty, A., *Closed Borders: The Contemporary Assault on Freedom of Movement*, Yale University Press, New Haven, 1987.

D'Souza, F., *The Refugee Dilemma: International Recognition and Acceptance*, Minority Rights Group, Report no. 43, London, 1980.

Evans, R., Saunders, K., and Cronin, K., *Race Relations in Colonial Queensland: A History of Exclusion, Exploitation, and Extermination*, University of Queensland Press, St Lucia, 1975.

Falk, R., *On Humane Governance: Towards a New Global Politics*, Polity Press, Cambridge, 1995.

Fitzgerald, S., *Is Australia an Asian Country? Can Australia Survive in an East Asian Future?* Allen & Unwin, St Leonards, NSW, 1997.

Fontaine, P. M., 'The Comprehensive Plan of Action (CPA) on Indochinese Refugees: Prospects for the Post-CPA, and Implications for a Regional Approach to Refugee Problems', paper presented at *United Nations: Between Sovereignty and Global Governance?*, 2–6 July 1995, Melbourne.

Foster, L., and Stockley, D., 'Multiculturalism: The Changing Australian Paradigm', *Multilingual Matters*, no. 16, 1984.

Freeman, G. P., and Jupp, J. (eds), *Nations of Immigrants: Australia, the United States, and International Migration*, Oxford University Press, Melbourne, 1992.

Frideres, J. S., 'Canada's Changing Immigration Policy: Implications for Asian Immigrants', *Asian and Pacific Migration Journal*, vol. 5, no. 4, 1996, pp. 449–70.

Gallagher, D., 'The Evolution of the International Refugee System', *International Migration Review*, vol. 23, no. 3, Fall 1989, pp. 579–98.

Gibney, M., *Open Borders, Closed Societies? The Ethical and Political Issues*, Greenwood Press, New York, 1988.

Giroux, H. A., 'Living Dangerously: Identity Politics and the New Cultural Racism: Towards a Critical Pedagogy of Representation', *Cultural Studies*, vol. 7, no. 1, January 1993, pp. 1–27.

Goddard, J., 'What the *Migration Reform Act* Really Means', *Law Society Journal*, vol. 32, no. 2, March 1994, pp. 33–6.

Goodwin-Gill, G., 'International Law and the Detention of Refugees and Asylum-Seekers', *International Migration Review*, vol. 20, no. 2, Summer 1986, pp. 193–219.

—— 'Non-refoulement and the New Asylum-seekers,' *Virginia Journal of International Law*, vol. 26, Summer 1986, pp. 897–920.

—— 'International Law and Human Rights: Trends Concerning International Migrants and Refugees', *International Migration Review*, vol. 33, no. 3, Fall 1989, pp. 526–46.

Grahl-Madsen, A., *The Status of Refugees in International Law*, 2 vols, Leyden, Sijhoff, 1966–72.

Grant, B., *The Boat People: An 'Age' Investigation*, Penguin, Ringwood, Vic., 1979.

Grant, B. (ed.), *Pauline Hanson: One Nation and Australian Politics*, University of New England Press, Armidale, 1997.

Gray, G., and Winter, C. (eds), *The Resurgence of Racism: Howard, Hanson and the Race Debate*, Monash Publications in History, no. 24, Monash University, Melbourne, 1997.

Green, M., SJ, 'Boat People in Australia: An Ethical Perspective', *Uniya Occasional Paper*, no. 65, 28 April 1994.

Habermas, J., 'Citizenship and National Identity: Some Reflections on the Future of Europe', *Praxis International*, vol. 12, no. 1, April 1992, pp. 1–19.

Hammer, T., *Democracy and the Nation State: Aliens, Denizens and Citizens in a World of International Migration*, Avebury, Aldershot, 1990.

Hargreaves, A. G., *Immigration, 'Race' and Ethnicity in Contemporary France*, Routledge, London, 1995.

Hargreaves, A. G., and Leaman, J., *Racism, Ethnicity and Politics in Contemporary Europe*, Edward Elgar, Aldershot, 1995.

Hathaway, J. C., *The Law of Refugee Status*, Butterworths, Toronto, 1991.

Hawkins, F., *Critical Years in Immigration: Canada and Australia Compared*, New South Wales University Press, Sydney, 1989.

Helsinki Rights Watch, *Foreigners Out: Xenophobia and Right-Wing Violence in Germany*, New York, 1992.

Helton, A. C., 'Making Refugee Detention Policy More Rational and Compatible with International Human Rights Standards: Reforming Alien Detention Policy in the United States: A Case Study', *Migration Monitor*, October 1993, pp. 13–18.

Hosking, P., 'The Debate on Immigration and Asylum,' *Uniya Occasional Paper*, no. 38, August 1992.

—— 'Australian Immigration Policy: Some Ethical Dimensions for Refugees and Asylum Seekers: Our Refugee Intake: Towards an Ethical Analysis', *Uniya Occasional Paper*, no. 49, June 1993.

—— 'Refugees, 'Human Trafficking', and Asylum Seekers: A Perspective on the Detention of the Cambodian Boat People', *Uniya Occasional Paper*, no. 74, May 1994.

Hoskings, P., and Murphy, K., 'Forced Migration: Objective Causes and Subjective Motivations and the Control Mentality: Recent Australian On-Shore Refugee Processing', *Uniya Occasional Paper*, no. 81, November 1994.

Inglis, C., *et al.*, *Asians in Australia: The Dynamics of Migration and Settlement*, Institute of Southeast Asian Studies, Singapore, 1992.

International Council of Voluntary Agencies, 'The Pursuit and Implementation of Durable Solutions', presented as part of the NGO Statement to the *47th Session of the Executive Committee of the UNHCR*, Geneva, 1996.

Jakubowicz, A. (ed.), *Racism, Ethnicity and the Media*, Allen & Unwin, St Leonards, NSW, 1994.

James, P., 'Reconstituting the Nation-State: A Postmodern Republic takes Shape', *Arena*, no. 4, 1994–95, pp. 69–90.

James, P. (ed.), *Critical Politics: From the Personal to the Global*, Arena Publications, Melbourne, 1994.

Jorden, A., *Redefining Australians: Immigration, Citizenship and National Identity*, Hale & Iremonger, Sydney, 1995.

Jupp, J. *Exile or Refuge?: The Settlement of Refugee, Humanitarian and Displaced Immigrants*, AGPS, Canberra, 1994.

—— *Understanding Australian Multiculturalism*, Centre for Immigration and Multicultural Studies, Australian National University, ANU, AGPS, Canberra, 1996.

Jupp, J. (ed.), *The Challenge of Diversity: Policy Options for a Multicultural Australia*, AGPS, Canberra, 1989.

Jupp, J., and Kabala, M. (eds), *The Politics of Australian Immigration*, AGPS, Canberra, 1993.

Kalin, W., 'Troubled Communication: Cross-Cultural Misunderstandings in the Asylum Hearing', *International Migration Review*, vol. 20, no. 2, Summer 1986, pp. 230–41.

Keely, C. B., 'How Nation-States Create and Respond to Refugee Flows', *International Migration Review*, vol. 30, no. 4, Winter 1996, pp. 1046–66.

King, D., and Waldron, J., 'Citizenship, Social Citizenship and the Defence of the Welfare State', *British Journal of Political Science*, no. 18, 1988, pp. 415–43.

Knowles, V., *Strangers at Our Gates: Canadian Immigration Policy, 1540–1990*, Dundurn Press, Toronto, 1992.

Kovacs, M. L., and Cropley, A., *Immigrants and Society: Alienation and Assimilation*, McGraw-Hill, Sydney, 1975.

Kritz, M., Keely, C., and Tomasi, S. (eds), *Global Trends in Migration: Theory and Research on International Population Movements*, Center for Migration Studies, New York, 1981.

Kukathas, C. (ed.), *Multicultural Citizens: The Philosophy and Politics of Identity*, Centre for Independent Studies, Sydney, 1993.

Kymlicka, W., *Multicultural Citizenship: A Liberal Theory of Minority Rights*, Clarendon Press, Oxford, 1995.

Lack, J., and Templeton, J., *Bold Experiment: A Documentary of Australian Immigration Since 1945*, Oxford University Press, Melbourne, 1995.

Laquian, E., *et al.*, *The Silent Debate: Asian Immigration and Racism in Canada*, Institute of Asian Research, University of British Columbia, Vancouver, 1998.

Laster, K., 'Geoffrey Blainey and the Asianisation of Australia: A Debate Half Won', *Migration Action*, vol. 7, no. 2, 1984.

Lawton, M., and Murphy, K., 'The Detention of Asylum Seekers in Australia', *Uniya Occasional Paper*, no. 67, July 1994.

Legomsky, S. H., 'The New Techniques for Managing High-Volume Asylum Systems', *Iowa Law Review*, no. 81, 1996.

Le May, M. C., *Anatomy of a Public Policy: The Reform of Contemporary American Immigration Law*, Praeger, Westport, 1994.

Lester, E., 'Arbitrary Detention of Boat People', *Uniya Focus*, no. 7, May 1997.

—— 'Who Is a Refugee? How Do We Decide?' *Uniya Focus*, no. 9, June 1997.

Lester, E., and Vinson, T., 'The Twilight Zone of Human Rights', *Uniya Focus*, no. 13, August 1997.

Lewis, F., 'Borderline Insanity', *Arena*, August–September 1994, pp. 8–9.

Lewis, J., 'Government Passes the Buck on Asylum-Seekers', *Migration News*, no. 41, June 1996.

Loescher, G., *Refugee Movements and International Security*, Adelphi Papers, no. 268, Brassey's, London, 1992.

—— *Beyond Charity: International Cooperation and the Global Refugee Crisis*, Oxford University Press, New York, 1993.

Loescher, G., and Monahan, L., *Refugees and International Relations*, Oxford University Press, 1989.

London, H. I., *Non-White Immigration and the 'White Australia' Policy*, Sydney University Press, 1970.

Lowenstein, W., and Loh, M., *The Immigrants*, Hyland House, Melbourne, 1977.

Luke, T. W., 'Televisual Democracy and the Politics of Democracy', *Telos*, no. 70, Winter 1986–87, pp. 59–79.

—— 'Discourses of Disintegration, Texts of Transformation: Re-Reading Realism in the New World Order', *Alternatives*, no. 18, 1993, pp. 229–58.

Lyons, A. 'Some Good News about Refugees', *Uniya Focus*, no. 29, August 1998.

Lyons, A. (ed.), *Voices, Stories, Hopes: Cambodia and Vietnam, Refugees and Volunteers*, Collins Dove, Melbourne, 1993.

Mackay, H., *Reinventing Australia: The Mind and Mood of Australia in the 90s*, Angus & Robertson, Sydney, 1993.

McGillivray, M., and Smith, G., *Australia and Asia*, Oxford University Press, Melbourne, 1997.

McLaren, P., 'Multiculturalism and the Postmodern Critique: Towards a Pedagogy of Resistance and Transformation', *Cultural Studies*, vol. 7, no. 1, January 1993.

Malkki, L., 'National Geographic: The Rooting of Peoples and the Territorialization of National Identity among Scholars and Refugees', *Cultural Anthropology*, vol. 7, no. 1, February 1992, pp. 24–44.

Manne, R., 'Indochinese Refugees and the Australian Political Culture', *Migration Action*, vol. 3, 1978, pp. 10–14.

Markus, A., *Fear and Hatred: Purifying Australia and California, 1850–1901*, Hale & Iremonger, Sydney, 1979.

—— *Australian Race Relations, 1788–1993*, Allen & Unwin, Sydney, 1994.

Markus, A., and Rasmussen, R. (eds), *Prejudice in the Public Arena: Racism*, Centre for Migrant and Intercultural Studies, Monash University, Melbourne, 1987.

Markus, A., and Ricklefs, M. C. (eds), *Surrender Australia? Essays in the Study and Uses of History*, Allen & Unwin, Sydney, 1985.

Marrus, M. R., *The Unwanted: European Refugees in the Twentieth Century*, Oxford University Press, New York, 1985.

Marshall, T. H., *Citizenship and Social Class, and Other Essays*, Cambridge University Press, 1950.

Martiniello, M., *Migration, Citizenship and Ethno-National Identities in the European Union*, Avebury, Aldershot, 1995.

Melander, L., 'Responsibility for Examining an Asylum Request, Asylum Seekers *vs* Quota Refugees', *International Migration Review*, vol. 20, no. 2, Summer 1986, pp. 220–9.

Merritt, G. J., *Pauline Hanson: The Truth*, St George Publications, SA, 1997.

Milne, F., and Shergold, P. (eds), *The Great Immigration Debate*, FECCA, Sydney, 1984.

Miyoshi, M., 'A Borderless World? From Colonialism to Transnationalism and the Decline of the Nation-State', *Critical Inquiry*, no. 19, Summer 1993, pp. 726–51.

Murphy, B., *The Other Australia: Experiences of Migration*, Cambridge University Press, 1993.

Murphy, K., 'Australia's Refugee and Humanitarian Program', *Uniya Occasional Paper*, no. 61, April 1994.

—— 'Who's Afraid of the Big Bad Courts? Detention of Asylum Seekers', *Law Society Journal*, vol. 32, no. 9, October 1994, pp. 60–1.

—— 'Are We Being Swamped?', *Uniya Focus*, no. 9, October 1996.

Muus, P. (ed.), *Exclusion and Inclusion of Refugees in Contemporary Europe*, European Research Centre on Migration and Ethnic Relations, The Netherlands, 1997.

Nile, R. (ed.), *Immigration and the Politics of Ethnicity and Race in Australia and Britain*, Bureau of Immigration Research, Melbourne, 1991.

—— *Australian Civilisation*, Oxford University Press, Melbourne, 1994.

Northern Territory University, *Retreating from the Refugee Convention, Conference Proceedings*, Northern Territory University, Darwin, 7–10 February 1997.

Ogata, S., 'Refugees: Lessons from the Past', *The Richard Storry Memorial Lecture*, no. 6, 5 May 1993, St Antony's College, Oxford, pp. 1–16.

Palfreeman, A. C., *The Administration of the White Australia Policy*, Melbourne University Press, 1967.

Poynder, N., 'Marooned in Port Hedland', *Alternative Law Journal*, vol. 18, no. 6, December 1993, pp. 272–4.

Pranger, R. J., *The Eclipse of Citizenship: Power and Participation in Contemporary Politics*, Holt, Rinehart & Winston, New York, 1968.

Quick, J., and Garran, R., *The Annotated Constitution of the Australian Commonwealth*, Angus & Robertson, Sydney, 1901.

Reilly, A., 'Incarcerating Refugees: From Killing Fields to Killing Time', *Alternative Law Journal*, vol. 18, no. 3, June 1993, pp. 126–9.

Riesenberg, P., *Citizenship in the Western Tradition: Plato to Rousseau*, University of North Carolina Press, London. 1992.

Rivett, K., *A Refugee Policy for Today and Tomorrow*, Institute of Public Affairs, Sydney, 1980.

Rivett, K. (ed.), *Immigration: Control or Colour Bar? The Background to 'White Australia' and a Proposal for Change*, Melbourne University Press, 1962.

—— *Australia and the Non-White Migrant*, Melbourne University Press, 1975.

Rogers, R., 'The Future of Refugee Flows and Policies', *International Migration Review*, vol. 26, no. 4, Winter 1992, pp. 1112–43.

Said, E. W., *Orientalism*, Penguin, New York, 1978.

—— 'The Mind of Winter: Reflections on Life in Exile', *Harpers Magazine*, September 1984, pp. 49–55.

Saikal, A., *Refugees in the Modern World*, Australian National University, Canberra, 1989.

Selby, H., (ed.), *Tomorrow's Law*, Federation Press, Sydney, 1995.

Shacknove, A. E., 'Who Is a Refugee?', *Ethics*, no. 95, December 1985, pp. 274–84.

Shawcross, W., 'Mass Migration and the Global Village', *Refugees*, no. 88, January 1992, pp. 26–9.

Sherington, G., *Australia's Immigrants: 1788–1978*, Allen & Unwin, Sydney, 1980.

Silverman, M., *Deconstructing the Nation: Immigration, Racism and Citizenship in Modern France*, Routledge, London, 1992.

Singer, R. (ed.), *The Immigration Debate in the Press 1984*, Clearing House on Migration Issues, Richmond, Vic., 1984.

Sluga, G., *Bonegilla: 'A Place of No Hope'*, History Department, University of Melbourne, 1988.

Smith, J. W. (ed.), *Immigration, Population and Sustainable Environments: The Limits to Australia's Growth*, Flinders Press, Adelaide, 1991.

Taylor, C., and Gutmann, A., *Multiculturalism and 'The Politics of Recognition'*, Princeton University Press, 1992.

Taylor, P., *The European Union in the 1990s*, Oxford University Press, 1996.

Taylor, S., 'The Meaning of 'Social Group': The Federal Court's Failure to Think beyond Social Significance', *Monash University Law Review*, vol. 19, no. 2, 1993.

Theophanous, A. C., *Understanding Multiculturalism and Australian Identity*, Elikia, Melbourne, 1995.

Thompson, E., *Fair Enough: Egalitarianism in Australia*, New South Wales University Press, Sydney, 1994.

Tomasi, L. F. (ed.), *In Defense of the Alien*, vols 17, 18, Center for Immigration Studies of New York, New York, 1996.

Triandafyllidou, A., 'National Identity and the "Other" ', *Ethnic and Racial Studies*, vol. 21, no. 4, July 1998, pp. 593–612.

Tucker, R. T., *et al.*, *Immigration and US Foreign Policy*, Westview, Boulder, 1990.

Turner, B. S., *Citizenship and Capitalism: The Debate over Reformism*, Allen & Unwin, London, 1986.

—— *Theories of Modernity and Postmodernity*, Sage, London, 1990.

—— *Orientalism, Postmodernism and Globalism*, Routledge, London, 1994.

Turner, B. S. (ed.), *Citizenship and Social Theory*, Sage, London, 1994.

Turner, G., *Making It National: Nationalism and Australian Popular Culture*, Allen & Unwin, Sydney, 1994.

Ungar, S. J., *Fresh Blood: The New American Immigrants*, Simon & Schuster, New York, 1995.

UNESCO, *Human Rights; Comments and Interpretations*, Greenwood Press, Connecticut.

UNHCR, *Collection of International Instruments Concerning Refugees*, Geneva, 1979.

—— *Guideline on Detention of Asylum-seekers*, UNHCR, 1996.

—— *Resettlement Handbook, 1996 Version: Division of International Protection*, Geneva, 1996.

Van Gunsteren, 'Admission to Citizenship', *Ethics*, vol. 98, no. 4, 1988. pp. 731–41.

Van Steenbergen, B. (ed.), *The Condition of Citizenship*, Sage, London, 1994.

Van Tran, M., 'The Long Journey: Australia's First Boat People', *CSAAR Research Paper*, no. 15, Griffith University, June 1981.

Vasta, E., and Castles, S. (eds), *The Teeth are Smiling: The Persistence of Racism in Multicultural Australia*, Allen & Unwin, St Leonards, NSW, 1996.

Vinson, T., 'The Hanson Effect', *Uniya Focus*, no. 8, May 1997.

Vinson, T., Leech, M., and Lester, E., 'The Number of Boat People: Fact and Perception', *Uniya Brief Research Report*, no. 1, 1997.

Viviani, N., *The Long Journey: Vietnamese Migration and Settlement in Australia*, Melbourne University Press, 1984.

—— *The Indochinese in Australia, 1975–1995: From Burnt Boats to Barbecues*, Oxford University Press, 1996.

Viviani, N., and Lawe-Davies, J., *Australian Government Policies on the Entry of Vietnamese Refugees, 1976 to 1978*, CSAAR Research Paper, no. 2, Griffith University, February 1980.

Walzer, M., *Spheres of Justice: a Defence of Pluralism and Equality*, Martin Robertson, Oxford, 1983.

Webb, J., and Enstice, A., *Aliens and Savages*, HarperCollins, Pymble, NSW, 1998.

Whelan, F. G., 'Citizenship and the Right to Leave', *American Political Science Review*, vol. 75, no. 3, September 1981, pp. 636–53.

Willard, M., *History of the White Australian Policy to 1920*, Melbourne University Press, 1974.

Wooden, M., *et al.*, *Australian Immigration: A Survey of the Issues*, AGPS, Canberra, 1994.

Xenos, N., 'Refugees: The Modern Political Condition', *Alternatives*, no. 18, 9, 1993, pp. 419–30.

Yarwood, A., 'The Dictation Test: A Historical Survey', *Australian Quarterly*, no. 30, June 1958.

—— *Asian Migration to Australia: The Background to Exclusion, 1896–1923*, Melbourne University Press, 1964.

Yarwood, A., and Knowling, M. J., *Race Relations in Australia: A History*, Methuen, North Ryde, NSW, 1982.

Yuan Chung-Ming, *Awakening Conscience: Racism in Australia*, Lung Men Press, Hong Kong, 1983.

Zelinka, S., *Understanding Racism in Australia*, Human Rights and Equal Opportunity Commission, AGPS, Canberra, 1996.

Zolberg, A., 'The Next Waves: Migration Theory for a Changing World', *International Migration Review*, vol. 23, no. 3, Fall 1989, pp. 403–30.

—— 'International Migrants and Refugees in Historical Perspective', *Refugees*, December 1992 – April 1993, pp. 36–42.

Zolberg, A., *et al.*, 'International Factors in the Formation of Refugee Movements', *International Migration Review*, vol. 20, no. 2, Summer 1986, pp. 121–69.

Zolberg, A., Suhrke, A. and Aguayo, S., *Escape from Violence: Conflict and the Refugee Crisis in the Developing World*, Oxford University Press, New York, 1989.

## Online Sources

Amnesty International, *Home Page, United Kingdom: Arbitrary detention of asylum-seekers*, 30 January 1997, <www. oneworld.org/amnesty/press/30Jan-ukasulum. html>.

Australian National Audit Office, *Audit Report no. 32: The Management of Boat People*, 1997–98, <www.anao.gov.au/rptsfull_98audrpf32/contents.html>.

Austcare Australia, aulca@unhcr.ch.

Department of Immigration and Multicultural Affairs, Fact Sheet 1, 'Immigration-the background', <www.immi.gov.au/facts/01backgd.htm >.

—— Fact Sheet 2, 'Key facts in immigration', <www.immi.gov.au/facts/02keyfac.htm>.

—— Fact Sheet 3, 'Recent developments in the Immigration and Multicultural Affairs portfolio', <www.immi.gov.au/facts/03recent.htm>.

—— Fact Sheet 20, '1998–99 Migration Program planning levels', <www.immi. gov.au/facts/20progra.htm>.

—— Fact Sheet 82, 'Immigration Detention', <www.immi.gov.au/facts/82detain. htm>.

—— Fact Sheet 81, 'Boat Arrivals since 1989', <www.immi.gov.au/facts/81boats. htm>.

Canada, Department of Justice, *Immigration Act*, <www.canada.justice.gc.ca/ STABLE/EN/Laws/Chap/I/1–2>.

European Commission, *Maastricht Treaty: Final Act*, <www.europa.eu.int/en/record/mt/final>.

—— *Background Report, Brussels: Myths and Realities*, <www.cec.org.uk/pubs/br/br97/br9706>.

—— *Background Report, The Growth of the EU, I*<bib10.sub.su.se/sam/euguide/eueng2>.

European Council on Refugees and Exiles Report, 1996, *Arrivals/Statistics*, part 3, Legal Developments, no. 3, Detention, ecre@gn.apc.org.

Immigration and Refugee Board of Canada, *Convention Refugee Determination*, <www.irb.gc.ca/crdd/default>.

—— *Convention Refugee Determination Division Process*, <www.irb.gc.ca/process/crdpro_e>.

—— *Guidelines on Detention*, <www.irb.gc.ca/guidline/detention%20review/detrev>.

Refugee Review Tribunal, *Homepage*, <www.austlii.edu.au/au/other/rrt/>.

UNHCR, *Country Updates*, <www.unicc.org/unhcr/news/cupdates/9811lakes>.

—— *Speeches of the High Commissioner*, The Ramon Magsaysay Award Forum: 'Human Displacement in the Decades to Come: Meeting the Needs of Refugees', Manila, 7 January 1998, <www.unhcr.ch/refworld>.

—— *Statistics*, <www.unhcr.ch/un&ref/un&ref>.

—— 'Global Statistics; Populations of Concern to UNHCR, 1995', *UNHCR Refworld*, <www.unhcr.ch/refworld/refbib/refstat; pp. 1–17>.

—— Executive Committee of the High Commissioner's Programme, *Conclusion No. 44 (37) 1986 Detention of Refugees and Asylum-seekers*, <www.unhcr.ch/refworld/unhcr/excom/xconc/excom44.htm>.

United States, Bureau of Population, Refugees, and Migration, Department of State, *Fact Sheet: Who is a Refugee?*, <www.state.gov/global/prm/fs_refugee.html>.

——, —— *Overview on Population, Refugee, and Migration*, 1996, <www.state.gov./global/prm/Oakley121996.html>.

—— Immigration and Naturalization Service, *Fact Sheet: Illegal Immigration Reform and Immigrant Responsibility Act of 1996*, <www.ins.USdoj.gov/public_affairs/press_releases/953>.

——, —— *Highlights*, <www.ins.USdoj.gov/stats/annual/fy96/977>.

——, —— *The Illegal Immigration Reform and Immigrant Responsibility Act of 1996*, <www.ins.USdoj.gov/public_affairs/press_releases/953>.

——, —— *Illegal Alien Resident Population*, <www.ins.USdoj.gov/stats/illegalalien/index>.

—— *International Policy: 1996 Overview on Population, Refugees, and Migration*, <www.state.gov/global/ptm/Oakley121996.html>.

# Index

Aboriginal people *see* Indigenous people
access and equity, 49, 165, 175
Adams, Phillip, 5
adjudicative system, 80, 96, 123, 125, 126; model, 117, 118
*Afghan* (ship), 129
Africa, 8–35 *passim*, 102, 109
*Age*, 136
alien(s), 4, 43, 83, 84, 107, 108, 111, 112, 113, 116, 128, 133, 161, 162, 163, 165, 168, 185; alienage, 23, 28, 83
Alternative Detention Model, 97
Amnesty International, 95, 101, 189
Anderson, Benedict, 133, 170
Anglo-Celtic, 5
anti-alien, 99
anti-immigrant, 99, 102, 106; anti-immigration, 62
*apatrides*, 19
Arendt, Hannah, 18, 20, 184
Aristotle, 163

ASEAN, 31
Asian, 2, 3, 5, 6, 22, 39, 42, 44, 47–58 *passim*, 63–4, 67, 70, 73, 82, 89, 127–8, 130–42 *passim*, 145–62 *passim*, 171, 188–91; Asianisation, 39, 52, 134, 145–7, 149, 160
assimilation, 6, 19, 43–7, 138, 140, 153, 158; policy, 145
assisted passage, 39
AustralAsia Centre of the Asia Society, 154
Australia Council, 144
Australia Day, 67
Australia–China Council, 149
*Australian Citizenship Act 1948*, 162
Australian Ethnic Affairs Council, 143
Australian Institute of Multicultural Affairs, 144
Australian Labor Party, 48–50, 53–5, 130, 141, 142
Australian Natives Association, 140

Australian Population and Immigration Council, 143

Australians Against Further Immigration, 152

'back door' entry, 107, 113, 114, 116

Barton, Edmund, 130

*Beagle* (ship), 73, 74, 84

Behai, 90

belonging, 6, 161, 163, 165, 166, 169, 170, 175, 177, 178, 185–7

Bereson, I. and Matheson, A., 130

Betts, Katherine, 52, 53, 146, 157

Bill C-86 (Canada), 122

Blainey, Geoffrey, 5, 52, 56, 127, 146–60 *passim*

boat people, 2–7, 13, 24, 35–9, 48–59, 64–82, 87–96, 109–16, 121–32, 141–6, 152–69, 180–91; first wave, 72, 73, 174; second wave, 73, 89, 174; third wave, 89, 91–4, 175

Bolkus, Nick, 61, 79, 88–94 *passim*

Bonegilla (camp), 47

Bosnia, 25, 185

Bracero (scheme), 113

Bradshaw rock paintings, 127

Britain, 5, 13, 15, 34–47, 98–9, 105, 135, 149–58, 167–72

Buckland River, 129

*Bulletin*, 131

Bureau of Immigration, Multicultural and Population Research, 62

Cadman, Alan, 150

Calavita, Kitty, 113

Calvinists, 13

Calwell, Arthur, 43–6, 138–9, 157

Cambodia, 22, 31, 32, 74–8, 88, 152; Cambodians, 54, 73–5, 78–83, 88–9, 146; Peace Plan, 96

Camilleri, J. A., 157

Campbell, G., 152

Canada, 5, 7, 32–6, 55, 85, 99, 102, 117–25; refugee policy 119

Cartagena Declaration, 27, 28, 37

Castles, S. and Miller, M. J., 32, 33, 35

Catholics, 12, 13

Chamarette, Christabel, 85, 87

Chang, David, 66, 67, 89

Charles, Prince of Wales, 67

Chifley, Ben, 43, 138

China, 11, 31, 44, 68, 78, 90–4, 130, 149, 152; Chinese, 2–5, 11, 30, 39–42, 48, 57, 64, 68, 74, 78–80, 89–96, 117, 127–40, 156, 159, 190, 191; Chinese Question, 129, 132, 134; coolies; 40, 128; labourers, 39, 128, 136; one-child policy, 92, 93; Tiananmen Square, 30, 57, 78, 91, 96

*Chinese Restriction Act*, 129

Chu Kheng Lim, 83

Chung Teeong Toy, 68

Chung-Ming, Yuan, 134, 135

citizenship, 2–7 *passim*, 17, 20, 30, 35, 46, 48, 84, 93, 105–9, 136, 140, 143, 161–90; civil, 186; consumer, 180–7; cultural, 174, 175, 180, 186, 187; political, 164; politics of, 162; semiotic, 180–7; social, 4, 7, 163–9, 173, 175, 179–86, 188, 190

Cold War, 32, 35, 45, 73, 107, 108, 116, 141, 160

Colombo Plan, 44, 45

colonisation, 5, 16, 19, 31, 32, 131, 158

'coloured', 3, 41–2, 99, 128, 130–4, 136, 138, 155, 159

Commonwealth Immigration Advisory Council, 43

*Commonwealth of Australia Constitution Act 1900*, 40

community parole system, 4

Comprehensive Plan of Action (CPA), 90, 91, 111, 122

convicts, 39; *see also* penal system

Cook, Matthew, 153

Cooney, Senator Barney, 85, 87

Cooney, Sean, 80

cosmopolitan, 5, 21, 53, 161, 162

criminal justice, 84

Crock, Mary, 59, 69, 82, 83

Cronin, K., 60

crypto-refugees, 30

Cubans, 107, 109, 112, 125

cultural diversity, 6, 142, 146, 171; pluralism, 142, 143

culture of control, 60, 81–2, 85, 89, 97

Curtin air force base, 94

Darwin, 70, 92

Davidson, Alastair, 4

de facto (refugees), 29, 30

*de jure* (refugees), 29

decolonisation, 19, 32, 102

'defend, deter, detain', 87

Defoe, Daniel, 99

denizens, 4, 98, 185, 186, 188

Department of Immigration and Ethnic Affairs (DIEA), 86, 90, 144

Department of Immigration and Multi-cultural Affairs (DIMA), 62, 69

detention, 2–10, 14, 32, 35, 39, 45, 59–101 *passim*, 106, 111–16, 121–6, 152, 156–69 *passim*, 176, 185–91 *passim*; camps, 8, 14, 32, 90; of children, 85; clause, 3; regime, 126; *see also* detention centres; mandatory detention

detention centres, 77, 79, 125; *see also* Port Hedland; Villawood

Determination of Refugee Status Committee (DORS), 52, 71, 72, 77, 78

deterrence, 67, 116, 125; policy, 50, 70

dictation test, 45, 47, 62, 135, 139

discrimination, 4, 7, 19, 67, 70, 78, 79, 89, 125, 127, 141, 157, 161–4, 182, 185, 190, 191; discriminatory practices, 7, 10, 85, 126, 187

displaced persons, 14, 19–25 *passim*, 31, 34, 37, 44, 45, 58, 94, 119; Scheme, 44

dispossessed people, 9, 24

Don Quixote, 148

Donati, P., 173

Dowty, A., 15

East Timor, 27, 58, 152

Eccleston, R., 2

economic rationalism, 53, 54, 167

economic refugees, 35, 53, 57, 72, 79, 112

egalitarianism, 135

Einfeld, Marcus, 87

Eliot, George, 15

émigrés (French Revolution), 16

Empire Settlement Scheme, 40

Ethnic Affairs Council, 143

ethnic lobby groups, 55–7, 147

Europe, 5–9, 12–19, 22, 28, 34–6, 43, 45, 98, 103–8, 122, 125–6, 138–9, 154–9, 173; European Union, 34, 99, 104–6, 185–8

Evans, Gareth, 74, 75, 76

Evian Conference, 42

exclusion, 4, 5, 129, 135, 157, 161–4, 185, 190

Falk, Richard, 182, 183

family reunion, 3, 34–5, 49–56 *passim*, 61, 62, 99, 114

Federal Court, 75, 79, 82, 84, 86, 92, 94, 97, 120

Federation, 5, 130, 132, 133

Fisher, Tim, 61

Fitzgerald, Report, 56, 61, 63, 150, 151

Fitzpatrick, Brian, 138

foreign policy, 9, 45, 48, 75–6, 96, 107–8, 110–11, 114, 116, 119, 124–5

former Soviet Union, 28, 32, 33, 58, 108, 124, 173

former Yugoslavia, 14, 25, 32, 35, 58

Fortress Europe, 106

'forum shopping', 91

France, 12–13, 34, 36, 98–107 *passim*, 126, 158

Fraser, Nancy and Gordon, Linda, 167, 185, 186

Fraser, Malcolm, 49, 55, 62, 145, 146, 151

Fraser Liberal–Country Party Coalition Government, 50, 52, 70, 71, 141, 144–6 *passim*

Freeman, G. and Jupp, J., 47, 151

'front door' entry, 107, 114

Front National, 36, 102, 107

Galang (camp), 90

Galbally Report, 144, 145

Geneva Convention, 104, 106

Germany, 34, 42, 104, 105, 107, 121, 158, 171

global village, 9

globalisation, 114, 155, 158, 163, 168–80, 184, 187; cultural, 171, 172; Western, 172

goldfields, 5, 40, 129

Good Neighbour Councils, 46, 47

Gorton, John, 142

Grassby, Al, 49, 143

Greece, Ancient, 163

guest-workers, 102, 113

Habermas, Jurgen, 168, 176

Haitians, 107, 110–12 *passim*

Hall, Stuart, 176

Hancock, W. K., 41

Hand, Gerry, 57, 79, 86, 87

Hanson, Pauline, 5, 63, 127, 148, 152–7 *passim*, 160, 173; *see also* One Nation Party

harmonisation, 105, 106, 126

Harradine, Senator B., 92

Hathaway, J. C., 23

Hawke, Bob, 49, 53, 55–7, 61, 75, 78–9, 91, 147, 149, 151

Hawke Labor Government, 55, 147, 149, 151

Hayden, Bill, 54, 149

*heimatlosen*, 19

Helton, Arthur, 113, 115, 116

Henn, Percy, 2

High Commissioner for Refugees, 18, 20, 25

High Court, 83, 84, 85, 87, 97

Hodgman, Alan, 149

Hollifield, J. F., 102

homeland, 1, 18, 20–1, 38, 40, 52, 183

homeless people, 9, 18

Hong Kong, 90

'hordes from the north', 3, 4, 7, 40, 49, 67, 70, 73, 75, 127, 129, 137, 145–6, 158–9, 182; *see also* 'yellow peril'

Hosking, P. and Murphy, K., 60

Howard, John, 5, 56, 61, 63, 127, 150–5 *passim*, 189

Howard Coalition Government, 61, 62, 152, 153, 156, 189

Hughes, Billy, 130, 137

Huguenots, 13, 14, 99

human rights, 3–7 *passim*, 18, 21–8, 55–67, 74, 83–97, 100–16, 126, 152, 162–70, 174–90; abuse of, 110; concerns about, 68, 106, 116; requirements for, 83; violations of, 4, 6, 27, 61, 74, 84, 86, 87, 91, 94,

111, 116, 126, 152, 156, 162, 166, 169, 188, 190

Human Rights Commissioner *see* Sidoti, Christopher

Human Rights and Equal Opportunity Commission (HREOC), 95, 97, 189

human trafficking, 2, 91, 94

Humanitarian Programs, 54, 58, 62, 63; aid, 24

Hurford, Chris, 55, 56

icons, 184

identity, 4, 6, 17, 19, 20, 21, 31, 53, 168, 174, 181, 184, 187, 190; Australian, 127, 133–6, 141, 145, 147, 152–3, 156–7, 159–60, 187; cosmopolitan, 161–2; crisis of, 21; federation, 130; insecure, 5; national, 5, 11, 21, 49, 146, 158, 161, 168, 173, 178; non-identity, 20, 32; politics of, 4, 156–9, 184; and republic debate, 158; settler, 153, 157, 158, 161

imagined community, 133, 170

immigration: club, 87; control of, 18, 82, 89, 94, 96, 134; debate about, 3, 6, 7, 52, 56, 127, 140, 146–53 *passim*, 155; industry, 61; policy, 3, 6, 38, 43, 44, 50, 52, 64, 82, 96, 137, 140, 141, 146, 150

Immigration and Naturalization Service (INS), 108, 111, 112, 114, 116

Immigration Reform Group, 47, 140

*Immigration Restriction Act 1901*, 5, 41, 42, 47, 130, 133, 134, 135, 136, 159

Immigration Review Tribunal, 57, 81, 85

Independent and Concessional Category, 56

Indigenous people, 38, 128, 131–5, 136, 145, 153, 155, 157–9, 179

Indochinese refugees, 22, 50–4 *passim*, 70, 72, 73, 78, 90, 146

Indonesia, 27, 74, 90

industrial capitalism, 15; and democracy, 98

INS Pilot Parole Project, 115–16

integration of immigrants, 6, 13, 35, 47, 140, 181, 187

Interdiction Program, 110, 111

internally displaced persons, 9, 22, 24, 25, 26, 37

international law, 29, 59, 67, 69, 81, 115; conventions, 21, 84; treaties, 16; obligations, 96, 98

*Inverell Times*, 128

Iran, 33, 124

Islamic tradition, 11, 12

James, Paul, 5, 23, 140, 169, 187

Janus nature, 26

Japan, 17, 31, 40, 137

Jews, 12, 42, 45, 137–8, 149

Joint Standing Committee on Migration, 60, 63, 84

Jupp, James, 5, 140

Kalantzis, Mary, 5, 187, 188

Kamenka, Eugene, 8

Kanakas, 40

Keating, Paul, 49, 79

Keating Labor Government, 61, 137

Keely, Justice J. A., 75

Kompong Som, 74

Kosovars, 2, 190, 191

Kovacs, M. L. and Cropley, A., 46

Kurds, 20

Lack, J. and Templeton, J., 46

Lambing Flat, 129

Langton, Marcia, 155

language test, 62

Laos, 22

Laster, Kathy, 149

Lawton, Maria, 86

Le, Marion, 92, 102

Le Pen, J.-M., 102

League of Nations, 18

League of Rights, 152

leapfrogging, 121; *see* queue-jumping

Lester, Eve, 92

liberal cosmopolitanism, 157

liberal democracy, 7, 67, 143

*Lim v Minister for Immigration*, 83, 86

lobby groups, 52, 61, 108, 175–9

Luke, T., 180–1

Maastricht Treaty, 34, 105, 185

McAllister, Ian, 143

McEwen, John, 138

MacKellar, M. J. R., 50–4, 71, 72, 145

McKiernan, Jim, 87

Macphee, Ian, 53, 54, 72

Malaysia, 33, 51, 52, 73, 74

mandatory detention, 63, 67, 79, 81, 82, 97, 126, 186, 189, 190; *see also* detention

Mann, Robert, 167

Mariel boatlift, 109

Markus, A., 45, 137, 145

Marshall, T. H., 164–9, 173–5, 179, 180, 185, 188

Marx, Karl, 15

mass migration, 9, 31, 35, 124, 183

Melanesians, 40, 128, 130

Menzies, Robert, 157

mercantilism, 12, 14

Mexicans, 107

Middle East, 11, 28, 32, 44

Migrant Resource Centres, 144

*Migration Act 1958*, 47, 67–9, 71, 74, 79, 139

*Migration Action*, 149

*Migration Amendment Act 1992*, 59, 81

*Migration Legislation Amendment Act (No. 4)*, 90

Migration Program (Howard Government), 61, 62, 63

ministerial discretion, 47, 52, 57, 68, 78–80, 89, 95–6, 119

Mitterand, President François, 102

Moriscos, 12

multiculturalism, 5, 6, 46–9, 53, 56–63, 64, 127, 140–60 *passim*, 170–6 *passim*, 183, 187

Murphy, K., 86, 87

Nantes, Edict of, 13

Natal, Government, 135

nation-state, 7–10, 18–20, 26, 31, 35, 37, 96, 106, 161–4, 168–76, 182, 184–90; nationalism, 134

National Action, 152, 173; National Front, 99

National Population Council, 59, 120

*Nationality and Citizenship Act 1948*, 46, 162

natural justice, 7, 123

naturalisation, 81, 143; ceremonies, 46

Nazi, 42, 138; neo-Nazi, 107, 171

'New Australians', 43

New South Wales, 39, 40, 77, 129

New World Order, 35

New Zealand, 5, 32, 154

Nile, R., 132

non-citizens, 4, 83, 84, 163, 164, 169, 179

non-refoulement, 22

Norris, R., 134

O'Donaghue, Anne, 62
offshore refugee program, 73
Ogata, Sagato, 25
One Nation Party, 64, 154, 155, 173;
    see also Hanson, Pauline
Organisation of African Unity (OAU),
    27, 28
Orientalism, 3, 146, 148, 150, 157–9
*Orientalism*, 3
the 'other', 1–4, 6, 7, 18, 19, 26, 37,
    39, 42, 44, 59, 64, 68–71, 79, 82,
    98, 99, 127, 132, 134, 136, 148,
    150, 158–64, 167, 170, 171, 180,
    181, 187–91; otherness, 6, 171
overstayers, 35, 68, 69, 79, 85, 89

Pakistan, 9, 33
Palestine, 32; Palestinians, 20
Palmer River, 129
Paris Peace Agreements, 75
Parkes, Henry, 129, 130, 131, 157
parole system, 112, 125
Peacock, A., 151
penal system, 16, 39, 126
*Pender Bay* (ship), 73, 74
persecution, 2, 9–17, 20–30, 40, 44,
    55, 60, 66–78, 83, 91–101, 109–
    14, 119
political correctness, 153
politics of blame, 64, 153, 158; race,
    153
'Populate or Perish', 43, 138
Port Hedland detention centre, 77, 80,
    91, 94, 95, 191
postmodernism, 171, 172, 175
Pranger, R. J., 168
pro-democracy movement, 78
prohibited non-entrants, 76
protest, 94, 140, 177
Protestants, 12, 13

Protocol Relating to the Status of
    Refugees, 20, 44; Protocol, 20–5,
    31, 37, 44, 50, 53, 58, 60, 71–2,
    81, 84, 99, 108, 113, 119

quarantine, 54, 74, 132
Queensland, 40, 129, 130, 154
queue-jumping, 2, 67

*Racial Discrimination Act 1975*, 49,
    141
racial equality, 130, 139
racism, 39, 44, 52–4, 62, 64, 107,
    127–8, 130–1, 135, 139, 142, 148,
    149–55 *passim*, 160, 172; racist
    attitudes, 7, 49, 151, 156
Ray, Robert, 56, 57
reffos, 42, 45
Reformation, 12, 13
refoulment, 13, 29, 30
Refugee Convention *see* United Nations
    1951 Convention
Refugee Council of Australia (RCOA),
    78, 81, 87
Refugee Review Tribunal, 60–2, 80,
    81, 85, 90, 95, 97
Refugee and Special Humanitarian Pro-
    gram, 55
Refugee Status Review Committee, 77,
    78, 81
refugees: crypto-, 30; definition of, by
    Refugee Convention, 22–8, 58, 63,
    81; determination of, 7, 87, 89,
    119; flows of, 9; policy on, 2, 48,
    61, 67–8, 70–1, 82, 89, 95–6,
    119, 125, 141, 190–1; Refugee
    Fund, 27; refugeehood, 21, 23, 28;
    status of, 19, 22–5, 28, 36, 37, 52,
    53, 59, 61, 68–83, 90–7, 111,
    118–20, 124, 180, 190–1
Returned Servicemenís League (RSL),
    140

revolutions: American, 16, 164; French, 102, 164; Russian, 18
Ricklefs, Merle, 149, 150
rights: civil, 102, 173; social, 99, 102, 162, 169, 173; *see also* human rights
Ruddock, Philip, 61, 63, 86, 97
Rusden, H. K., 131
Russia, *see* former Soviet Union
Ruxton, Bruce, 148
Rwanda, 22, 32, 185

Sackville, Justice R., 92
Said, Edward, 3, 18
Saikal, Amin, 24, 25, 27
St Vincent de Paul Society, 88
sameness, 6, 135
sanctuary, 2, 10, 51, 71
Schengen Agreement, 34, 105
Shacknove, A. E., 21, 23, 27, 28
Short, Senator, 94
Sidoti, Christopher, 95, 191
'significant other', 3, 4, 6, 18, 37, 38, 67, 182, 190
signs, 152, 181, 182
Sikhs, 121
Sino-Vietnamese, 94
skilled migration, 53
slaves, 12, 163
Snowy Mountain Scheme, 45
social cohesion, 6, 56, 146, 147, 150–1, 155, 187
Social Darwinism, 131, 159; Darwinist, 132, 134
social movements, 157, 174–83; struggle, 174, 175, 179, 183
South Australia, 39, 40, 77, 129
South-East Asia, 14, 16
sovereignty, 10, 18, 21, 26, 34, 67, 84, 96, 145, 163, 170, 172, 173, 182, 184
Societ Union *see* former Soviet Union
Special Assistance Program, 58

Special Broadcasting Service (SBS), 144
Spencer, Herbert, 131
Spender, Percy, 45
Spybey, T., 184
stateless persons, 20, 29, 185
strangers, 7, 9, 17, 38, 127, 128, 156, 162, 181, 182
*Sun Herald*, 148

Tamils, 121, 125
Taylor, C., 170
Thailand, 33, 52
Thatcher, Margaret, 99
Thompson, Elaine, 135
tourist visas, 68
trade unions, 43, 47, 136
trafficking, 2, 94; *see also* human trafficking
transit refugee, 31; zones, 106, 126
transnational companies, 35, 172
Turner, Bryan, 131, 169–88 *passim*
Turner, H. G., 131

UNESCO, 139
UNHCR, 9, 20, 22–31 *passim*, 50, 53, 58–72, 78, 90, 93, 96, 106, 124, 189
*Unicorn* (ship), 91
United Nations, 9, 10, 20–2, 25, 27, 44, 58, 61, 69, 121, 139, 169, 176, 184
United Nations 1951 Convention Relating to the Status of Refugees, 20, 22, 24, 25, 31, 37, 44, 50, 60, 82, 84, 99, 108, 113, 119
United States, 5, 7, 32–6, 47, 53, 68, 85, 99, 102, 107–17, 122, 136, 172, 180; detention policy, 113, 125; immigration policy, 107; refugee policy, 107, 108, 114, 116, 125

universal visa system, 67
unlawful non-citizens, 2, 59–61, 67–8
unwanted migration, 35

*Vagabond* (ship), 90
Victoria, 68, 77, 128, 129
Vietnam, 3, 22, 39, 48–53, 64, 70–8, 90, 141, 157–9, 179; Vietnam War, 3, 39, 48–9, 53, 64, 70, 141, 157–9; Vietnamese, 54, 70–6, 90–4, 112, 125, 141–6
Villawood detention centre, 66, 77
Viviani, Nancy, 54, 72–8, 89, 145–6

Walzer, Michael, 170, 178
Watson, J. C., 130
welfare state, 10, 163, 165, 166, 167, 173
West, Stewart, 147, 149
Western Australia, 39, 77, 80
Wexler, Philip, 180, 181, 184, 187
White Australia policy, 3–6 *passim*, 39, 40, 41, 42, 44, 45, 47, 50, 54, 64, 127, 130, 132–42 *passim*, 147, 157, 159, 160, 161, 162
Whitlam, Gough, 55, 142
Whitlam Labor Government, 47, 49, 50, 141, 143
World War I, 18, 19, 40; World War II, 5, 10, 19, 20, 28, 43, 44, 45, 64, 99, 102, 113, 138, 158, 160, 166, 167, 173

xenophobia, 102, 107, 153, 154, 171
Xenos, Nicholas, 184

Yarwood, A. T. and Knowling, M. J., 134
'yellow peril', 3, 73, 137, 146, 157, 182; *see also* 'hordes from the north'
Young, Mick, 56
Yugoslavia *see* former Yugoslavia

Zolberg, Aristide, 12, 14
Zubrzycki, J., 52